Daniel V. Pitti
Wendy M. Duff
Editors

Encoded Archival Description on the Internet

Encoded Archival Description on the Internet has been co-published simultaneously as *Journal of Internet Cataloging,* Volume 4, Numbers 3/4 2001.

Pre-publication REVIEWS, COMMENTARIES, EVALUATIONS . . .

"A BROAD OVERVIEW OF EAD: how it came to be, what it does, where it fits with other descriptive standards, and what its future might hold. THOUGHT- PROVOKING articles explore EAD's potential impact on reference service, archival information systems, and museum descriptive practices–areas that have not yet been fully explored or exploited by the archival community."

Kris Kiesling, MILS
Head, Department of Manuscripts and Archives
Harry Ranson Humanities Research Center
University of Texas at Austin

More pre-publication
REVIEWS, COMMENTARIES, EVALUATIONS . . .

"A THOROUGH INTRODUCTION TO EAD. . . . Provides valuable background information on the history and development of EAD. USEFUL AS A TEXTBOOK in professional training seminars on archival description and online presentation. Readers will profit from the profound expertise of the authors and their experience in the field."

Dr. Angelika Menne-Haritz, PhD
Director
Archives School
Phillips-Universität
Marburg, Germany

"ESSENTIAL READING FOR ALL ARCHIVISTS, callow or seasoned, concerned with improving on their basic archival skills. . . . The knights of the EAD roundtable– Duff, Fox, Gilliland-Swetland, Hensen, Pitti, Pollock, Ruth, Szary, and Sweet–are joined by other champions of virtual archive initiatives. . . . Eleven informative essays by leading exponents, theoreticians, and practitioners."

Lesley M. Richmond, MA
Acting University Archivist
University of Glasgow, Scotland

"ONE OF THE MOST IMPORTANT BOOKS YET WRITTEN ON EAD. The introduction by Pitti and Duff gives a precise and brilliant overview of the current scene, how it has come about, and where it is likely to lead. The essays themselves SHOULD BE REQUIRED READING FOR ALL ARCHIVISTS."

Paul Watry, DPhil
Infrastructure Provider
The Archives Hub
Projects Manager for Special Collections and Archives
Liverpool University Library
United Kingdom

Encoded Archival Description on the Internet

Encoded Archival Description on the Internet has been co-published simultaneously as *Journal of Internet Cataloging*, Volume 4, Numbers 3/4 2001.

The *Journal of Internet Cataloging* Monographic "Separates"

Below is a list of "separates," which in serials librarianship means a special issue simultaneously published as a special journal issue or double-issue *and* as a "separate" hardbound monograph. (This is a format which we also call a "DocuSerial.")

"Separates" are published because specialized libraries or professionals may wish to purchase a specific thematic issue by itself in a format which can be separately cataloged and shelved, as opposed to purchasing the journal on an on-going basis. Faculty members may also more easily consider a "separate" for classroom adoption.

"Separates" are carefully classified separately with the major book jobbers so that the journal tie-in can be noted on new book order slips to avoid duplicate purchasing.

You may wish to visit Haworth's Website at . . .

http://www.HaworthPress.com

. . . to search our online catalog for complete tables of contents of these separates and related publications.

You may also call 1-800-HAWORTH (outside US/Canada: 607-722-5857), or Fax 1-800-895-0582 (outside US/Canada: 607-771-0012), or e-mail at:

getinfo@haworthpressinc.com

Encoded Archival Description on the Internet, edited by Daniel V. Pitti, CPhil, MLIS , and Wendy M. Duff, PhD, (Vol. 4, No. 3/4, 2001). *A broad overview of EAD: how it came to be, what it does, where it fits with other descriptive standards, and what its future might hold. Thought-provoking articles explore EAD's potential impact on reference service, archival information systems, and museum descriptive practices–areas that have not yet been fully explored or exploited by the archival community." (Kris Kiesling, MILS, Head, Department of Manuscripts and Archives, Harry Ranson Humanities Research Center, University of Texas at Austin)*

CORC: New Tools and Possibilities for Cooperative Electronic Resource Description, edited by Karen Calhoun, MS, MBA, and John J. Riemer, MLS (Vol. 4, No. 1/2, 2001). *Examines the nuts-and-bolts practical matters of making a cataloging system work in the Internet environment, where information objects are electronic, transient, and numerous.*

Metadata and Organizing Educational Resources on the Internet, edited by Jane Greenberg, PhD (Vol. 3, No. 1/2/3, 2000). *"A timely and essential reference. . . . A compilation of important issues and views . . . provides the reader with a balanced and practical presentation of empirical case studies and theoretical elaboration." (John Mason, Co-Chair, Dublin Core Education Working Group, and Technical Director, Education, Au LTD [Education Network Australia])*

Internet Searching and Indexing: The Subject Approach, edited by Alan R. Thomas, MA, and James R. Shearer, MA (Vol. 2, No. 3/4, 2000). *This handy guide examines the tools and procedures available now and for the future that will help librarians, students, and patrons search the Internet more systematically, and also discusses how Internet pages can be modified to facilitate easier and efficient searches.*

Encoded Archival Description on the Internet

Daniel V. Pitti
Wendy M. Duff
Editors

Encoded Archival Description on the Internet has been co-published simultaneously as *Journal of Internet Cataloging*, Volumc 4, Numbers 3/4 2001.

The Haworth Information Press
An Imprint of
The Haworth Press, Inc.
New York • London • Oxford

Published by

The Haworth Information Press®, 10 Alice Street, Binghamton, NY 13904-1580

The Haworth Information Press®, is an imprint of The Haworth Press, Inc., 10 Alice Street, Binghamtom, NY 13904-1580 USA.

Encoded Archival Description on the Internet has been co-published simultaneously as *Journal of Internet Cataloging*™, Volume 4, Numbers 3/4 2001.

Cover design by Thomas J. Mayshock Jr.

Library of Congress Cataloging-in-Publication Data

Encoded Archival Description on the Internet / Daniel V. Pitti, Wendy M. Duff, editors.
p. cm.
Co-published simultaneously as Journal of Internet cataloging, v. 4, nos. 3/4, 2001.
Includes bibliographical references and index.
ISBN 0-7890-1397-5 (alk. paper) --ISBN 0-7890-1398-3 (pbk. : alk. paper)
1. Encoded Archival Description (Document type definition) I. Pitti, Daniel V. II. Duff, Wendy M. III. Journal of Internet cataloging.
Z695.2 .E63 2001
025.3'24--dc21 2001039984

Indexing, Abstracting & Website/Internet Coverage

This section provides you with a list of major indexing & abstracting services. That is to say, each service began covering this periodical during the year noted in the right column. Most Websites which are listed below have indicated that they will either post, disseminate, compile, archive, cite or alert their own Website users with research-based content from this work. (This list is as current as the copyright date of this publication.)

Abstracting, Website/Indexing Coverage . . . . Year When Coverage Began

- *AGRICOLA Database* **1997**
- *Applied Social Sciences Index & Abstracts (ASSIA) (Online: ASSI via Data-Star) (CDRom: ASSIA Plus)* **1997**
- *BUBL Information Service, an Internet-based Information Service for the UK higher education community <URL: http://bubl.ac.uk/>* **1999**
- *CNPIEC Reference Guide: Chinese National Directory of Foreign Periodicals* **1997**
- *Combined Health Information Database (CHID)* **1997**
- *Computer Literature Index* **1997**
- *Current Awareness Abstracts of Library & Information Management Literature, ASLIB (UK)* **1997**
- *Current Cites (Digital Libraries) (Electronic Publishing) (Multimedia & Hypermedia) (Networks & Networking) (General)* **1998**
- *Current Index to Journals in Education* **1999**

(continued)

- *FINDEX <www.publist.com>* **1999**
- *FRANCIS.INIST/CNRS <www.inist.fr>*. **2001**
- *Index to Periodical Articles Related to Law* **1997**
- *Information Science Abstracts*. **1997**
- *INSPEC <www.iee.org.uk/publish/>*. **1999**
- *Internet & Personal Computing Abstracts can be found online at: DIALOG, File 233; HRIN & OCLC and on Internet at: Cambridge Scientific Abstracts; Dialog Web & OCLC <www.infotoday.com/mca/default.htm>*. **1999**
- *Konyvtari Figyelo (Library Review)*. **1997**
- *Library & Information Science Abstracts (LISA)* **1997**
- *Library and Information Science Annual (LISCA) <www.lu.com/arba>* **1999**
- *Management & Marketing Abstracts*. **2000**
- *MLA International Bibliography (available in print, on CD-ROM and Internet) <www.mla.org>*. **1997**
- *OCLC Public Affairs Information Service <www.pais.org>*. **1999**
- *PASCAL, c/o Institute de L'Information Scientifique et Technique. Cross-disciplinary electronic database covering the fields of science, technology & medicine. Also available on CD-ROM, and can generate customized retrospective searches <http://www.inist.fr>*. **1998**
- *Referativnyi Zhurnal (Abstracts Journal of the All-Russian Institute of Scientific and Technical Information– in Russian)* **1997**
- *Social Work Abstracts* **1997**
- *World Publishing Monitor*. **2000**

(continued)

Special Bibliographic Notes related to special journal issues (separates) and indexing/abstracting:

- indexing/abstracting services in this list will also cover material in any "separate" that is co-published simultaneously with Haworth's special thematic journal issue or DocuSerial. Indexing/abstracting usually covers material at the article/chapter level.
- monographic co-editions are intended for either non-subscribers or libraries which intend to purchase a second copy for their circulating collections.
- monographic co-editions are reported to all jobbers/wholesalers/approval plans. The source journal is listed as the "series" to assist the prevention of duplicate purchasing in the same manner utilized for books-in-series.
- to facilitate user/access services all indexing/abstracting services are encouraged to utilize the co-indexing entry note indicated at the bottom of the first page of each article/chapter/contribution.
- this is intended to assist a library user of any reference tool (whether print, electronic, online, or CD-ROM) to locate the monographic version if the library has purchased this version but not a subscription to the source journal.
- individual articles/chapters in any Haworth publication are also available through the Haworth Document Delivery Service (HDDS).

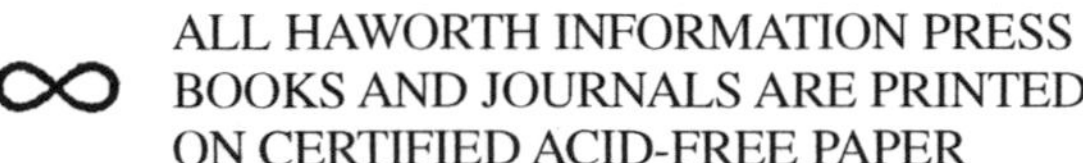
ALL HAWORTH INFORMATION PRESS BOOKS AND JOURNALS ARE PRINTED ON CERTIFIED ACID-FREE PAPER

Encoded Archival Description on the Internet

CONTENTS

ABOUT THE EDITORS

Daniel V. Pitti, CPhil, MLIS, is Project Director at the Institute for Advanced Technology in the Humanities (IATH) at the University of Virginia. His responsibilities include project design in general, and SGML and XML development in particular. Before coming to IATH in 1997, Mr. Pitti was Librarian for Advanced Technologies Projects at the University of California at Berkeley Library. For the past seven years, he has participated in a national and increasingly international effort to develop an encoding standard for library and archival finding aids known as Encoded Archival Description.

Wendy M. Duff, PhD, is Assistant Professor at the University of Toronto, Faculty of Information Studies. While doing her doctoral work, Dr. Duff was the project coordinator for the University of Pittsburgh Electronic Recordkeeping Project. She is Chair of the Canadian Committee on Archival Description, a member of the Encoded Archival Description Working Group, and was a member of the International Archival Description Adhoc Commission on Descriptive Standards. Dr. Duff's primary research interests include metadata, user studies, archival description, and electronic records.

Introduction

Daniel V. Pitti
Wendy M. Duff

Archives differ from libraries in the nature of the materials held. Libraries collect individual published books and serials, or bounded sets of individual items. The books and journals libraries collect are not unique, at least not in ways that are of general interest. Multiple copies of one publication exist, and any given copy will generally satisfy as well as any other copy. The materials in archives and manuscript libraries are the unique records of corporate bodies and the papers of individuals and families. The records and papers are the organic byproducts of corporate bodies carrying out their functions and responsibilities, and of individuals or families living their lives. In contrast to the published items collected by libraries, the identifiable object of interest in the archive is a complex body of *interrelated,* unique materials that provide legal or historical evidence of the activities of the creator. All records or documents created, accumulated, or used by one corporate body or individual or family are referred to as a collection, or *fonds*. The *fonds* coheres and is identifiable because all of its records or papers share a common provenance, which is to say, derived from one source. While a *fonds* may contain just one item, it fre-

---

Daniel V. Pitti is Project Director at the Institute for Advanced Technology in the Humanities, Alderman Library, 3rd Floor, University of Virginia, Charlottesville, VA 22903 (E-mail: dpitti@Virginia.edu).

Wendy M. Duff is Chair of the Canadian Committee on Archival Description, and Assistant Professor, Faculty of Information Studies, University of Toronto, 140 St. George Street, Toronto, Ontario M5S 3G6 (E-mail: duff@fis.utoronto.ca).

[Haworth co-indexing entry note]: "Introduction." Pitti, Daniel V., and Wendy M. Duff. Co-published simultaneously in *Journal of Internet Cataloging* (The Haworth Information Press, an imprint of The Haworth Press, Inc.) Vol. 4, No. 3/4, 2001, pp. 1-6; and: *Encoded Archival Description on the Internet* (ed: Daniel V. Pitti, and Wendy M. Duff) The Haworth Information Press, an imprint of The Haworth Press, Inc., 2001, pp. 1-6. Single or multiple copies of this article are available for a fee from The Haworth Document Delivery Service [1-800-342-9678, 9:00 a.m. - 5:00 p.m. (EST). E-mail address: getinfo@haworthpressinc.com].

quently comprises hundreds or thousands, and sometimes millions. Many *fonds* are current, with additional materials added over time. The items in a *fonds* are frequently manuscripts and typescripts, but they may be in any form or medium: plans, drawings, charts, maps, photographs, audio, video, or electronic records of all kinds.

Because published materials differ fundamentally from the complex collections of unique materials found in archives, there are major differences in bibliographic and archival description. A bibliographic description, such as that found in many MARC records, represents an individual published item, and thus is item-level. There is a one-to-one correspondence between the description and the item. The description is based on, and is derived from, the physical item. Archival description represents a *fonds,* a complex body of materials, frequently in more than one form or medium, sharing a common provenance. The description involves a complex hierarchical and progressive analysis. It begins by describing the whole, then proceeds to identify and describe sub-components of the whole, and sub-components of sub-components, and so on. Occasionally the description extends to the level of individual items. The description emphasizes the intellectual structure and content of the material, rather than their physical characteristics.

Archivists have designed Encoded Archival Description (EAD) to accommodate the unique qualities and characteristics of archival description. Given the history of archival repositories, there are significant differences both among the repositories in a given country, and among different national practices. Nevertheless, archivists internationally share fundamental principles and practices that transcend these differences and provide a solid foundation for a common, standardized approach to archival description.

The Society of American Archivists and the Library of Congress Network Development and MARC Standards Office formally released EAD Version 1.0 in the fall of 1998. Even before its official release, EAD had generated enthusiastic interest and a number of major institutional "early implementers." The initial interest in EAD came from archivists in the United States, but soon Canadian and British colleagues joined them. Interest in EAD has continued to spread around the world. While many of those looking at EAD have been merely curious, taking a cautious or skeptical wait-and-see position, many others have taken substantial steps towards implementation, investing significant human and monetary resources. What accounts for EAD's remarkable early success?

The most significant reason for EAD's success is that archivists recognize in EAD their shared principles and practice, and have embraced EAD not as a full realization of all of their expectations, but as common ground on which they can negotiate and realize the future of one of the profession's central responsibilities. EAD has certainly sparked an important, international, professional dialogue. While the "familiarity" of EAD is central to its initial success, two other factors also stand out as significant.

First, as a standardized electronic representation of archival description, EAD makes it possible to provide union access to detailed archival descriptions and resources in repositories distributed throughout the world. Users will be able to discover or locate archival materials no matter where they are located in the world, and they will be able to do this at any time of the day or night, and from any place. Researchers will no longer need to know *a priori* where they are likely to find relevant materials. They will simply be able to ask if the resources exist, and if they do, where they exist, and how to get access to them. Such union access will benefit not only public users, but also librarians and archivists. Libraries and archives will be able to easily share information about complementary records and collections, and to "virtually" integrate collections related by provenance, but dispersed geographically or administratively. Much of EAD's appeal springs from the possibility of realizing this longstanding dream of union access.

Second, the attempt to facilitate networked access to archival description through the development of EAD benefited from fortunate timing. EAD grew out of the Berkeley Finding Aid Project, which was conceived in 1993 and initiated in 1994. At that time, archivists and librarians were increasingly using email and the Gopher, a simple though powerful technology for indexing and providing access to flat ASCII textual files. Both technologies demonstrated the power of the Internet for providing access to and delivering information. The World Wide Web (WWW) and HTML, which ultimately replaced the Gopher, and profoundly transformed almost every facet of our lives, was then a curious and little known experiment being conducted at CERN, the European Organization for Nuclear Research in Switzerland.

Just before the WWW exploded on the scene, archivists began experimenting with Standard Generalized Markup Language (SGML) as a means to publish electronically archival description or finding aids on the global network. Had these efforts preceded email and the Gopher, they would not have been easily understood, even abstractly. Had development of EAD followed the astonishing and seemingly instantaneous success of the WWW and HTML, it would have been difficult to explain why the effort was even necessary. As it was, during the early stages of the development of EAD, many asked why it was necessary, arguing that HTML appeared to be "good enough" to do the job. Fortunately, the academic, commercial, and government organizations that embraced and were developing the Internet and the WWW, realized that HTML was insufficient to realize the full potential of Internet communication. They supported the development of Extensible Markup Language (XML), a simplified version of SGML. The effort to develop XML began in 1996, and the World Wide Web Consortium (W3C) approved version 1.0 in February 1998. The archivists developing EAD did not have to argue for SGML over HTML, the developers of HTML did it for them. The rapid adoption of EAD can be attributed to this timely transition.

The papers in this volume are intended to provide an introduction to archival description and EAD, examples of its use in various contexts, and its impact and potential impact on users and reference services.

The first two papers provide an introduction to archives and archival description, and a detailed history and overview of EAD. In the first paper, Kent Haworth discusses the nature of archives and the central role that description plays in archival work. In particular Haworth focuses on the key archival principle of *respect de fonds* and its application in multilevel or hierarchical description, and argues that EAD for the first time provides an electronic representation that accurately accommodates the intellectual content and structure of archival description. In the second paper, Janice Ruth describes the traditional characteristics and role of finding aids. Building on this description, Ruth traces the origin and history of EAD, and further describes its intellectual content and structure.

Following are two papers that situate EAD in the complex world of descriptive standards and discuss the relationship between MARC collection-level summary descriptions and the detailed and full descriptions found in finding aids. In the first of these two papers, Michael Fox compares and contrasts EAD with several longstanding and emerging descriptive standards, and argues that EAD finds a clear place among them as a data structure standard. Steven Hensen argues that EAD complements, rather than replaces MARC collection-level description. Hensen maintains that MARC records serve the function of representing archival materials in online catalogs that increasingly provide access to all cultural heritage resources and not just published materials.

Application of EAD, like any complex technology, can be a challenge. To meet this challenge, archives increasingly are forming consortia. Two papers discuss the Online Archive of California (OAC) and the American Heritage Virtual Archive Project, and a third, the role of the Research Libraries Group (RLG) in providing union access to primary resources throughout the world. In the first paper, Charlotte Brown and Brian Schottlaender describe the formation and administration of the OAC. Brown and Schottlaender argue that the consortial approach, among other benefits, offers efficiencies, a new sense of community and dialogue, and the means to provide union access to geographically related records. Timothy Hoyer, Stephen Miller, and Alvin Pollock describe their experience in developing a shared approach to EAD in the OAC and American Heritage Virtual Archive Project consortia. Hoyer, Miller, and Pollock describe the practical implementation of EAD to retrospective conversion in the two consortia and the need to develop a shared and consistent approach. Negotiating such an approach, they argue, leads to a fruitful tension between the past and the future that is laying the groundwork for transforming archival description. In her paper, Anne Van Camp describes the role that the Research Libraries Group has played on behalf of libraries, archives, and museums, with particular attention given to providing access to primary resources. Within the context of RLG's overall mission, Van Camp describes RLG's important early efforts to provide EAD training, and its unique effort to provide universal, union access to finding aids from all over the world in their groundbreaking Archival Resources.

While much of the literature to date has addressed the application of EAD in research archives and manuscript libraries, EAD has an important role to play in government and corporate archives. Meg Sweet, Matthew Hillyard, Derek Breeden, and Bill Stockting describe the use of EAD in the Public Record Office in the United Kingdom. The authors describe the relational database that serves as the primary management tool for describing 150 kilometers of material dating to the 11th century, and the supporting role that EAD plays in public access to this foundation collection in the English speaking world.

Interest in EAD has not been limited to archives. In his paper, Richard Rinehart argues that EAD appears to offer museums the possibility of complementing traditional item descriptions found in museum management systems with collection information that provides context for enhancing the appreciation and understanding of the items. Based on a description of early experiments, Rinehart argues that EAD offers museums many advantages, but also, given its provenance, presents many challenges.

Traditionally finding aids have only been available on site or through the mail. Making finding aids available via the Internet will expand access to archives and archival resources to new users, enhance access for traditional users, and have an impact on those who mediate use of the resources, the reference archivists. Richard Szary evaluates the potential impact EAD will have on archival reference service. Anne Gilliland-Swetland argues that EAD can play an important role in an online archival information system that can provide access to archival materials, ancillary materials, and paths into other online archival and bibliographical information to a vast range of users beyond the traditional. Gilliland-Swetland describes in detail a model for enhancing archival information discovery and retrieval, and argues for rethinking the role of description within the context of the new possibilities offered by the technology.

The editors hope that the eleven papers presented here will provide an effective introduction to archival description and EAD, a useful overview of its use in various contexts, and an insight into its potential to revolutionize archival practices and services and to democratize and extend access to archival resources.

Archival Description: Content and Context in Search of Structure

Kent M. Haworth

SUMMARY. This essay focuses on the nature of archives, the function of description and how the former governs the requirements of both the content and structure of descriptive products. Archival description is at the heart of archival work and is informed by the archival principle of *respect des fonds,* which in turn governs the way archives are arranged and made accessible. Descriptions of archival records must represent both the content and the context of their creation in order to convey to users two essential qualities: their impartiality and authenticity as evidence of actions and transactions by individuals and organizations. The application of the technique of multilevel description as it is prescribed in the General International Standard Archival Description (ISAD) structures an archival description in such a way that the lowest level of description can be linked to successively higher levels of descriptions. For the first time, Encoded Archival Description (EAD) provides a data structure standard to accommodate hierarchies of archival descriptions and for this reason is being adopted by several archives in North America and Europe. The development of a similar SGML/XML data structure for archival authority records is essential in order to capture contextual information about the creators of archival records. With the application of both these standards around the world, archivists will be in a

---

Kent M. Haworth is University Archivist and Head of Special Collections at York University, 305 Scott Library, 4700 Keele Street, Toronto, ON, M3J 1P3 (E-mail: khaworth@yorku.ca).

[Haworth co-indexing entry note]: "Archival Description: Content and Context in Search of Structure." Haworth, Kent M. Co-published simultaneously in *Journal of Internet Cataloging* (The Haworth Information Press, an imprint of The Haworth Press, Inc.) Vol. 4, No. 3/4, 2001, pp. 7-26; and: *Encoded Archival Description on the Internet* (ed: Daniel V. Pitti, and Wendy M. Duff) The Haworth Information Press, an imprint of The Haworth Press, Inc., 2001, pp. 7-26. Single or multiple copies of this article are available for a fee from The Haworth Document Delivery Service [1-800-342-9678, 9:00 a.m. - 5:00 p.m. (EST). E-mail address: getinfo@haworthpressinc.com].

position to build archival information systems and exchange archival descriptions in much the same way librarians have been able to do since the adoption of MARC and the Z39.50 data exchange protocol.

KEYWORDS. APPM, archival description, archival descriptive standards, Encoded Archival Description, EAD, finding aids, ISAD(G), multilevel description, RAD

INTRODUCTION

> Accurate description gives users a tool to help them to understand the material that they are using. It creates a consciousness about the coherence of fragmented bits of information. It creates the potential to understand the value of acts and data as evidence, not as the disembodied stuff of confusion and alienation.
>
> –Liv Mykland, "The Archivist's Identity and Professionalism"[1]

Archival description is at the heart of archival work.[2] It is informed by archival principles of arrangement and, when correctly carried out, it represents and safeguards the two essential archival qualities that Sir Hilary Jenkinson believed characterized archival material: impartiality and authenticity.[3] According to Jenkinson, archives are impartial because they were created without thought to any particular research interest, but instead, were "drawn up for purposes almost infinitely varying . . . the only safe prediction, in fact, concerning the Research ends which Archives may be made to serve is that . . . these will not be the purposes which were contemplated by the people by whom the Archives were drawn up and preserved."[4] Hence, the concepts of a natural process of creation, sometimes expressed as an "unselfconscious accumulation" or "automatically and organically created and/or accumulated and used," are incorporated into various definitions of archives.[5]

This quality of impartiality is both significant and challenging for librarians and archivists who describe archives. The potential research uses to which an archive might be put can neither be anticipated by their creator, nor the archivist who describes them. For example, a government creates a birth register to document all births that take place within a certain jurisdiction as "proof" or evidence of citizenship. This is its primary value. It will have different residual or secondary values including being a valuable source for genealogists interested in tracing family histories. The birth register was not created in the first instance to serve the interests of genealogical research, but rather to serve the administrative need to document citizenship and protect all the rights and privileges associated with it. To interpret a record and judge its authenticity, one must understand its primary value. Thus, the content of an archival description (e.g., a fonds, series, and so on) must contain information about the context of its creation as well as information transcribed and taken from the unit of description. For this reason, archivists describe the content, structure and context of records and thereby protect the impartiality and authenticity of *evidence*. This essay focuses on the *nature* of archives, the *function* of description and how the former governs the requirements of both the content and structure of descriptive products.

Librarians select and create representations of *information products* to make them available. In other words, the nature of the material informs their cataloging or description. In addition to being sensitive to the nature and quality of archives, librarians approaching the description (or cataloging, in bibliographic terminology) of archival material need to be cognizant of the differences between cataloging "the book," that is, an item, and describing archival material, an aggregate, group, or collection of documents. The book (traditionally) contains information on a particular subject, produced and distributed by publishers, with a title page that serves as a source of information about the item and therefore the primary source for the purposes of cataloging. On the other hand, archival material contains evidence of actions and transactions of a records creator and comprises multiple documents or records, frequently in different media. The documents or records are usually related by form or function to other documents, and are often grouped into identifiable subgroups. These groups document how the records were "automatically and organically created/and or accumulated and used." To represent the creation or provenance of records, which is essential for an understanding of those records, the archivist must describe all of the documents or records generated by one creator, as well as the groups of related items within the whole, and the items themselves. Therefore, before the formal process of description of archives can take place the related groups of materials must be identified and arranged. Furthermore, the description must reflect both the provenance (the context of creation) of the records and their original order. As our Australian colleagues point out:

> The documentation processes involved in arrangement and based on provenance and original order are of great importance because archives, unlike books, draw much of their meaning from their context. Books, being discrete items, complete in themselves, can be catalogued and used and understood individually. However, archives, being the organic products of continuing work or life activities, can only be fully understood through a knowledge of why and how they were created and used over time. As one's life or business changes, these new directions are reflected in the records and provide important evidence for the researcher.[6]

Given the nature of archives, the act of describing archival material occupies a large portion of the archivist's time. But it is only recently that the attention of archivists interested in making their descriptions more widely available to users has focused on standardizing archival description.[7] Accordingly, archivists have given considerable thought to how they describe archives, why they describe them the way they do, and by what means they might use automated systems to enhance access to the materials in their repositories. Their analysis of the descriptive function inevitably led archivists to consider standardizing both the contents of an archival description and the descriptive products they produce (e.g., an inventory, a list, a "catalog" record, and so on). This new attention to archival description resulted in the development, application, and maintenance of descriptive standards at both the national and international level. The genesis for these developments is well documented.[8]

DEFINITIONS OF ARCHIVAL DESCRIPTION

It is worth noting that in recent years archivists have developed several different definitions of archival description.[9]

> The creation of accurate representation of a unit of description and its component parts, if any, by the process of capturing, collating, analyzing, and organizing any information that serves to identify archival material and explain the context and records systems which produced it.
>
> *ISAD(G): General International Standard Archival Description*
> Glossary (International Council of Archives, 1993)

> (1) The process of analyzing, organizing, and recording information that serves to identify, manage, locate, and explain the holdings of archives and manuscript repositories and the contexts and records systems

from which those holdings were selected. (2) The written representations or products of the above process.

A Glossary for Archivists, Manuscript Curators, and Records Managers
(Society of American Archivists, 1992)

The recording in a standardized form of information about the structure, function, and content of records.

Rules for Archival Description
Glossary (Bureau of Canadian Archivists, 1992)

The process of recording information about the nature and content of the records in archival custody. The description identifies such features as provenance, arrangement, format and contents, and presents them in a standardised form.

Keeping Archives
Glossary (Australian Society of Archivists, 1993)

All of these definitions embody important concepts relating to the nature of archives and the functions of archival description. Furthermore, they are fundamental to the primary mission of the archivist: to describe archival materials and to make them available for use. To realize this mission, the archivists must provide effective and efficient reference service for users seeking access to archival materials. Efficient reference service depends upon effective archival description. A careful analysis of the various definitions noted above might produce the following functional definition of archival description that synthesizes concepts inherent in these definitions: *the presentation of an accurate representation of archival documents so that users can, as independently as possible, locate them.*[10] Three concepts are embedded in this functional definition of archival description:

- the provision of accurate descriptions in the form of a variety of types of finding aids;
- the provision of effective and efficient access for users;
- the independence of finding aids from archivists.

If an archival description is an accurate representation of content and context, then the user should be able to retrieve information relevant to his or her research. This constitutes an effective finding aid. If the user can retrieve what he or she is looking for with as little mediation as possible from the archivist, this constitutes an efficient finding aid.

PRINCIPLES GOVERNING ARCHIVAL DESCRIPTION

Archival description represents the content and context of the records, through which the archivist documents the essential qualities of archival records, that is, their impartiality and their authenticity. As Michael Cook notes, "By placing the archives in an order which is the same as, or which corresponds to, or reflects, that of the original system, an archivist is providing a statement on meaning and authenticity: this statement is the main strongpoint of the moral defense of the archives, for it ensures that the evidential meaning of the archives will be understood forever afterwards."[11] Information concerning the content and context of records is conveyed to users by representing the arrangement of the materials in a multilevel description. Archival arrangement is governed by the principle of *respects des fonds*. This principle states that "the records of a person, family, or corporate body must be kept together in their original order, if it exists or has been maintained, and not be mixed or combined with the records of another individual or corporate body."[12] This principle encompasses two subsidiary principles commonly known as the principle of original order and the principle of provenance. The archivist's analysis of provenance, that is, its external context, and the original order of the records, that is, its internal structure, will produce information essential for an understanding of both context and content. Figure 1 illustrates these two principles.[13]

The archivist documents the context of creation of the records being described (the external context of their creation) by providing a biographical sketch or administrative history and a custodial history of the records in the archival description. For example, a biographical sketch will provide an account of the various activities of an individual that may or may not be revealed in the records constituting their archives, including their education, place(s) of residence, occupation(s), offices held, and significant accomplishments. This sketch can be part of the description of archival records or it can reside in an authority file that is linked to the description.

A history of custody will indicate either that the records remained in the control of their creator until being transferred to the archives, thereby enhancing their value as authentic evidence, or, on the other hand, it will indicate a change of custody which could have resulted in the disruption of their provenance, thereby calling into question their reliability as authentic evidence.

FIGURE 1

PRINCIPLE OF RESPECT DES FONDS

PRINCIPLE OF PROVENANCE

Analysis of ***external structure*** (order) and ***external context*** revealed through an analysis of provenance and represented in archival description will reveal:

- archival quality of authenticity: custody, control, and use
- context and functional responsibilities: "records follow function"
- authority relationships: superior subordinate relationships
- administrative structure and relationships: predecessor /successor agencies
- functional responsibilities and contextual activities

and characterized in archival description as:

- administrative history / biographical sketch
- custodial history

PRINCIPLE OF ORIGINAL ORDER

Analysis of ***internal structure and internal content*** revealed through an analysis of original order and represented in archival description will reveal:

- archival quality of impartiality: records speak for themselves
- content
- documentary form
- documentary relationships, processes and procedures
- organization and arrangement of the documents

and characterized in archival description as:

Scope, as an analysis of:

- function
- activities
- dates
- geographical areas

and:

Content, as an analysis of:

- documentary arrangement
- documentary forms
- subject

An analysis of the internal structure and content of the records being described provides information about the scope and content of the records. Has the original order of the archives been maintained or has an order been imposed where none existed? Are the records organized chronologically, by subject, or by documentary form? What specific activities resulted in the accumulation of a particular set of records? What are the principal documentary forms (for example: correspondence, reports, minutes of meetings, drawings) and their relationship to the activities of the records-creator? The content of the unit of description should reveal the subject matter of the records, the time period of records comprising the unit of description, and the geographical area to which the records relate.

The writing of a good biographical sketch or administrative sketch, and a scope and content note is an art, based on a careful analysis of the sometimes intricate and complex relationships between a records-creator and the records they generate. As can be seen, the task of archival description is substantially removed from the more mechanical process of compiling information for a catalog record derived from the title page of a publication.

MULTILEVEL DESCRIPTION

Describing archival material is further complicated by the fact that the description may reflect the records' arrangement. The way a record-creator organizes records (for example, into series or files) will affect the way the records are described. As Hugo Stibbe notes,

> all archival description is fundamentally [a] description of collectivities and . . . these collectivities may be organized in sub-collectivities which may be further subdivided . . . Each collectivity or unit of arrangement becomes [potentially] a unit of description. Thus, there may be many "units of description" in a collectivity of archival material. These units of description, being divisions and subdivisions of the whole collectivity [and] naturally have a hierarchical structure, and group themselves into hierarchical levels that have as a common characteristic, the structure of a tree.[14]

Preparing a multilevel descriptive record of a fonds and its parts can thus be defined as "the preparation of descriptions that are related to one another in a part-to-whole relationship and that need complete identification of both parts and comprehensive whole in multiple descriptive records."[15]

The analysis and description of the external structure and internal structure must be represented to facilitate understanding of context, content, and arrangement (structure) and to enable access to records that document evidence of actions and transactions. This is accomplished through the application of the following rules governing the preparation of a multilevel description specified in the *ISAD(G)* as follows:[16]

1. Description must proceed from the general (highest) level of description to successively more specific (lower) levels of description;
2. Information in the description must be provided that is relevant to the level of description;
3. Each lower level of description must be identified and linked to its immediate higher level so that the unit of description is displayed in the context of the full hierarchy of descriptions;
4. Information given at a higher level should not be repeated at lower levels to avoid redundancy.

The hierarchical descriptive model prescribed by ISAD(G) is illustrated in Figure 2.[17]

The following example of a multilevel description illustrates the application of ISAD (G)'s multilevel rules represented in Figure 2. It is important to note that the highest (e.g., fonds) level description, together with the subsequent series, sub-series, file and item descriptions form *one* archival descriptive record. The relative relationship of each unit of description is distinguished by layout. Moreover, because information at higher levels is not repeated at lower levels, the lower-level description is dependent on the higher level of description. In other words, all descriptive records for the fonds, series, sub-series, file, and item must be displayed together to be comprehensible.

FIGURE 2

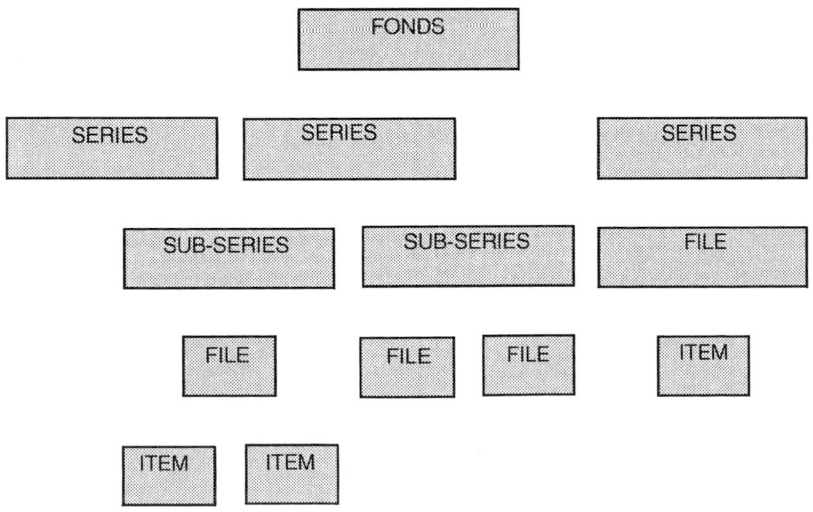

FONDS-LEVEL DESCRIPTION

John Smith fonds.–1951_1994.–4.8 m of textual records.–202 videocassette tapes.–3 audio cassette tapes.–3 boxes of graphic materials.

John Smith is a Canadian film-maker whose films include *Dieppe* and *The Boys of St. Vincent,* which he both directed and co-wrote, the latter gaining for him the 1994 Gemini award for Best Direction in a Dramatic Program. Smith was born in Montreal in 1943 and obtained a B.A. in 1964 from McGill University. While studying for a Master's degree in Political Science he became involved with a group of film-makers, and as a result of this association produced his first film with a fellow-student for the CBC in 1967. In 1968 he went to work for CBC Toronto as a researcher and a year later moved to Hobel-Leiterman Productions as a producer/director for television series on the CTV network. In 1972 he joined the National Film Board as executive producer of the television unit. With the closure of the NFB's television unit in the mid-1970s, Smith turned his attention to drama, with the result that he produced several films, including *Acting Class* (a view of the workings of the National Theatre School), *The First Winter* (a dramatic account of Irish settlers in the Ottawa Valley in the 1880s), and *For the Love of Dance* (a backstage look at the world of dance through the activities of seven Canadian Dance Troupes). His most recent film (1995) is *Dangerous Minds,* starring Michelle Pfeiffer.

The fonds consists of a wide variety of documentation in a variety of formats relating to Smith's personal life and professional career as writer, producer and director. The documentation includes screenplays, draft notes for works in progress, shot lists, story boards, call lists and shooting schedules, casting and contact lists, correspondence, research files, and press clippings; incomplete printing elements for 16mm and 35mm productions, rough assemblies, rushes and outs on VHS and Beta video cassettes for film productions. The fonds is arranged into the following six series: Series #S1014: Production files; Series #S1015: Scripts; Series #S1016: National Film Board files; Series #S1017: Canadian Broadcasting Corporation files; Series #1018: Business files; and Series #S1019: Personal files.

Title supplied from contents of the fonds.–Access to some textual records is restricted. Written permission to consult must be obtained from John N. Smith. All moving image material is accessible only for research use. Copies of moving image material in the fonds is made for study purposes on an as-requested basis.–File lists available with series level descriptions.–Further accruals are expected.

S1014
Series Production files.–2.7 m of textual records.–2 folders of photographs.–61 video cassettes.–Series consists of research files, successive drafts of scripts, casting lists, and other documentation related to films produced by John Smith. Films included in this series include *The Boys of St. Vincent* (1992), *Dieppe* (1993), and *My Posse Don't Do Homework* (1994?). Other production files include such award winning films as *Bargain Basement* (1976), *Revolution's Orphans* (1979), and *First Winter* (1980).–Sub-series within this series are arranged alphabetically by the title of the production.–Some sub-series level descriptions available.

S1014.1
Sub-series *Boys of St. Vincent* productions files.–1990-1993.–1.24 m (ca. 7 boxes) of textural records.–2 video cassettes.–Sub-series consists of research files, time lines, successive drafts of the screenplay, script revisions, and publicity files relating to the release of the film. Files pertaining to the Supreme Court case preventing the film from being shown in Montreal and in Ontario are in the series titled CBC files (Series #1017).–File list of textual records and item level descriptions of release version of the production is available.

File level *Boys of St. Vincent* release versions.–2 video cassettes (185 min.).–1992.–File consists of video cassettes of the release version of *Boys of St. Vincent* and *The Boys of St. Vincent: 15 years later*. a two-part production entitled The Boys of St. Vincent produced by John N. Smith.–Title supplied from contents of the file.–Item level descriptions available.

Item level *The Boys of St. Vincent* [videorecording]/produced by Les Productions T l _Action Inc. in co-production with the National Film Board of Canada, in association with the Canadian Broadcasting Corporation.–Canada: Productions T l _Action, Inc.–1 videocassette (92 min.): sd., col.; 1/2 in.–Performers: Henry Czerny, Brian Dooley, Philip Dinn, Johnny Morina.–Directed by John N. Smith; director of photography, Pierre Letarte; edited by Werner Nold.–VHS. Closed_captioned for the hearing impaired.–Item is a fictional account of the emotional and sexual humiliation experienced by boys in a Newfoundland orphanage run by the All Saints Brothers. Tells the story of ten-year-old Kevin who rebels against the authoritarian rule.

Item level *The Boys of St. Vincent* [videorecording]: 15 years later/produced by Les Productions T l _Action Inc. in co-production with the National Film Board of Canada, in association with the Canadian Broadcasting Corporation.–Canada: Productions T l _Action, Inc.–1 videocassette (93 min.): sd., col.; 1/2 in.–Performer(s): Henry Czerny, Sebastian Spence, David Hewlett.–Directed by John N. Smith; director of photography, Pierre Letarte; edited by Andre Corriveau.–VHS. Closed_captioned for the hearing impaired.–Item is a fictional account of a public inquiry into the physical and sexual abuse reported by former residents of a Newfoundland orphanage run by the All Saints Brothers. Kevin recounts his torment at the hands of Brother Lavin, who is now married and the father of two children.

S1015 Scripts.–1989_1994.–1.08 m of textual records.–Series consists of scripts sent to John Smith in the course of his film making career for which there are no production notes, just screenplays. Scripts are arranged alphabetically by the title of the script.–File list available.

S1016 National Film Board files.–1982_1994.–24 cm. of textual records.–Series consists of files John Smith incurred in the course of his work with the NFB. Included are advertisements, production press releases, newsletters, Committee 200 files, reports and other staff related files.–File list available.

S1017 Canadian Broadcasting Corporation files.–1982_1992.–42 cm. of textual records.–Series consists of files accumulated by John Smith in the course of his work with the CBC and include telecast schedules and correspondence for the Children's Television Department (1982-1987), contractual agreements, and files pertaining to the CBC's court case with the Supreme Court of Canada relating to the release of *The Boys of St. Vincent* in Ontario and Montreal.–File list available.

Note that there are two item descriptions under sub-series 1014.1. These descriptions are for films produced by the creator of the records, in this case John N. Smith. Each of these descriptions would exist as a separate record in a MARC bibliographic data base. Here, however, these two descriptions are parts of a sub-series that is part of a series that is part of a fonds. Standing by themselves, independent of the higher level units of description of which they form a part, the item descriptions would provide no contextual information to a user. Therefore, these descriptions must be presented together with the higher-level descriptions upon which they depend to be fully understandable.

In addition, if we wish to provide a list of files (shown below) associated with a particular fonds/collection, series/sub-series level of description in this multilevel description the archivist must link such a list to a formal, ISAD(G)-compliant multilevel description. The linked description will provide users with more details of the contents of a particular unit of description. In order for users to understand the *context of creation* of the archival materials described in the box, file or item list, it is essential to provide the *context of that material.*

FILE LIST LINKED TO THE SERIES-LEVEL DESCRIPTION

S1014.1 *Boys of St. Vincent* production files.–1990-1993.–1.24 m (ca. 7 boxes) of textual records.–Sub-series consists of research files, time lines, successive drafts of the screenplay, script revisions, and publicity files relating to the release of the film.–Title supplied from contents of the sub-series.–Files pertaining to the Supreme Court case preventing the film from being shown in Montreal and in Ontario are in the series titled CBC files (Series #1018).–File list of textual records and item list of moving image records is available.

FILE LIST: TEXTUAL RECORDS

Call Number
1994-039/001

(01) "The Boys of St. Cashel," Newfoundland Project, Story, Time Lines, Scenes, (First Draft.)
(02) "The Boys of St. Cashel," Incomplete Draft Synopsis, March 30, 1990.
(03) "The Boys of St. Cashel," Story Outline For a Film, April 1990.
(04) "Les Garcons de Mount Cashel," Synopsis, le 15 avril, 1990.
(05) "The Boys of St. Cashel," Story Outline, (First Revision), June 1990.
(06) "The Boys of St. Cashel," Screenplay, (First Draft), July 1990.

(07) "The Boys of St. Cashel-15 Years Later," Story Outline, (First Draft), October 1990.
(08) "The Boys of St. Vincent," Part One, Screenplay, (Third Draft), March 1991.
(09) "The Boys of St. Vincent," Part One, Screenplay, (Fourth Draft), May 1991.
(10) "The Boys of St. Vincent," Part One, Screenplay, (Fifth Draft), June 1991.
(11) "The Boys of St. Vincent," Part One, Screenplay, (Sixth Draft), June 1991.

THE PRODUCTS OF ARCHIVAL DESCRIPTION

Since multilevel description is integral to the accurate representation of successive units of description, as demonstrated in the previous example, MARC, a data structure standard designed primarily for representing AACR2-based description of *individual items,* has proven less than adequate as the carrier of these descriptions. While archivists in both the United States and Canada adopted the bibliographic model and ISBD structure when they developed their respective rules for archival description, Canadians differed from their colleagues in the United States because they included rules for multilevel description in their content standard. This may explain, in part, why many Canadian archivists rejected the use of the MARC-AMC format as a data structure standard for descriptions prepared in accordance with the Canadian *Rules for Archival Description* (*RAD*).

Steven Hensen, the author of *Archives, Personal Papers and Manuscripts (APPM),*[18] has noted the inadequacies of the "In" Analytic technique, a method used in APPM to links descriptions of a fonds to its parts, and acknowledged in 1990 that "[w]hile it is true that there may be better ways to describe complex hierarchical relationships, it is nonetheless a reality that to a large degree these descriptive rules are constrained by the fact of their implementation within specific bibliographic software and systems."[19] In fact, few Canadian archives–the chief exception being university archives–had access to bibliographic software and systems. This may be why Canadian archivists have never demonstrated the same enthusiasm for using the MARC-AMC format for the description of archival material as their American colleagues. Moreover, there is little doubt that our colleagues in Europe have even less enthusiasm for bibliographic models and systems for conveying archival description.[20] Given its hierarchical structure, archival description presents complex challenges that the MARC data structure was never designed to accommodate.

THE ARRIVAL OF EAD: A DATA STRUCTURE STANDARD FOR ARCHIVAL DESCRIPTION

Given the inadequacies of MARC for carrying archival descriptions beyond the fonds/collection-level descriptive (catalog) record, archivists began seeking ways to exploit the new technologies offered by the Internet environment. In retrospect, the emergence of EAD was an inevitable development. The plethora of finding aids generated by archivists (MARC collection/item-level catalog records, inventories of fonds/collection-level and series-level descriptions with associated box and files lists) were contained in a variety of software-dependent systems which could not be easily linked or exploited. Clearly there was a pressing need for an Internet-accessible archival description system that integrated and linked all of the descriptive records that make up a fonds/collection description. To this end, the EAD development team assembled by Daniel Pitti proposed the following set of functional requirements for a wide range of archival finding aids which, to a greater or lesser degree, possessed similar data elements and related data structures:

- presentation of comprehensive and inter-related descriptive information;
- preservation of hierarchical relationships existing between levels of description;
- representation of descriptive information inherited by one level of description from another;
- navigation within a hierarchical information architecture;
- element-specific indexing and retrieval.[21]

The rapidity with which EAD was developed and subsequently adopted by archival institutions, not only in the United States, but internationally, has been phenomenal. Canadian archivists are considering its adoption as a data structure standard for archival description. The Public Record Office in Great Britain has adopted it, and the Swedish National Archives has incorporated the capability to export and import archival descriptions using the EAD into its Archival Information Management System (ARKIS II). German, Italian, French and Spanish archivists are also investigating its applicability. EAD workshops have been presented in Australia, Ireland, and South Africa, in addition to numerous venues in the United States, the United Kingdom, and Canada.

What accounts for this sudden and active international interest in EAD by archivists? First and foremost, EAD is based on an internationally recognized standard for markup languages: Standard Generalized Markup Language (SGML), and the related and derivative standard, Extensible Markup Language (XML).[22] For the first time, archivists have been offered a data structure standard that accommodates a hierarchical structure for the presentation of a variety of finding aids. EAD enables archivists to be standards compliant and software independent. Just as bibliographic records are contained in a stable internationally recognized standard (the MARC record), so too can archival descriptions encoded with EAD be contained in an equally stable standardized container. There is no doubt that EAD will evolve and enjoy enhancements, just as the MARC record has evolved over the last thirty years. And like catalog records stored in a MARC data structure, archival descriptive records that are stored in an EAD container will not have to be re-keyed in the course of migration from one software system to another. Software vendors seeking to house archival descriptions marked up in EAD will ensure that their programs can accommodate EAD in the same way that bibliographic utilities and vendors ensure that their systems are MARC compliant. For this reason alone, the cost savings that will accrue to archives using EAD are self-evident and a reason for institutions to carefully scrutinize their existing automated systems for SGML and XML compliance. Further, and perhaps most important, EAD enables a semantic and structural representation of archival material that is faithful to archival principles. It enables archivists to instruct automated systems to exploit encoded data to serve a variety of purposes (e.g., searching, display, navigation, access, print, and so on), and it provides the capability of universal access to the world's archival resources. The development and on-going maintenance of EAD should give archivists cause for satisfaction and optimism that, as they enter the third millennium, they have available to them a stable, internationally recognized data structure standard to contain their archival descriptions.

THE FUTURE

As significant as the development of EAD is for archival description and for the benefits that users, keepers, and sponsors of archives will derive from its application, much work needs to be done at both the national and international levels. A select group of archivists in the United States has developed EAD, which in turn is being maintained by the Society of American Archivists and the Library of Congress. At the same time, the development of EAD has made American archivists aware that *APPM* is not an adequate data content standard for finding aids. In recognition of this inadequacy, United States and Canadian archivists have entered into discussions with a view to determining the extent to which the Canadian *Rules for Archival Description,* which is ISAD(G) compliant, could serve as data content standard, with modifications as required, for EAD.[23]

Archivists from Canada and the United States met at the Bentley Library in July 1996 to consider ways in which Canadian and American rules for archival description might be harmonized. At a subsequent meeting in Toronto in March 1999 this objective was advanced and a set of principles agreed upon for presentation to the governing bodies for descriptive standards in the respective countries for endorsement.[24] Canadian archivists mapped their *Rules for Archival Description* to EAD and found that there are few instances where any significant modifications have to be made to the EAD to accommodate *RAD.*

In addition, an international mechanism for monitoring the development of EAD as a data structure standard capable of accommodating national and local conventions governing the description of archival materials needs to be established. It would be unfortunate indeed if EAD became fragmented to meet national conventions in the way that the MARC format was divided into national MARC structures. Such fragmentation would make it difficult, if not impossible, to provide universal access through archival information networks such as those currently being developed in Sweden, Scotland and Canada, thus eliminating one of the compelling reasons for standardization. One means of avoiding this course might be for the International Council of Archives' Descriptive Standards Committee to undertake a review of EAD and to establish an acceptable international version of it. This Committee is presently reviewing guidelines for the format and presentation of finding aids and this review might also include a review of the applicability of EAD as a recommended data structure standard. Whatever mechanism is established to develop international consensus and agreement, it is essential that resources are made available to each participant to ensure that the revision process takes place in a structured, representative environment, in much the same way that AACR and the MARC format are maintained at the international level.

In addition, the development of an SGML/XML-based schema (or Document Type Definition) for the International Standard Archival Authority Record for Corporate, Personal and Family Names (ISAAR (CPF) is integral to the success of EAD. Like ISAD(G), EAD is only half a standard because it is a standard for the description of archival material. What is also required is a companion standard that captures contextual information about the creators of those archival records. Archival authority records contain this contextual information and therefore authority records must be linked to the descriptive records to which they pertain. In other words, an encoding schema for archival authority records (based on ISAAR (CPF) would enable providing contextual information essential to the understanding of the records described in EAD.[25]

CONCLUSION

In an exchange in 1990 between Steven Hensen and Heather MacNeil noted above (see note 18), MacNeil agreed with Hensen "that agreement on a North American standard for archival description is in the long-term interests of the Canadian and American archival communities."[26] Three years later, Luciana Duranti echoed this sentiment when she stated that "[i]t is very possible that the new technologies and records created will bring about both a reintegration of the three activities [preservation of meaning, exercise of control, and provision of access] into a unified concept of description which has entirely absorbed arrangement, and the production of one principal, multipurpose descriptive instrument."[27] Can we hope that EAD, in combination with the flexibility of the new technologies available to us, has at last provided us with that "principal, multipurpose descriptive instrument" encased in an internationally recognized data structure standard?

NOTES

1. Liv Mykland, "Protection and Integrity, The Archivist's Identity and Professionalism," paper presented to the XIIth International Congress on Archives (Montreal, 1992), 4.

2. "All else in the archival world, except appraisal," Rich Berner claims "is a matter of philosophy and attitude, or is part of a body of theory from another field." *Archival theory and practice in the United States: A Historical Analysis* (Seattle: University of Washington Press, 1983), 5.

3. Hilary Jenkinson, *A Manual of Archive Administration* (London: Percy Lund, Humphries & Co. Limited, 1965), 12.

4. Ibid., 12.

5. Most Canadian, Australian, and European archivists make a distinction between an "archive" (known in French as a "fonds" or "archief" in other European languages) and a collection, which may be considered an "artificial assemblage of documents accumulated on the basis of some common characteristic without regard to the provenance of those documents. Not to be confused with an "archival fonds." See Judith Ellis, editor, *Keeping Archives,* 2nd edition (Australia: Australian Society of Archivists, Inc., 1993), 4; *Rules for Archival Description* (Ottawa: Bureau of Canadian Archivists, 1990), rule 0.1, fn.; and ISAD(G): General International Standard Archival Description (Stockholm: International Council of Archives, 1999), Glossary. Manuscript curators and archivists in the United States have not made this distinction in their descriptive practices and most often use the term "collection" to refer to both archives

(a fonds or archief) and collections. In this paper, for the benefit of an American audience, a "collection" may be used interchangeably with the term "archive" or "fonds" when referring to the highest unit of description in a multilevel descriptive unit.

6. Ellis, *Keeping Archives,* 223.

7. Hugo Stibbe, "Standardizing Description: The Experience of Using ISAD(G)," *Janus* 1 (1998): 132-133.

8. See particularly *Archivaria* 34 (Summer 1992) and *Archivaria,* 35 (Spring 1993), which devote several articles to the subject of archival description from a variety of national perspectives.

9. Luciana Duranti provides an analysis of several definitions of archival description, noting that these definitions can be associated with "(1) a process of analysis, identification and organisation; (2) purposes of control, retrieval and access; and (3) a final product which illustrates archival material, its provenancial and documentary context, its interrelationships and the ways it can be identified and used." "Origin and Development of the Concept of Archival Description," *Archivaria* 35 (Spring 1993): 47-48.

10. Kent M. Haworth, "Standardizing Archival Description in the Information Age," paper presented to the XIIth International Congress on Archives (Montreal, 1992), 2. See also *Toward Descriptive Standards, Report and recommendations of the Canadian working group on archival descriptive standards* (Ottawa: Bureau of Canadian Archivists, 1985), 9: "Description is a major function in the processing of archival materials, and the products of this function are finding aids of various sorts which give administrators control over their holdings and enable users and archivists to find information about particular topics."

11. Michael Cook, *The Management of Information from Archives* (England: Gower Publishing Company Limited, 1986), p. 80.

12. *Rules for Archival Description* (Ottawa: Bureau of Canadian Archivists, 1992), Glossary, D-6.

13. For a more thorough explanation of the relationship of archival arrangement to the description of archival materials see Heather MacNeil, "The Context Is All: Describing a Fonds and Its Parts in Accordance with the *Rules for Archival Description*" in Terry Eastwood, Editor, *The Archival Fonds: From Theory to Practice* (Ottawa: Bureau of Canadian Archivists, 1992), 205-213.

14. Hugo Stibbe, "Standardizing Description: The Experience of Using ISAD(G)," *Janus* 1 (1998): 136.

15. *Rules for Archival Description* (Ottawa: Bureau of Canadian Archivists, 1992), Glossary, D-5.

16. See ISAD(G), 2: Multilevel description rules, at http://www.archives.ca/ica/CDS/isadg(e).html.

17. ISAD(G), Appendix A2.

18. Steven L. Hensen, *Archives, Personal Papers and Manuscripts: A Cataloging Manual for Archival Repositories, Historical Societies, and Manuscript Libraries* (Washington, DC: 1983).

19. See the exchange between Steven Hansen and Heather MacNeil regarding the adequacy of the rules in *APPM* to construct a multilevel description in *Archivaria,* Number 31 (Winter 1990-91), pp. 5-9.

20. Kent M. Haworth, "The Voyage of *RAD*: From the Old World to the New," *Archivaria* 36 (Autumn 1993): 7, and Elio Lodolini, "The War of Independence of Archivists," *Archivaria* 28 (Summer 1989): 41.

21. *Encoded Archival Description Tag Library, Version 1.0* (Chicago: Society of American Archivists, 1998), 1-3.

22. See *The XML Cover Pages,* at http://www.oasis-open.org/cover/sgml-xml.html, for more information on SGML and XML.

23. Wendy M. Duff and Kent M. Haworth, "Advancing Archival Description: A Model for Rationalising North American Descriptive Standards," *Archives and Manuscripts* 25, no. 2 (November 1997): 210-211.

24. Known as the "Toronto Accords," participants at the meeting acknowledged that a common North American descriptive standard would be of great benefit to users both in the United States and Canada, and that a common descriptive standard would be more cost-effective since archivists in both countries would only have to develop and maintain one set of standards, not two.

25. A graphic illustration of the integral relationships between authority records and descriptive records in a complete archival description is given by Hugo Stibbe in "Standardising Description . . . " op. cit., 149.

26. Heather MacNeil, "The Reviewer Responds," *Archivaria* 31 (Winter 1990-91): 9.

27. Luciana Duranti, "Origin and Development of the Concept of Archival Description," *Archivaria* 35 (Spring 1993): 52.

The Development and Structure of the Encoded Archival Description (EAD) Document Type Definition

Janice E. Ruth

SUMMARY. Although there has been recent speculation about applying the Encoded Archival Description (EAD) Document Type Definition (DTD) to a host of descriptive outputs, including catalog records and subject guides, its perceived need, design, and development emerged from the American archival community's focus on that special subset of finding aids known as collection inventories and registers. This article briefly analyzes the traditional function and structure of these finding aids in a paper-based form and explores how longtime interest in disseminating these guides electronically led to the formation of the Berkeley Finding Aid Project in 1993, and five years later, to the version 1.0 release of EAD. The author provides a basic outline of EAD's structure and demonstrates that although much of its design stems from American archival practice, its developers tried from the outset to create a data model that would merit international support and address the needs of a wide variety of archival institutions both in the United States and abroad.

Janice E. Ruth is Writer/Editor and Manuscript Specialist in Women's History, Manuscript Division, Library of Congress, Washington, DC 20540-4680 (E-mail: jrut@loc.gov).

[Haworth co-indexing entry note]: "The Development and Structure of the Encoded Archival Description (EAD) Document Type Definition." Ruth, Janice E. Co-published simultaneously in *Journal of Internet Cataloging* (The Haworth Information Press, an imprint of The Haworth Press, Inc.) Vol. 4, No. 3/4, 2001, pp. 27-59; and: *Encoded Archival Description on the Internet* (ed: Daniel V. Pitti, and Wendy M. Duff) The Haworth Information Press, an imprint of The Haworth Press, Inc., 2001, pp. 27-59. Single or multiple copies of this article are available for a fee from The Haworth Document Delivery Service [1-800-342-9678, 9:00 a.m. - 5:00 p.m. (EST). E-mail address: getinfo@haworthpressinc.com].

KEYWORDS. Archival description, Berkeley Finding Aid Project, Encoded Archival Description, EAD, finding aids

INTRODUCTION TO FINDING AIDS

Is there a guide to the materials? This simple question, as reference archivists the world over know, is frequently asked by experienced researchers who have discovered that archival repositories routinely create detailed guides to the larger collections or fonds under their control. These researchers know that such guides, commonly called handlists, inventories, registers, or finding aids, are essential access tools for conveying information about the arrangement and content of often large and complex bodies of personal papers, corporate archives, and government records. They have learned that such finding aids contain far more information about a collection than can be captured in a summary catalog record. In fact, a catalog record, if it exists at all, is simply an abstract of the longer, more detailed analysis and description found in the finding aid.

Finding aids are generally created in the course of processing a collection and usually reflect the hierarchical arrangement of the materials. They embody the archival view of the materials not as discrete, individually described items but as groups of related documents that are arranged and analyzed collectively in an effort to preserve their context and reflect the relationships between items. Often, many finding aids start by describing a large group of materials, usually the entire collection or record group, and then move to a description of the series or first-level components, followed by descriptions of smaller and smaller components, such as subseries, files, and possibly even items. The description at the lower levels inherits the description of the preceding levels so as to minimize the need to repeat shared information. Although finding aids vary in length and format according to the repository and the nature of the materials, many finding aids contain similar types or categories of information. Some portion of the finding aid usually includes information about the collection's provenance (or source) and the conditions under which it may be consulted, reproduced, or quoted. A biographical note or organizational history lists the important dates and events in the life of the individual or group featured in the collection. A scope and content note describes the arrangement of the materials, the topics covered, and any notable gaps or weaknesses in the collection. A description of the series may outline the major groups or divisions within the collection, and a hierarchical list often identifies in progressive detail the contents of the papers, usually down to the file (and sometimes item) level, together with each file's corresponding microfilm or box number.

Because of the importance of finding aids to the research process, archivists have been eager for many years to find an effective means of searching them online and disseminating them electronically to distant users. This desire to provide structured and predictable remote access to finding aids fueled the development of Encoded Archival Description (EAD), a data structure standard or encoding scheme based on the rules of Standard Generalized Markup Language (SGML) and Extensible Markup Language (XML). This article briefly explores the origins, growth, and structure of EAD. It suggests that EAD's development not only stems from recent technological advances but also from the archival and library communities' longtime interests in access, descriptive standards, and information storage and retrieval. EAD's structure reflects these traditional archival concerns and practices, and hopefully paves the way for improvements and electronic enhancements to that valuable class of documents known as finding aids.

EARLY EFFORTS TO DISTRIBUTE SUMMARY DESCRIPTIONS OF ARCHIVAL MATERIALS

EAD is the latest in a series of efforts by archivists to help remote researchers identify collections relevant to their topics. Especially before the advent of online catalogs and finding aids, researchers learned of pertinent collections by word-of-mouth from colleagues, by scanning footnotes and bibliographical references, by addressing numerous letters and telephone inquiries to multiple repositories, and by undertaking time-consuming and expensive research trips. Archivists assisted prospective researchers by issuing press releases about new acquisitions, putting notices in historical journals, and publishing repository guides which summarized their institution's holdings. Although all these methods were helpful, they were not always the most efficient or cost-effective strategy for identifying pertinent research holdings scattered across multiple institutions. At the urging of historians, archivists, and other interested parties, two complementary projects arose in the United States in the early 1950s to address the need for a national union listing or catalog of archival materials.[1]

In 1951, the National Historical Publications Commission (NHPC, later renamed the National Historical Publications and Records Commission, NHPRC) began to compile collection-level descriptions of archival and manuscript holdings in more than thirteen hundred American repositories. A decade later, the commission published its work as *A Guide to Archives and Manuscripts in the United States,* edited by Philip Hamer.[2] Also in the early 1950s, the Library of Congress, which had previously developed the *National Union Catalog* for printed works, began planning a comparable union listing for manuscript holdings, whereby individual institutions could submit descriptive summaries of important single manuscripts or entire collections to the Library's Descriptive Cataloging Division, which in turn would publish the submissions annually or biannually in book form for distribution to subscribing institutions. The first volume of this new *National Union Catalog of Manuscript Collections* (NUCMC) was published in 1962, with twenty-eight subsequent volumes appearing during the next thirty-two years.[3]

Shortly after these print publications appeared, a new corollary development in library cataloging surfaced, which would have important ramifications for the archival world, particularly in the United States. In 1966, with a grant from the Council on Library Resources, the Library of Congress developed a pilot project named MARC (for Machine-Readable Cataloging) to test the feasibility and utility of distributing cataloging data in machine-readable form (magnetic tapes at the time) from the Library of Congress to sixteen participating libraries throughout the country. The content of the new, machine-readable cataloging record was similar to that found on the traditional paper catalog card, in that it included information about a work's title, author, edition, publication information, physical description, access points, subject headings, and call number, but each piece of data was presented in a discrete segment known as a field or subfield, which was preceded by brief numbers, letters, symbols or other "signposts" that helped the computer recognize where the field began and to anticipate the type of data it contained. By consistently assigning the information typically found on catalog cards into uniform fields across records, the new MARC system allowed for predictable exchange of data from one institution's computer system to another. It also permitted the development of computer programs that could search for and retrieve certain types of information within specific fields and that would format the information correctly for either online display or printed output.[4] These benefits of consistent descriptive markup did not go unnoticed by EAD's developers thirty years later.

The success of the MARC pilot project led to the establishment of the MARC Distribution Service at the Library of Congress in early 1969. It also resulted in the development among college and university libraries of joint bibliographic utilities designed to encourage the creation and exchange of shared cataloging data for copies of works held by multiple repositories.[5] These online databases, in turn, helped to foster the continued growth of the original MARC format and led to its subsequent revision and adoption by many archivists and manuscript curators. In the first few years after its creation, the original LCMARC format evolved into a national USMARC standard, and the initial focus on English-language book materials was expanded to include other languages and types of material. In 1973, the first MARC format for manuscripts was published. Unfortunately, its emphasis on item-level description made it unsuitable for the type of collection-level cataloging undertaken by most American archivists. Eight years later, however, the Library of Congress expressed a willingness to revise the manuscript format, and the Society of American Archivists' National Information Systems Task Force (NISTF) took the lead in developing a new data structure standard, which became known as the USMARC Archival and Manuscripts Control (MARC AMC) format, released by the library in 1984.[6]

In the fifteen years since the development of MARC AMC, archivists have created and distributed to the RLIN and OCLC databases nearly 800,000 collection-level catalog records providing important access to archival and manuscript holdings scattered throughout the United States.[7] The creation of these records has been aided, in part, by the community-wide adoption of *Archives, Personal Papers, and Manuscripts* (APPM), a set of cataloging rules and content guidelines first developed in 1983 at the Library of Congress as a supplement to the second edition of the *Anglo-American Cataloging Rules* (AACR2).[8] The use of APPM, AACR2, and the Library of Congress Subject Headings (LCSH) all helped to standardize the content of archival catalog records. The MARC AMC format provided the framework for organizing and exchanging this standardized data, while OCLC, RLIN, and other nationally networked computer databases provided the technical means for building the kind of centralized union catalog envisioned by archivists since the beginnings of the NHPC and NUCMC projects thirty years earlier. In addition to the immediate benefits of widely distributing information about archival and manuscript holdings, the successful implementation of the MARC AMC format also taught American archivists the value of community-based descriptive standards, a lesson that would bear fruit a decade later during the development of EAD.

As important as MARC AMC has been, it nevertheless fell short of full descriptive access. Despite creative efforts to stretch its limits, the MARC format could not contain the wealth of information residing in collection inventories, registers, and other finding aids. The collection-level catalog record, whether captured on card stock or in a MARC AMC-compliant system, continued to be only an abstract of the fuller description found in the finding aid. At best, the MARC AMC system helped researchers identify the titles and locations of relevant collections. It also, through a note field on an individual record, alerted the researcher to the existence of a fuller finding aid. Most such finding aids, however, were available until recently only in paper form and could be obtained only by visiting the holding institution or by ordering a copy by mail. What was needed was a union database of finding aids.

PROVIDING REMOTE ACCESS TO FINDING AIDS

The first such attempt to provide union access to finding aids coincided with the development of the MARC AMC format. In the early to mid-1980s, Chadwyck-Healy released the microfiche publication *National Inventory of Documentary Sources in the United States* (Teaneck, NJ: Chadwyck-Healy, 1983). As part of this commercial endeavor, participating archives and libraries submitted finding aids to the publisher to be reproduced on microfiche and distributed to purchasing institutions. Printed indices provided access to more than fifty thousand finding aids contributed by more than three hundred repositories. The significance of such widespread participation and remote access notwithstanding, the limitations of non-searchable, non-machine-readable finding aid data captured on static microfiche soon became apparent as more and more institutions began creating and storing their finding aids electronically in word processing software and database systems.

A potential solution presented itself in the early 1990s with the emergence of the Internet and the development of the Gopher technology at the University of Minnesota. Shortly thereafter, many archival institutions began establishing Gopher sites and mounting their finding aids on them. These ASCII finding aids provided both advantages and disadvantages to existing paper versions. On the plus side, the Gopher environment presented the first real opportunity to provide readily available remote access to these important descriptive tools. It also offered the unprecedented potential to conduct keyword (character-string) searching both within and across finding aids. Saved as simple ASCII files, the documents could be mounted with relatively little effort and technical expertise, and the files could be easily downloaded, printed, and mailed around. Moreover, the displayed documents preserved the indentation used in many finding aids to reflect the intellectual hierarchy of the collection arrangement and description. They also retained the blank line spaces that suggested breaks in either the physical or intellectual structure of the materials, and they recreated the columnar layout of paper finding aids that was used for the simultaneous display of dual hierarchies, i.e., the intellectual organization of a collection is represented by text running down one column, while the physical arrangement is indicated through box, folder, or item numbers descending an opposite column.

Accompanying these notable advantages, however, were several significant drawbacks to the Gopher finding aids. Many of the navigational clues embedded in paper-based finding aids did not transcend this new online environment. Users could no longer skim the document as easily as in paper form, where tables of contents, indices, page numbers, and page and column headings helped provide context to often complex arrangements of materials.

The lack of hyperlinks in Gopher documents also meant that jumping from section to section in a large guide was often easier in paper form than scrolling or paging through the same-sized document online. Also unsupported by the Gopher technology were various typographical conventions, such as boldface, italics, and font sizes, which had helped in the paper guides to indicate hierarchical levels within the collection and to alert readers to information of special significance.

Many of the problems associated with Gopher finding aids disappeared a few years later with the development of the World Wide Web, the Internet's new graphical interface. Documents intended for Web distribution could now be encoded with HyperText Markup Language (HTML), an SGML document type definition designed to facilitate online display and hypermedia. Using HTML, archivists could regain some of the typographical and navigational aspects of their paper-based finding aids. Colors, fonts, italics, and boldface helped to differentiate types of information within HTML-encoded finding aids. Linking capabilities permitted easier navigation within large files and facilitated dividing big documents into smaller, more manageable files which could be accessed through electronic tables of contents or links from one file to another. This same linking capability, coupled with the development of Web-based interfaces to repositories' online public access catalogs (OPACs), made it possible to jump directly online between a collection's summary catalog record and its more detailed finding aid. Further linking could be employed to retrieve other Web documents or related digital images, including digital surrogates of the archival materials described within the finding aid.

Despite the benefits of these newer Web-based finding aids, certain limitations soon surfaced as well. HTML provided no means for encoding the intellectual structure or content of the finding aids. It consisted of a small set of procedurally oriented markup tags that control only the presentation and display of the document. As was the case with both the MARC format and the earlier Gopher technology, HTML could not adequately represent the hierarchical structure of finding aids. Its limited tag set precluded descriptive markup, making it even less suitable than MARC for designating the content of finding aids. For example, HTML allowed the encoder to identify and then control the font size, color, and other presentation of certain structural elements of finding aids such as paragraphs, headings, and so on, but it could not distinguish a scope and content note from a biographical summary, a personal name from a geographic name, or a series title from a file heading.[9] Without the ability to assign the data to discrete fields based on descriptive content, as MARC does for catalog records, HTML could not support element-specific searching or other complex processing of the text. Furthermore, this lack of descriptive markup, coupled with the fact that HTML is not a fully accepted standard, presented potential problems for formal interchange and migration of finding aid data over time.

BERKELEY FINDING AID PROJECT

At about the same time that many institutions were first beginning to experiment with HTML markup of their finding aids, researchers at the University of California, Berkeley, had already begun to seek an alternative approach that would overcome the inherent limitations of HTML and Gopher delivery of finding aid data. In 1993, Berkeley library staff, under the direction of Daniel Pitti, had received a grant from the Department of Education's Title IIA Program, to investigate the possibility of developing a nonproprietary encoding standard for machine-readable finding aids. Pitti quickly established that, at a minimum, any proposed standard would need to be able to do the following: present the extensive descriptive information found in archival finding aids; preserve the hierarchical relationships that exist between levels of descriptive detail; represent descriptive information that is inherited by one hierarchical level from another; navigate within a hierarchical information architecture; and conduct element-specific indexing and retrieval.[10]

Gopher and HTML presentation of ASCII text were both inadequate in fulfilling these requirements. Pitti thus turned his attention to the MARC format as a possible encoding structure for finding aids. He was aware that the archival community in the United States was already heavily invested in using MARC for collection-level cataloging, and he was attracted to MARC's focus on descriptive markup and its status as a publicly owned international standard. Nevertheless, further examination of MARC led Pitti to eliminate it as an option for three reasons: MARC could not handle a finding aid longer than 100,000 characters (approximately thirty printed pages of text); its flat database design made it a poor vehicle for conveying the hierarchical relationships between materials in an archival collection; and the MARC user community was too small to command the attention of most commercial software developers.[11] In analyzing MARC's advantages and disadvantages, Pitti became aware of Standard Generalized Markup Language (SGML) as a viable alternative that shared MARC's "strengths of descriptive markup and public ownership" but overcame "its weaknesses of limited record and field length, hierarchical poverty, and small market appeal."[12]

SGML, a registered international standard since 1987, is a public, nonproprietary technique for defining and expressing the logical structure of documents.[13] It is the metalanguage or grammar used to write Document Type Definitions (DTDs), which are sets of rules for marking up and encoding classes of documents so that the text therein may be searched, retrieved, displayed, and exchanged in a predictable, platform-independent manner. A DTD identifies portions of text commonly found in a class of documents and assigns to each portion a unique element name and definition. It also establishes the relationship between those portions of text. In the same way that the MARC format divides the information in a catalog record into various descriptive fields or data categories, an SGML DTD can designate or specify the elements of information in a finding aid. It can provide a uniform data structure that encourages consistent markup across finding aids and enables more successful machine processing (searching, retrieval, display, and so on) of the data.

All text in an SGML document is bound within at least one element. Every element within a DTD can be represented in the document by a short alphanumeric word (or "tag") captured as simple ASCII characters that surround the text (or content) being designated. These tags, which are enclosed in angle brackets, indicate to a computer where the text of an element begins and ends. For example, the beginning of a paragraph may be marked as <p> and the end of the same paragraph as </p>. Similarly, the beginning of a scope and content note within a finding aid may be identified with the element tag <scopecontent>, and the end of that same note with the close tag </scopecontent>.

Elements may also be nested inside of other elements, making SGML particularly well suited for the hierarchical data structure of finding aids. Thus within the <scopecontent> element, structural elements such as paragraphs <p> and lists <list>, or content elements such as personal names <persname> or subjects <subject>, may be further designated. Even more importantly, the description of an archival file may be nested inside the description of its parent subseries, which in turn may be nested inside the description of the archival series. This nesting establishes the hierarchical links between elements and allows for data from the parent element to be inherited by the subelements. Also inherited are attribute values. Attributes modify element definitions and frequently provide further information about the contents of an element or aspects of its display or retrieval. For example, if the intention is to identify a birth date in a document, a DTD may permit the general designation <date>1929</date>, or it may allow a more precise designation using an attribute named TYPE, e.g., <date TYPE = "birth">1929</date>.

One of the most familiar DTDs in existence is HTML, which, as noted earlier, is designed primarily for procedural markup of documents for presentation and display on the World Wide Web. HTML does not utilize SGML's ability to support full descriptive content designation. The latter liberates a document for multiple purposes. In an SGML document, you need not hard-code how you want the elements to display. Instead, you can simply identify the contents and use an external program called a stylesheet to specify how those contents should be displayed and printed, including whether portions of the text should appear in a dynamically generated navigator frame or table of contents, which provide context when maneuvering long documents. By separating the content of the document from its formatting, SGML allows greater flexibility in using the data. It also makes global display changes easier to implement.

In addition to its ability to handle archival hierarchies and descriptive markup, SGML also appealed to Pitti because it is both a standard and is generalized, meaning that it is endorsed by government and industry groups worldwide and can be applied to any type of document. Because it is a standard, SGML documents are easily interchanged, and software manufacturers are more likely to develop tools and programs for standards. Anyone who has tried to retrieve and revise a document created on a defunct database system or outmoded word processing software knows firsthand the problems with data migration. As a platform-independent, internationally recognized standard, SGML helps to ensure that the data created and encoded today is not rendered useless by the acquisition of new hardware and software tomorrow. Thus, standardized data encoded in SGML should be easier to maintain, upgrade, and migrate to new systems.

Having decided on SGML as the environment for their proposed encoding standard, Pitti and his colleagues set about the task of creating a draft DTD. They began by consulting with various archival experts at other institutions and by analyzing numerous finding aid examples forwarded to them by institutions anxious to cooperate in this new initiative. From their analysis, Pitti's team began to consider how the parts of a finding aid relate to one another, identified some of the basic elements, and started to subdivide the larger parts into smaller and smaller units or subelements. They developed a rudimentary data model, for which Pitti wrote a DTD, and they began the process of encoding representative finding aids and creating a prototype database for searching and display. Throughout the process, Pitti disseminated information about the project and encouraged the participation of a wide cross section of the archival and library worlds, maintaining on numerous occasions that "standards are the products of communities, not of individuals working in splendid isolation."[14]

By March 1995, Pitti and his Berkeley colleagues had drafted a preliminary DTD (called FindAid), encoded nearly two hundred finding aids from fifteen repositories, and created a prototype database for searching and retrieval. Eager to share their results with representatives from the archives and library communities, they convened a three-day Finding Aids Conference in early April, which was jointly sponsored by the Library of the University of California, Berkeley, and the Commission on Preservation and Access. Conference participants reacted favorably to the project's use of SGML, and they agreed that the Berkeley team had achieved its goal of demonstrating that an encoding standard for finding aids was both desirable and feasible. The attendees also noted, however, that additional testing of the DTD was needed, and they recommended that interested institutions forward feedback to Pitti and to members of a research fellowship team which he had recently assembled to evaluate and revise the data model.

BENTLEY FELLOWSHIP FINDING AID TEAM

The research team, consisting of seven archivists and one expert in SGML, met briefly at the conclusion of the Berkeley conference and spent a day exploring the prototype database, discussing design principles, and planning an agenda for a week-long meeting to be held in July at the Bentley Historical Library in Ann Arbor, Michigan.[15] In preparation for their July meeting, team members also read selections from several introductory texts on markup theory and SGML, reviewed design principles for other DTDs (especially those written for the Text Encoding Initiative (TEI) and the USMARC format), studied examples of representative finding aids, and began to experiment with the Berkeley data model and DTD. Most members of the group had little or no experience with SGML, or even HTML, but they were knowledgeable about archival descriptive practices and shared a common understanding of how and why finding aids are constructed, the kinds of information they contain (or should contain), and the uses to which they have been put. It was this knowledge and appreciation of traditional finding aid practices that Pitti hoped to tap when he assembled the team in Ann Arbor.

In creating the FindAid DTD, Pitti felt that it would be inappropriate and premature for him to create a prescriptive or normative model that enforced his own subjective judgments about good descriptive practices. He strived to accommodate all the finding aids that had been submitted to him throughout the course of the Berkeley project. But the steady receipt of new and different finding aids led to frequent revisions to the data model and resulted in a DTD driven as much by the exceptions as by the commonalities among finding aids. The flexibility of the FindAid DTD allowed it to handle the considerable inconsistency and variety in the project's sample finding aids, but Pitti became rightly concerned that this unrestrained permissibility would pose long-term problems for data exchange, DTD upkeep, and search and retrieval capabilities. Anxious for input from the larger archival community, he encouraged the Bentley team to undertake a rigorous critique of the Berkeley model.[16] Team members quickly agreed that his spirit of accommodation and desire to handle every conceivable finding aid, both good and bad, led Pitti to create a model that was somewhat cumbersome and problematic. The number of elements in the FindAid DTD was daunting, and their specificity seemed unnecessary in many instances. Also, in an effort to preserve the physical layout of various finding aids, the FindAid DTD integrated too closely the content of the data with its formatting, a relationship the Bentley team, including Pitti, felt should be more distinct in an SGML environment.

Before systematically reviewing all the elements in the FindAid DTD, however, the Bentley team spent the first part of their week in Ann Arbor creating a set of design principles and goals to guide their work. Named for the meeting site, these principles or accords stated the group's philosophy and outlined the new DTD's intent, parameters, and structural features.[17] Responding first to confusion over the meaning and scope of the term "finding aid," the group decided to limit its focus to that class or subset of documents known specifically as archival inventories and registers. It also determined that, although the DTD should be able to handle most legacy finding aids, its design would be optimized for authoring new guides.

Having thus limited the document class, the design team then confined itself to developing an archetypical data structure, resisting efforts to specify or prescribe the intellectual content that would reside inside that structure. The task was not to develop a data content standard, but to create instead a content designation or encoding standard. The group felt that subsequent content guidelines should be developed to address questions of "best practice" and to do for finding aids what the AACR2 and APPM accomplished for catalog records. The team hoped that by reducing the data model to key elements and structural components and by restricting the use of certain elements to specific locations in the document, the DTD would begin to encourage greater consistency and good practice by not intentionally supporting poor descriptive choices.

Led by Pitti and the other team members most knowledgeable about SGML, the group began tackling three of the most important steps in building the DTD: naming and defining the elements, naming and defining attributes for each element, and determining where and in what sequence elements may appear. To accomplish these tasks, group members analyzed the structure and functionality of traditional finding aids and evaluated existing standards, especially the MARC AMC format and the General International Standard Archival Description (ISAD(G).[18] The latter, as explained more fully in Kent M. Haworth's and Michael J. Fox's articles in this issue, was endorsed by the International Council of Archives (ICA) in 1994 as a guideline to be followed in the preparation of archival finding aids. The Bentley team accepted the following ISAD(G) assumptions: (1) a finding aid consists of hierarchically organized information describing a unit of records or papers along with its component parts, (2) information in the finding aid is inherited from one descriptive level to another, (3) information given at a higher level should not be repeated at lower levels, and (4) descriptions of both the whole and the various component parts each comprise the same essential data elements.

The design group was also cautious about adding to the DTD every element a team member could identify. Each proposed element was expected to support one of the following functions: description, control, navigation, indexing, or online and print presentation. The intellectual order of the archival materials was also given precedence over the physical arrangement of the items.

The DTD that emerged from the week's deliberations was renamed Encoded Archival Description, or EAD. It differed from the earlier FindAid model in several ways, some of which are discussed more fully later in this article. Essentially, it separated information about the finding aid from information about the body of archival materials being described. It replaced the FindAid's collection divisions and materials lists with the more open-ended concept of recursive "component descriptions." This created a model more analogous to the hierarchical, multilevel approach outlined in ISAD(G), in that the EAD finding aid could begin with a summary description of the whole unit and proceed to descriptions of the component parts using the same essential descriptive elements at each level. The group eliminated many elements, which were found to be duplicative or unnecessary, while at the same time it increased the use of attributes to permit more specific content designation when needed. Also at this early stage of EAD's development, preliminary discussions occurred concerning various ideas for electronic enhancements to finding aids and for creating linking, reference, and display elements that were in accordance with existing hypertext and hypermedia conventions and that could be supported by current or anticipated software.

EARLY WORK ON THE ALPHA VERSION OF THE DTD

The annual meeting of the Society of American Archivists, held in late August 1995, provided an opportunity for Pitti and members of the Bentley development team to report on their progress to a large group of interested colleagues. It also marked the establishment of the EAD Working Group under the auspices of the society's Committee on Archival Information Exchange (CAIE). The EAD Working Group accepted responsibility for monitoring and supporting the ongoing development of the EAD DTD and its necessary documentation. Equally important, it expanded the development team's membership to involve an even broader range of archivists and information professionals, including a leading archival educator and representatives from the Library of Congress Network Development and MARC Standards Office, the Research Libraries Group (RLG), and the Online Computer Library Center (OCLC).[19] Shortly after the SAA meeting, Pitti released for review an early version of the EAD data model and prototype DTD based on the work accomplished in Ann Arbor by the Bentley team. Known colloquially as the "straw man DTD," this early version was distributed to a small group of "early implementors" who had agreed to review and test it.

Two weeks later, in early November 1995, the Library of Congress National Digital Library Program (NDLP) sponsored a meeting of the original Bentley team in Washington, D.C., to refine the data model and to meet with Debbie Lapeyre, an SGML expert with ATLIS Consulting Group, who had been retained by the Library of Congress to assist in revising the "straw man" DTD and to create an EAD tag library which would explain to users the purpose and valid application of all the DTD's elements and attributes. The NDLP, which was then grappling with ways to manage large numbers of digital items collectively, was interested in EAD's potential for situating finding aids in a tiered online access system, "in which collection-level [catalog] records lead to finding aids, and finding aids lead to computer surrogates of primary source materials that exist in a variety of native formats: pictorial materials, graphics, three-dimensional objects, manuscripts, typescripts, printed texts, sound recordings, motion pictures, and so on."[20]

In early January 1996, a subset of the Bentley team met in Los Angeles, California, to review the DTD and tag library prepared by Lapeyre and Pitti. Also at this gathering, which was sponsored by the Council on Library Resources (later Council on Library and Information Resources), the team met with Anne Gilliland-Swetland and Thomas La Porte to outline the content of EAD application guidelines, which the two had been hired to write. Following that meeting, Pitti and Lapeyre made additional changes to the DTD, and Bentley team member Janice Ruth edited and revised the draft tag library. As this work was nearing completion, the Library of Congress Network Development and MARC Standards Office (ND/MSO) responded favorably to SAA's request that it serve as the maintenance agency for EAD. Under their agreement, the Library would make the DTD and support documentation available and act as a clearinghouse for communications on EAD, chiefly through the establishment of a Listserv and Web site. SAA, in turn, would retain intellectual control and remain responsible for ongoing development of the standard. Thus, in its new role, the ND/MSO posted on its EAD Web site the first official or "alpha" version of the DTD on 26 February 1996. To ensure the broadest possible access, mirror copies of both the DTD and tag library were also made available at the University of California, Berkeley, Web site.

PREPARATION AND RELEASE OF THE BETA VERSION

Within a few weeks of the alpha release, various institutions and consortia began implementing EAD, notably the Library of Congress, the Berkeley and San Diego campuses of the University of California, Duke, Yale, and Harvard universities, the SOLINET Monticello Project, and the NEH-funded Dance Heritage Coalition. These and other institutions gathered important feedback about the DTD's strengths and weaknesses, and within two months, the EAD developers began planning for a revised beta version at a meeting in late April 1996, which also included a review of the draft application guidelines prepared by Gilliland-Swetland and La Porte.[21] In the months following the April meeting, EAD team members engaged in lengthy email discussions concerning proposed changes to the DTD. Pitti completed a new draft in mid-June 1996, which was modified slightly after SAA's annual meeting in late August and was then publicly released as the beta version of the DTD in mid-September 1996.[22] A beta version tag library, prepared by Gilliland-Swetland and La Porte, appeared in October 1996, and draft application guidelines followed two months later.

Release of the beta DTD and its documentation generated increased interest in EAD among institutions that had previously worked with the alpha version as well as among newcomers with little prior knowledge of the encoding standard. Major implementation projects were undertaken by consortia and small and large institutions throughout the United States and abroad.[23] To help foster this interest, the Research Libraries Group (RLG) obtained funding from the Delmas Foundation to develop EAD training classes for its member institutions.[24] Since the first EAD workshop in July 1996, instructors Kris Kiesling, Michael J. Fox, Jackie Dooley, and Richard Szary have taught more than thirty workshops throughout the United States and in Canada, England, Ireland, and Australia. These hands-on workshops have introduced more than six hundred archivists, librarians, and systems administrators to EAD, first under the aegis of RLG and since September 1997 as part of SAA's continuing education program. Other archivists have received instruction through their institution's internal training and by attending classes and presentations given by various EAD Working Group members and early implementors. Supplementing these formal courses has been the generous exchange of ideas and advice disseminated via the official EAD Listserv maintained by the Library of Congress and the separate EAD Help Pages Web site created by SAA's EAD Roundtable in September 1998.[25]

PREPARATION AND RELEASE OF VERSION 1.0 OF THE EAD DTD

About a year after the beta release, the full EAD Working Group, which had been expanded by then to include two non-American archivists, assembled in Washington, D.C., in early November 1997 to discuss changes to the DTD, many of which had been proposed by early implementors during a formal comment period.[26] At this meeting, which was supported by a grant from the Delmas Foundation, the working group reviewed nearly fifty email messages sent from beta testers around the world, including the National Archives of Sweden, the British Public Records Office, the Bodleian Library (UK), Durham University (UK), and the University of Saskatchewan (Canada). The majority of the correspondents recommended changes to the DTD based upon their experience with the beta version or their analysis of its relationship to other archival data structures or content standards such as MARC, ISAD-G, and the Canadian Rules for Archival Description (RAD). Group members reached consensus after considering such factors as the global applicability of the proposed change, the amount of retrospective conversion a desired change would require, and whether other changes or existing DTD structures would achieve the same result more effectively.

In late January 1998, the working group prepared and released two detailed email messages to the EAD Listserv outlining the changes that it had agreed to incorporate in the DTD's next release (Version 1.0) and the proposals that it had declined to enact.[27] Although it was anxious to provide the community with a revised DTD, the group decided to postpone releasing Version 1.0 until later in the summer to ensure greater compatibility with the emerging Extensible Markup Language (XML) standard, which was just entering the final stages of development. As a more content-aware language than HTML, XML offered the potential for forthcoming versions of Web browsers like Netscape and Internet Explorer to display EAD-encoded finding aids in their native SGML without requiring helper applications like Panorama. Although parts of XML and its related standards, Extensible Stylesheet Language (XSL) and Extensible Linking Language (XLL), still remained unclear, Pitti and other team members felt that XML development had reached sufficient stability to proceed with releasing Version 1.0 of the EAD DTD at the end of August 1998 to coincide with the SAA annual meeting, held in Orlando, Florida. Accompanying Version 1.0 of the DTD was a completely revised and updated EAD tag library, which had been compiled by working group members during Spring and early Summer 1998.[28]

OVERVIEW OF THE EAD VERSION 1.0 STRUCTURE[29]

Although significant improvements occurred with each iteration of the EAD DTD, much of the Version 1.0 structure, released in 1998, resembles the model created during the design team's first meeting in Ann Arbor three years earlier. At that meeting, it was determined that the information within most finding aids could be divided initially into two broad categories: one that consists of information about the finding aid itself (its title, compiler, compilation date, and so on); and another that includes information about a body of archival materials (a collection, a record group, a fonds, or a series).[30] As shown in Figure 1, the EAD DTD splits the first category, consisting of metadata for the finding aid, into two high-level elements known as EAD Header <eadheader> and Front Matter <frontmatter>. The second category, consisting of information about the archival materials, is designated by a third high-level element named Archival Description <archdesc>. All three of these high-level elements are contained within the outermost element named Encoded Archival Description <ead>. Although the mandatory <eadheader> element and the optional <frontmatter> element would actually appear before the <archdesc> element in a valid EAD finding aid, this overview will begin with the <archdesc> element since it encompasses the bulk of the finding aid and contains the descriptive elements necessary for building a good archival inventory.

The <archdesc> element is an excellent example of how EAD exploits SGML's nesting capabilities to accommodate the hierarchical arrangement of archival materials and the finding aids that describe them. It allows for a description of the entire corpus of the materials at the highest or unit level followed by nested, detailed descriptions of the unit's parts, which are designated by Component <c> elements. The descriptions of the nested parts are bundled inside one or more Description of Subordinate Components <dsc> elements, thus mirroring the unfolding hierarchy of a finding aid that progresses from the broad summary descriptions of a collection, fonds, or record group to the progressively more detailed descriptions of lower-level series, subseries, files, and possibly even items. Following the ISAD (G) model, data elements used to describe the whole unit at the <archdesc> level are repeatable at all the <c> levels within the <dsc> as illustrated in Figure 1. In addition, at each level, information is inherited from the higher levels that precede it. This includes information about the content, context, and extent of the archival materials as

FIGURE 1. High-Level Model for the Encoded Archival Description (EAD) DTD

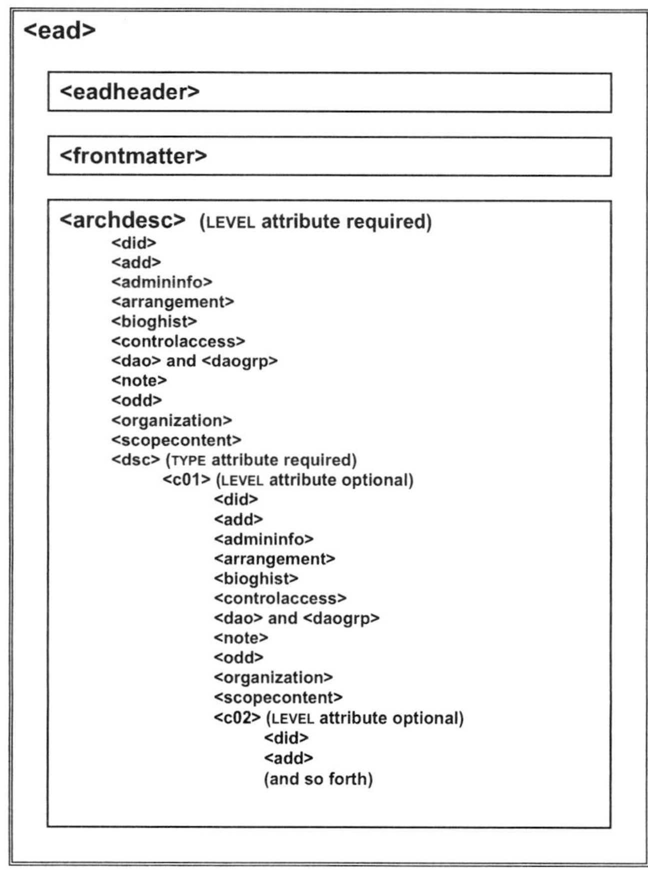

well as any optional supplemental information that facilitates their use by researchers.

For example, an archivist may begin to build an EAD finding aid by first determining the nature of the materials being described, i.e., do the items, in their entirety, constitute a record group, a collection, a fonds, a series, a subseries, and so on? The answer to this question is recorded with the required LEVEL attribute on the <archdesc> element so as to identify the highest tier of the materials being described. After identifying this first level of description, the archivist then proceeds to record some basic facts about the whole body of materials using the required Descriptive Identification <did> element. The

<did> is a "wrapper" or parent element that groups or bundles an optional Heading <head> element followed by twelve other (mostly optional) content-based elements that are thought to be among the most important for ensuring a good basic description of an archival unit or component. These core subelements identify such fundamental information as the creator of the materials; the title, dates, and extent of the materials; the repository where they are held; a short abstract of their contents; and any pertinent identification numbers or storage locations affiliated with them (see Figure 2).

Often the information captured in the highest-level <did> resembles the descriptive summary found in a collection-level catalog record. Appearing as it

FIGURE 2. Elements Under Descriptive Identification <did>

<did>

<head> Heading: Title or caption for a section of text

<abstract> Abstract: Brief summary of the materials being described, occasionally extracted from longer scope and content notes <scopecontent> and creator sketches <bioghist> elsewhere in the guide

<container> Container: Number of the carton, box, folder, or other holding unit in which the archival materials are arranged and stored

<dao> Digital Archival Object and <daogrp> Digital Archival Object Group: Used to link to digital surrogates of the material being described in the finding aid

<note> Note: General comments, citations, or annotations but not summary descriptive information about the archival materials

<origination> Origination: Individuals or organizations responsible for the creation or assembly of the archival materials

<physdesc> Physical Description: Extent, dimensions, genre, form, and other physical characteristics

<physloc> Physical Location: Stack number, shelf designation, or other storage location

<repository> Repository: Institution responsible for providing intellectual access

<unitdate> Date of the Unit: Creation dates of the archival materials

<unitid> Identification of the Unit: An accession number, classification number, lot number, or other such unique and permanent identifier

<unittitle> Title of the Unit: Title of the archival materials at whatever level they are being described, such as collection title, series title, subseries title, file title, or item title

does immediately inside the <archdesc> element, this high-level <did> enables a researcher to determine whether the materials are pertinent without having to read far into the finding aid. This is especially important online where retrieval of summary data helps the user interpret search results quickly and accurately. In addition to facilitating resource discovery and recognition at the highest-level, the gathering of descriptive subelements within the parent <did> insures that the same data elements and structure are available at every level of description within the EAD hierarchy and helps remind encoders to capture descriptive information they may otherwise overlook.

Not every <did> subelement is used at every level of description. For the high-level <did>, the elements <head>, <repository>, <origination>, <unittitle>, <unitdate>, <physdesc>, and <abstract> are most frequently used. The <unitid> and <physloc> elements may also be useful at this level when describing the materials as a whole, but the elements <container>, <note>, <dao>, and <daogrp> are more likely to appear in the <did> elements within lower Component <c> levels. Conversely, the <origination> and <repository> elements are rarely used at the <c> levels since the information they contain has been encoded at the <archdesc> unit level and inherited by the subordinate components.

Various attributes are associated with the <did> subelements to enable more specific content designation. Of particular significance is the optional ENCODINGANALOG attribute, which permits the designation of a comparable field or area in another descriptive encoding system, such as ISAD (G) or the USMARC format. By using ENCODINGANALOG attributes to designate applicable MARC fields or subfields together with the authoritative form of the data, archivists may be able to generate skeletal, collection-level MARC records automatically from EAD finding aids. Use of such analogs may also help retrieval and indexing systems identify comparable data elements that appear in both bibliographic records and finding aids. Figure 3 shows a fully encoded <archdesc> <did> with USMARC ENCODINGANALOG attributes.

After using the <did> subelements to capture a basic description at the <archdesc> level, the archivist may proceed directly to a description of the unit's component parts. More likely, however, the finding aid creator will provide additional narrative information about the content and extent of the archival unit as well as information that provides contextual details about the creation and function of the materials. This description usually appears in prose form within elements named Administrative Information <admininfo>, Biography or History <bioghist>, Scope and Content <scopecontent>, Organization <organization>, and Arrangement <arrangement>, which are suggestive of the categories of information traditionally found in archival finding aids. Structurally, from an SGML perspective, the content models for these

FIGURE 3. High-Level Unit Description with MARC Encoding Analogs

```
<archdesc level="collection" langmaterial="eng" type="register">
    <did>
        <head>Collection Summary</head>
        <origination label="Creator">
            <persname encodinganalog="100"> Stanton, Elizabeth Cady, 1815-
            1902</persname>
        </origination>
        <unittitle label="Title" encodinganalog="245">Elizabeth Cady Stanton Papers
            <unitdate label="Dates" type="inclusive" encodinganalog="260"> 1814-1946,
            bulk 1840-1902</unitdate>
        </unittitle>
        <physdesc label="Extent">
            <extent encodinganalog="300">4.3 linear feet; 1,000 items</extent>
        </physdesc>
        <repository label="Repository" encodinganalog="852">
            <corpname>
                <subarea>Manuscript Division,</subarea>Library of Congress
            </corpname>
        </repository>
        <abstract label="Abstract" encodinganalog="520">Reformer and feminist.
        Correspondence, speeches, articles, drafts of books, scrapbooks, and printed matter
        documenting Elizabeth Cady Stanton's career as an advocate for women's rights.
        Includes material on her efforts on behalf of women's legal status and women's
        suffrage, the abolition of slavery, rights for African Americans following the Civil War,
        temperance, and other nineteenth-century social reform movements.</abstract>
    </did>
```

Collection Summary

Creator:	Stanton, Elizabeth Cady, 1815-1902
Title:	Elizabeth Cady Stanton Papers
Dates:	1814-1946, bulk 1840-1902
Extent:	4.3 linear feet; 1,000 items
Repository:	Manuscript Division, Library of Congress
Abstract:	Reformer and feminist. Correspondence, speeches, articles, drafts of books, scrapbooks, and printed matter documenting Elizabeth Cady Stanton's career as an advocate for women's rights. Includes material on her efforts on behalf of women's legal status and women's suffrage, the abolition of slavery, rights for African Americans following the Civil War, temperance, and other nineteenth-century social reform movements.

narrative-based elements are "heads" and "text," meaning that an optional Heading <head> may be followed by text contained within Paragraphs <p> or Lists <list>. This differs in structure from the information within the <did> subelements, which is generally presented as short, labeled phrases or simple data strings not requiring paragraph formatting. Once text is wrapped within a <p> to facilitate online formatting and print output, a host of subelements becomes available within <p>, including various descriptive subelements, useful reference and linking elements, additional formatting elements, and ten controlled access elements (discussed later in this article).

Because it helps to illustrate EAD's accommodation of various degrees of content designation, let us consider in greater detail the <admininfo> element mentioned above. This element contains descriptive background information concerning an institution's acquisition, processing, and management of a body of archival materials. It designates facts about provenance, acquisition, access and reproduction restrictions, availability of microform and digital surrogates, preferred form of citation, and other descriptive details that help readers of the finding aid know how to approach the archival materials and make use of the information they find. All the specific descriptive details captured in <admininfo> have their own corresponding elements in the DTD–with tag names such as <custodhist>, <accruals>, <acqinfo>, <appraisal>, <accessrestrict>, <userestrict>, <altformavail>, <prefercite>, and <processinfo>–which may be applied individually if desired. Should such specificity in tagging not be needed or cannot be afforded, the archivist may elect to tag the entire body of information at the parent level, <admininfo>, and not to encode separately the text relating to each nested subelement.

DESCRIBING ARCHIVAL MATERIALS AT THE COMPONENT LEVEL

Once an archivist has completed the description of the records or papers at the highest (or unit) level, focus shifts to describing one or more of the unit's component parts. Although the concept of component descriptions is well grounded in ISAD(G) and RAD, some archivists, especially in the United States, have expressed confusion about how these components are represented in EAD. It is important to remember that components are intellectual, logical subdivisions of the previously described archival unit; they are not determined by their physical storage devices. In other words, the boxes and folders in which the materials are housed are not the components of the collection; instead components are entities like series, subseries, files, and items. Components are not only nested under the <archdesc> element, they are usually nested inside of one another. For example, series are parts of collections, record groups, and fonds. Similarly, subseries are parts not only of their parent series but of their "grandparent" unit as well. Subseries, in turn, are comprised of files, which subsequently consist of other files and/or items. The description of any single component inherits the description of its parents, grandparents, great-grandparents, and so on. Traditionally, in paper-based finding aids, this inheritance was conveyed typographically in outline form with staged indentations, as illustrated in Figure 4.

In this example, the file "Position paper, 1977" is a component of the parent file "Women's rights," part of the subseries "Compliance and Enforcement Committee," which is within the series "Administrative File," itself a component of the unit comprising the Records of the Leadership Conference on Civil

FIGURE 4. Example of Untagged Component Descriptions

Container List

Container Nos. *Contents*

ADMINISTRATIVE FILE, 1943-1989, n.d.

Correspondence, memoranda, notes, press releases, reports, minutes, newsletters, financial records, photographs, clippings, and miscellaneous background items. Arranged alphabetically by topic, organizational unit, or type of material, and chronologically therein.

Container Nos.	Contents
11	Articles and clippings, 1968-89, n.d.
	Chronological file, 1946-88
12	Compliance and Enforcement Committee
	— Annual report, 1967
	— Committee members, n.d.
	— Memoranda and correspondence, 1966-82, n.d. (2 folders)
	— Task forces
	— — Education
	— — — Mailing list, n.d.
	— — — Memoranda and correspondence, 1977-82
13	— — — Notes, 1982
	— — Employment
	— — — Members, 1978-83
	— — — Minutes, 1978-80, n.d.
14	— — Women's rights
	— — — Members, 1979-81, n.d.
	— — — Memoranda, 1978-85
	— — — Position paper, 1977
	Executive Committee
	Financial records

Rights (LCCR). Thus, a researcher interested in the 1977 position paper would follow the descriptive hierarchy up and deduce that the file was created by the women's rights task force of the Compliance and Enforcement Committee, the records of which are part of the Administrative File of the parent organization LCCR.

Regardless of their place in the hierarchy, all components share the same generic element name and tag <c>; a LEVEL attribute conveys any desired differentiation in tagging, such that "Women's rights" might be tagged as a <c level = "file"> and "Administrative File" as <c level = "series">. Since it is often difficult during encoding and editing to spot where one <c> begins and ends, the DTD permits use of numbered components (<c01>, <c02>, <c03>, and so on) to assist the finding aid author in nesting up to twelve component levels accurately. For example, the first series in a collection would be tagged as the first <c01>. The first <c02> is not the second series in the collection, but rather the first subseries or file within that first <c01>. The numbers carry no intellectual significance, and their values are not absolute; a <c02> in one part of the finding aid may be a file, while elsewhere, a <c02> may be a subseries. Figure 5 shows the correct tagging of the components outlined in Figure 4.

Once the components have been identified, their intellectual content may be described using the <did> subelements and other descriptive tags, such as <scopecontent>, <arrangement>, and <organization> discussed earlier. Often added to this intellectual description are shelf locations or container and folder numbers, which expand the role of the finding aid from an intellectual access tool to a device for also identifying the materials' physical location. This container information is linked to the intellectual hierarchy, i.e., the container information "follows" the intellectual component structure rather than the reverse. As shown in Figure 5, each new container is identified as part of the description of the first component housed in that container.

Also shown in Figure 5 and explained more fully in the *EAD Tag Library* and *EAD Application Guidelines* is the required Description of Subordinate Components <dsc> element, which must be opened before any <c> element is available. All components must be gathered in this "wrapper" element, which can assume several different forms identified by the element's TYPE attribute.[31] For the purposes of this article, we will examine only the "combined" form, which is the approach recommended in the *EAD Application Guidelines*. In this scenario, the following steps are taken:

1. The <dsc> is opened and its TYPE attribute is set to "combined."
2. A Component <c> element is then opened.
3. The LEVEL attribute of the first <c> is set to "series."
4. This first series-level component is then described using the same extensive set of elements that were previously available for describing the whole unit at the <archdesc> level, i.e., the <did> and its subelements, <scopecontent>, <arrangement>, and so on.
5. All subseries, files, or items nested within the first series-level component are tagged as recursive, nested components, possibly with optional LEVEL attributes set to identify their hierarchical order within the collection or record group.
6. As in the series description, unique information about each of these lower-level components may be identified by utilizing the full complement of descriptive elements.
7. Steps 2-6 are repeated for each remaining series-level component.

This structure of endlessly nested components inside a <dsc>, and further inside <archdesc>, illustrates EAD's ability to provide for descriptive information that is inherited from one level to another and that shares or repeats the same essential data elements.

FIGURE 5. Example of Tagged Component Descriptions

```
<dsc type="combined"><head>Container List</head><thead><row
valign="top"><entry colname="1">Container Nos. </entry><entry
colname="2">Contents</entry></row></thead>

<c01 level="series"><did><unittitle>Administrative File,<unitdate>1943-89,
n.d.</unitdate></unittitle></did> <scopecontent><p>Correspondence,
memoranda, notes, press releases, reports, minutes, newsletters, financial
records, photographs, clippings, and miscellaneous background items.
</p><arrangement><p>Organized alphabetically by topic, organizational
unit, or type of material, and arranged chronologically therein.</p>
</arrangement> </scopecontent>

<c02><did><container type="box">11 </container><unittitle>Articles and
Clippings, 1968-89, n.d.</unittitle></did></c02>
<c02><did><unittitle>Chronological File, 1946-88</unittitle></did></c02>
<c02><did><container type="box">12</container><unittitle>Compliance and
Enforcement Committee</unittitle></did>
<c03><did><unittitle>Annual report, 1967</unittitle></did></c03>
<c03><did><unittitle>Committee members, n.d.</unittitle></did></c03>
<c03><did><unittitle>Memoranda and correspondence, 1966-82, n.d.
</unittitle><physdesc><extent>(2 folders)</extent></physdesc></did></c03>
<c03><did><unittitle>Task forces </unittitle></did>
<c04><did><unittitle>Education</unittitle></did>
<c05><did><unittitle>Mailing list, n.d.</unittitle></did></c05>
<c05><did><unittitle>Memoranda and correspondence, 1977-
82</unittitle></did>
<c05><did><container type="box">13</container><unittitle>Notes,
1982</unittitle></did> </c05></c04>
<c04><did><unittitle>Employment</unittitle></did>
<c05><did> <unittitle>Members, 1978-83</unittitle></did></c05>
<c05><did><unittitle>Minutes, 1978-80, n.d.</unittitle></did></c05></c04>
<c04><did><container type="box">14</container><unittitle>Women's
rights</unittitle></did>
<c05><did><unittitle>Members, 1979-81, n.d.</unittitle></did></c05>
<c05><did><unittitle>Memoranda, 1978-85</unittitle></did></c05>
<c05><did><unittitle>Position paper, 1977 </unittitle></did></c05>
</c04></c03></c02>
<c02><did><unittitle>Executive committee</unittitle></did></c02>
<c02><did><unittitle>Financial records</unittitle></did></c02> . . . </c01> . . .
</dsc>
```

ADJUNCT DESCRIPTIVE DATA <ADD> *AND OTHER DESCRIPTIVE DATA <ODD>*

In addition to the descriptive elements already discussed, two others that are available within both <archdesc> and <c> deserve brief mention. The Adjunct Descriptive Data <add> element is designed to encode supplemental descriptive information that facilitates use of the materials featured in the finding aid. This includes additional access tools, such as bibliographies, indexes, file plans, and other finding aids, as well as descriptions or lists of materials separated from or related to those described in the finding aid. The Other Descriptive Data <odd> element helps to minimize problems converting existing finding aids to EAD by allowing an encoder to designate as "other" any information that may not fit into EAD's distinct categories. The <odd> element can be used when information does not correspond to another element's definition; when the information is of such mixed content as to make a single classification difficult; and when shifting the information to permit more specific content designation would be too costly or burdensome.

ENHANCED SEARCHING CAPABILITY THROUGH ACCESS TERMS

Aside from encoding the major structural parts of a finding aid and designating the core descriptive data about the unit and its components, EAD encoders also have the option of identifying character strings throughout the finding aid that are likely to be the objects of searches, such as personal, corporate, family, and geographic names; occupations; functions; form and genre terms; subjects; and titles. All of these elements (<name>, <persname>, <corpname>, <famname>, <geogname>, <occupation>, <function>, <genreform>, <subject>, and <title>) permit, through the use of attributes, the designation of encoding analogs and authorized forms. Additional optional attributes allow for specifying the role or relationship of persons and corporate bodies (e.g., author, editor, photographer) and the source of the controlled vocabulary terms used (e.g., *Library of Congress Subject Headings, Library of Congress Name Authority File, Art and Architecture Thesaurus, Dictionary of Occupational Titles*). Although the DTD permits liberal access to these elements throughout the finding aid, especially within the <p> and <unittitle> elements, bundling them together under the parent element Controlled Access Headings <controlaccess> helps facilitate authority-controlled searching across finding aids.

The EAD developers envisioned that users may approach online finding aids via a variety of avenues. Some may search a repository's online catalog, locate relevant entries, and follow links from those entries to online versions of finding aids. Others may start by searching the finding aids directly, bypassing the catalog and losing the advantage of the authority-controlled search terms contained therein. The <controlaccess> element is designed to replicate in a finding aid the collection-level search terms found in the 1xx, 6xx, and 7xx fields of MARC catalog records. Finding aid searches limited to the <controlaccess> element will improve the likelihood of locating strong sources of information on a desired subject, because access terms will have been entered in a consistent and authorized form across finding aids, and also because only the most significant terms are likely to have been selected for encoding.

POINTER, REFERENCE, AND LINKING ELEMENTS

One aspect of the EAD DTD which underwent considerable revision from the alpha to Version 1.0 releases centered on the DTD's hypertext and hypermedia capabilities and the need to bring EAD into conformity with XML. Most of EAD's linking and reference elements are standard in many DTDs, but a few were created specifically for EAD. These include the Archival Reference <archref> element, which provides for either an electronic link from the EAD finding aid to another archival description, or for a simple non-linked citation within the finding aid (usually in a bibliography) to another body of archival materials. Also unique to EAD are the Digital Archival Object <dao>, Digital Archival Object Description <daodesc>, Digital Archival Object Location <daoloc>, and Digital Archival Object Group <daogrp> elements, which are used to connect information in the finding aid to electronic representations (digital surrogates) of the archival materials described therein, a capability more fully explored in Steven L. Hensen's article in this issue.

ADDING METADATA TO DESCRIBE THE FINDING AID

Although finding aids are essentially metadata for the archival materials they describe, these same finding aids nevertheless have metadata of their own, usually in the form of title pages and prefaces. This documentation about the creation, revision, publication, and distribution of the finding aid is especially important in a machine-readable environment, given the difficulty of keeping track of electronic revisions. In EAD, information about the finding aid (as opposed to descriptive information about the archival materials) is contained within the optional Front Matter <frontmatter> element and the required EAD Header <eadheader>, which was modeled on the header element in the Text Encoding Initiative (TEI) (see Figure 1).[32] The sequence of elements and subelements in the <eadheader> is specified by the DTD, with the expectation that searches by finding aid title, date, repository, or language will be more predictable if the elements are uniformly ordered. The resulting <eadheader> contains four subelements, which must appear in the following order:

- EAD Identifier <eadid> provides a unique identification number or code for the finding aid and can indicate the location, source, and type of the identifier.
- File Description <filedesc> contains much of the bibliographic information about the finding aid, including the name of the author, title, subtitle, and sponsor (all contained in the Title Statement <titlestmt> element), as well as the edition, publisher, series, and related notes encoded separately.

- Profile Description <profiledesc> is used to record the language of the finding aid and information about who created the encoded version, and when it was created.
- Revision Description <revisiondesc> summarizes any revisions made to the EAD document.

POST VERSION 1.0 ACTIVITIES AND POSSIBLE FUTURE DEVELOPMENTS

Although the overview above provides a brief introduction to the EAD structure, much more extensive documentation is needed by those actually intending to encode finding aids with the Version 1.0 DTD. Anticipating this need for supplemental information, the EAD developers, shortly after releasing the new DTD and tag library in August 1998, turned their attention to revising and expanding the outdated beta application guidelines. During the first week in November 1998, with a grant from the Institute of Museum and Library Services (IMLS), a subset of the EAD Working Group reconvened at the Bentley Historical Library in Ann Arbor, Michigan, to begin outlining and drafting the EAD Version 1.0 Application Guidelines.[33] Over the next six months, the subgroup wrote, revised, and debated via email the content of those guidelines, which were reviewed at different points by other members of the EAD Working Group, members of SAA's Technical Subcommittee on Descriptive Standards (TSDS), three official "outside" reviewers, and several interested EAD implementors.[34] The final copy was published and released for sale in August 1999 at SAA's annual conference in Pittsburgh, Pennsylvania.[35]

The annual meeting also provided an opportunity for members of the working group, representatives from other SAA committees, and staff from American funding agencies to meet and discuss the continued development and maintenance of EAD, including ways to enhance international acceptance of the emerging standard and ideas for securing long-term financial support for future meetings and editorial revisions. Despite the almost breakneck speed at which EAD has developed, those gathered in Pittsburgh acknowledged that the DTD remains very much in its infancy and will undoubtedly grow in both expected and unanticipated ways.

A large part of EAD's future may ultimately be determined by the research community's response to how these encoded finding aids meet its needs. Future EAD developments may involve revisiting one of Pitti's original ideas for creating an interactive access system, in which researchers could add data about the materials to alternate versions of the finding aid. Although this author is unaware of any further work on this aspect of the Berkeley project, Pitti had originally envisioned that in an online finding aid system "it will be possible to create both private and public information spaces that reference the materials. In his or her private space, it will be possible for the individual researcher to attach notes and annotations to selected items in collections, and to establish and document relations between items and collections not made in the catalog and finding aids."[36]

Technological advancements and the emergence of new Web browsers and protocols will also undoubtedly affect EAD's development. Equally influential will be the important work undertaken by RLG and various consortia to build union databases of finding aids. These projects are bringing to fruition the developers' early goals of searching and retrieving finding aid data about archival materials scattered across multiple institutions. As these projects develop and as more archivists situated in diverse settings throughout the world begin to implement EAD, changes will undoubtedly occur to make the data structure standard a truly international vehicle for capturing and disseminating the wealth of information in archival finding aids.

NOTES

1. See Daniel V. Pitti, "Encoded Archival Description: The Development of an Encoding Standard for Archival Finding Aids," *American Archivist* 60 (Summer 1997): 268-83, for a fuller discussion of early print and online efforts at building union access to archival material and for an explanation of how these projects set the stage for EAD's development. Countries other than the United States also engaged in similar activities to produce union lists, including, for example, the Public Archives of Canada, *Union List of Manuscripts in Canadian Repositories = Catalogue collectif des manuscrits archives canadiennes,* ed. Robert S. Gordon (Ottawa: Public Archives of Canada, 1968).

2. United States. National Historical Publications Commission, *A Guide to Archives and Manuscripts in the United States,* ed. Philip M. Hamer (New Haven: Yale University Press, 1961).

3. In 1994 the Library of Congress ceased publishing the printed volumes, and NUCMC office staff redirected their energies to assisting mostly smaller repositories with creating cataloging records for online distribution via RLIN (Research Libraries Information Network), a national-level database.

4. Betty Furrie, "What is a MARC Record and Why Is It Important?" in *Understanding MARC Bibliographic: Machine-Readable Cataloging,* 5th ed., reviewed and edited by the Network Development and MARC Standards Office, Library of Congress (Washington, DC: Cataloging Distribution Service, in collaboration with The Follett Software Company, 1998), copy available online at http://lcweb.loc.gov/marc/umb/um01to06.html.

5. The Online Computer Library Center (OCLC), the first regional bibliographic utility, was established in 1967 as the Ohio College Library Center and later became a national and international cataloging database. Other bibliographic utilities followed,

including the Research Libraries Information Network (RLIN), the Washington Library Network (WLN), and the University of Toronto Library Automated System (UTLAS).

6. H. Thomas Hickerson, "Archival Information Exchange and the Role of Bibliographic Networks," *Library Trends* 36 (Winter 1988): 553-71; and Richard H. Lytle, "An Analysis of the Work of the National Information Systems Task Force," *American Archivist* 47 (Fall 1984): 357-65.

7. According to the Research Libraries Group's Archival Resources Web site, the RLIN database contained 500,000 records as of 1 November 1999. The 1998 annual report of OCLC, which is available online at http://www.oclc.org/ar98/wcat.htm, indicated that its mixed materials database contained 279,578 records.

8. For information on the development of APPM see the prefaces in both editions: Steven L. Hensen, *Archives, Personal Papers, and Manuscripts: A Cataloging Manual for Archival Repositories, Historical Societies, and Manuscript Libraries* (Washington, DC: Library of Congress, 1983), v-vi, and Hensen, *Archives, Personal Papers, and Manuscripts: A Cataloging Manual for Archival Repositories, Historical Societies, and Manuscript Libraries,* 2d ed. (Chicago: Society of American Archivists, 1989), v-viii. Also of interest is Hensen's "'NISTF II' and EAD: The Evolution of Archival Description," *American Archivist* 60 (Summer 1997): 288-91.

9. *Encoded Archival Description Application Guidelines, Version 1.0* (Chicago: Society of American Archivists, 1999), 6.

10. "Encoding Standard for Electronic Aids: A Report by the Bentley Team for Encoded Archival Description Development," *Archival Outlook* (January 1996): 10.

11. Pitti, *American Archivist,* 275-76.

12. Ibid., 279.

13. This summary of SGML is based, in part, on Janice E. Ruth, "Encoded Archival Description: A Structural Overview," *American Archivist* 60 (Summer 1997): 311-12, and Pitti, *American Archivist,* 276-78.

14. Pitti, *American Archivist,* 279.

15. The meeting in Ann Arbor occurred under the auspices of the Research Fellowship for Study of Modern Archives, a program supported by the Andrew W. Mellon Foundation, the Division of Preservation and Access of the National Endowment for the Humanities, and the Bentley Historical Library, University of Michigan. The participants were Steven J. DeRose (INSO, formerly Electronic Book Technologies), Jackie M. Dooley (University of California, Irvine), Michael J. Fox (Minnesota Historical Society), Steven L. Hensen (Duke University), Kris Kiesling (Harry Ransom Humanities Research Center, University of Texas at Austin), Daniel V. Pitti (University of Virginia, formerly University of California, Berkeley), Janice E. Ruth (Library of Congress Manuscript Division), Sharon Gibbs Thibodeau (National Archives and Records Administration), and Helena Zinkham (Library of Congress Prints and Photographs Division).

16. In a paper Pitti delivered in March 1995 at the RLG DIAP workshop, he wrote, "There is enough inconsistency in the logical order of finding aids, and in the relations of the various elements to one another, that it was necessary to make the first iteration of the Finding Aid DTD far more complicated and amorphous than it would need to be if there were more structural consistency and agreement on logical order." See Daniel Pitti, "Access to Digital Representations of Archival Materials: The Berkeley Finding Aid Project," in *RLG Digital Image Access Project: Proceedings from an RLG Symposium* (Palo Alto: The Research Libraries Group, 1995), 81; also available online at

http://sunsite.berkeley.edu/FindingAids/EAD/diap.html. Also in his application to the Bentley Historical Library's Research Fellowship Program for Study of Modern Archives, Pitti wrote that "it is essential that experts in archival processing and description engage in an informed, careful critique of the work of the Berkeley Finding Aid Project so that a truly community backed data model and standard can be arrived at." Daniel V. Pitti, "Encoding Standard for Electronic Archival Finding Aids: A Proposal to the Research Fellowship Program for Study of Modern Archives," 4, copy in author's possession.

17. "Ann Arbor Accords: Principles and Criteria for an SGML Document Type Definition (DTD) for Finding Aids," *Archival Outlook* (January 1996): 12.

18. For the full text of ISAD(G), see International Council on Archives, *ISAD(G): General International Standard Archival Description, adopted by the Ad Hoc Commission on Descriptive Standards, Stockholm, Sweden, 21-23 January 1993* (Ottawa, Ont.: International Council on Archives, 1994) or ICA's home page at http://www.ica.org.

19. The EAD Working Group, chaired by Bentley team member Kris Kiesling, initially consisted of all members of the original Bentley team (except Steven J. DeRose) as well as the following additional individuals: Randall Barry (Library of Congress Network Development and MARC Standards Office), Ricky Erway (Research Libraries Group), Anne Gilliland-Swetland (University of California, Los Angeles), Eric Miller (OCLC Online Computer Library Center), Robert Spindler (Arizona State University), and Richard Szary (Yale University). In August 1997, Meg Sweet (Public Record Office, United Kingdom) joined the group, and in November 1997, Wendy Duff (University of Toronto) was added and William E. Landis (University of California, Irvine) assumed Gilliland-Swetland's place.

20. Daniel V. Pitti, "The Berkeley Finding Aid Project: Standards in Navigation," paper delivered in September 1993 at the Society of American Archivists annual meeting in New Orleans, Louisiana, and revised and presented in November 1994 at the Symposium on Electronic Publishing on the Network, sponsored by the Association of Research Libraries and the Association of American University Presses in Washington, D.C., in November 1994, draft copy available online at http://sunsite.berkeley.edu/FindingAids/EAD/arlpap.html. Later published in *Filling the Pipeline and Paying the Piper: Proceedings of the Fourth Symposium, November 5-7, 1994, the Washington Vista Hotel, Washington, D.C.,* Ann Okerson, ed. (Washington, DC: Association of Research Libraries, 1995), 161-66.

21. This meeting was also sponsored by the Council on Library Resources (later Council on Library and Information Resources).

22. Several minor typographical modifications occurred in late November 1996, resulting in a date change to the September EAD files. Thus some references to the beta DTD list a November 1996 date.

23. Daniel Pitti and Kris Kiesling discuss some of these projects in their respective articles in the Summer 1997 issue of the *American Archivist.* See Pitti, *American Archivist,* 281-82, and Kris Kiesling, "EAD as an Archival Descriptive Standard," *American Archivist* 60 (Summer 1997): 351. Also see the case studies described in the *American Archivist* 60 (Fall 1997) issue and the implementation sites identified on the official EAD Web site at www.loc.gov/ead/eadsites.html.

24. EAD Working Group chair Kris Kiesling took a six-month leave of absence from her position at the Harry Ransom Humanities Research Center to advise RLG on EAD-related issues and to assist in creating a two-day workshop. Kiesling and co-instructor Michael Fox developed the initial course with contributions from Daniel Pitti,

Tim Hoyer, and Alvin Pollack at the University of California, Berkeley, and input from an advisory panel of early implementors consisting of Lisa Browar (New York Public Library), Steven L. Hensen (Duke University), Steven Mandeville-Gamble (Stanford University), Richard Szary (Yale University), Richard Masters (British Library), and Susan von Salis (Schlesinger Library) who joined Kiesling, Fox, Ricky Erway (RLG), and the Berkeley trio for a three-day meeting in Mountain View, California, on May 23-25, 1996, to discuss curriculum materials.

25. See EAD Help Pages Web site at http://jefferson.village.virginia.edu/ead/

26. The EAD Working Group sent out a formal request for comments via the EAD Listserv on 23 June 1997. See Kris Kiesling, "EAD Comment Period Opens," 23 June 1997, online posting, Encoded Archival Description Listserv, http://www.loc.gov/cgi-bin/lwgate/EAD/archives/. Although the formal comment period ended on 22 August 1997, the group considered all recommendations received before 31 October 1997. For a listing of working group members, see footnote 19.

27. Kris Kiesling, "EAD Beta–Version 1.0 Changes," 30 January 1998, online posting, Encoded Archival Description Listserv, http://www.loc.gov/cgi-bin/lwgate/EAD/archives/.

28. *Encoded Archival Description Tag Library, Version 1.0* (Chicago: Society of American Archivists, 1998).

29. Much of this structural analysis is based on Janice E. Ruth's "Encoded Archival Description: A Structural Overview," *American Archivist* 60 (Summer 1997): 310-29, and the author's contributions to the *Encoded Archival Description Tag Library, Version 1.0* (Chicago: Society of American Archivists, 1998) and the *Encoded Archival Description Application Guidelines, Version 1.0* (Chicago: Society of American Archivists, 1999).

30. "Encoding Standard for Electronic Aids: A Report by the Bentley Team for Encoded Archival Description Development," *Archival Outlook* (January 1996), 10.

31. The TYPE attribute can be set to a value of analytic overview ("analyticover"), to identify a set of series descriptions; "in-depth," to identify a listing of containers or folders, a calendar, or a listing of items; "combined," to identify instances in which the description of each series is followed immediately by a listing of subseries, files, and items for that series; and "other," to identify models that do not follow any of the above-mentioned formats.

32. The TEI is an international, humanities-based effort to develop a suite of DTDs for encoding literary texts or other objects of study. The EAD developers elected to use a TEI-like header in an attempt to encourage as much uniformity as possible in the provision of metadata across document types.

33. EAD Working Group members involved in the guidelines project included Jackie M. Dooley, who served as editor, and Michael J. Fox, Steven L. Hensen, Kris Kiesling, William E. Landis, and Janice E. Ruth. Also participating in the Ann Arbor meetings and writing sessions was Greg Kinney, a Bentley Historical Library staff member.

34. The Society of American Archivists Technical Subcommittee on Descriptive Standards is chaired by William E. Landis and includes Nicole Bouché (Yale University), Donna DiMichele (Mashantucket Pequot Museum and Research Center), Susan

Potts McDonald (Emory University), Dennis Meissner (Minnesota Historical Society), and Alden Monroe (Alabama Department of Archives). Outside reviewers were Elizabeth H. Dow (University of Vermont), Chris Powell (University of Michigan), and Kathleen Roe (New York State Archives).

35. *Encoded Archival Description Application Guidelines, Version 1.0* (Chicago: Society of American Archivists, 1999).

36. Daniel V. Pitti, "Setting the Digital Frontier: The Future of Scholarly Communication in the Humanities," paper presented at the Berkeley Finding Aids Conference, April 1995, available online at http://sunsite.berkeley.edu/FindingAids/EAD/dpitti.html.

Stargazing: Locating EAD in the Descriptive Firmament

Michael J. Fox

SUMMARY. Encoded Archival Description fits squarely into the common framework of standards for the documentation of cultural resources. As a communications tool, it operates in parallel to MARC 21. As a data structure standard, it overlaps the General International Standard Archival Description (ISAD(G)). They are not in conflict, however, because EAD is actually an implementation–an applied manifestation of the descriptive principles embodied in ISAD(G), enhanced through extensions that expand the latter's documentary core. *[Article copies available for a fee from The Haworth Document Delivery Service: 1-800-342-9678. E-mail address: <getinfo@haworthpressinc.com> Website: <http://www.HaworthPress.com> © 2001 by The Haworth Press, Inc. All rights reserved.]*

KEYWORDS. APPM, archival description, archival descriptive standards, Encoded Archival Description, EAD, finding aids, ISAD(G), MARC, RAD, USMARC

INTRODUCTION

Encoded Archival Description (EAD) first appeared publicly in 1995, but it was not born in isolation. It fit comfortably into a generally accepted, though

---

Michael J. Fox is Acting Assistant Director for Library and Archives, Minnesota Historical Society, 345 Kellogg Boulevard West, St. Paul, MN 55102 (E-mail: michael.fox@mnhs.org).

[Haworth co-indexing entry note]: "Stargazing: Locating EAD in the Descriptive Firmament." Fox, Michael, J. Co-published simultaneously in *Journal of Internet Cataloging* (The Haworth Information Press, an imprint of The Haworth Press, Inc.) Vol. 4, No. 3/4, 2001, pp. 61-74; and: *Encoded Archival Description on the Internet* (ed: Daniel V. Pitti, and Wendy M. Duff) The Haworth Information Press, an imprint of The Haworth Press, Inc., 2001, pp. 61-74. Single or multiple copies of this article are available for a fee from The Haworth Document Delivery Service [1-800-342-9678, 9:00 a.m. - 5:00 p.m. (EST). E-mail address: getinfo@haworthpressinc.com].

not fully codified, tradition of archival descriptive practice. It was compatible with new mechanisms for resource discovery and delivery that were evolving on the Web. It meshed with a suite of other standards for description that had arisen within the archival tradition or which archivists had come to share with librarians and museum curators. Unfortunately, its relationships to these protocols have not always been fully understood. The fact that many archivists in the United States have only a passing acquaintance with two of the most relevant codes, the Rules for Archival Description [1] (RAD) and the General International Standard for Archival Description (ISAD(G)[2], further complicates the general appreciation for the place the EAD occupies in standards-space. These associations are the subject of this paper, with particular emphasis on ISAD(G). The analysis begins with a review of archival descriptive practice, suggests a taxonomy for cataloging standards, and then correlates EAD with five related protocols–ISAD(G); the Anglo-American Cataloguing Rules (AACR); Archives, Personal Papers, and Manuscripts(APPM)[3], the USMARC Format for Bibliographic Data; and RAD–in order to fix EAD's location in the descriptive firmament.

DESCRIPTIVE CONTEXT

The need for description appears deceptively simple; its execution is more complex. Since the typical user cannot physically examine every manuscript collection, photograph, or book, it is necessary to create a surrogate for such objects. The publication *Functional Requirements for Bibliographic Records*[4] identifies four uses for the data that descriptive systems perform. **Find**–to serve as a tool for locating desired materials. **Identify**–to convey the unique and distinguishing characteristics of a particular entity so as to distinguish it from others. **Select**–to help users choose appropriate items. In an archival context, this may limit materials to those in a language the user understands or those whose use is not restricted in some way. **Obtain**–to enable the delivery of resources. There are differences in the methodologies that librarians and archivists use to facilitate the finding and identification functions. These are rooted in differences in the bibliographic and archival traditions and reflected in the type of access tools required for each. A brief review of the purposes of these archival access tools may help to understand their relationships to analogous library standards.

Library descriptive codes proceed from the premise that the descriptive surrogate, the virtual representation of a published work, consists of certain prescribed details of its publication, as transcribed from the physical item. The underlying assumption is that such data captures the information needed for finding and identifying, in conjunction with physical description and content analysis, for selection. Archival description takes a different tack both for conceptual and practical reasons.[5] As the output of an organic activity–the operations of a business or the life activities of an individual–and lacking the inherent identifying characteristics of published works, archival materials can only be found and identified on the basis of their origins, expressed by identifying both their creator and the functions that they document. There is another significant distinction. Bibliographic description almost always focuses on an individual item, a work, or at least a bounded set of objects. The nature of modern archives is that they usually are organized, described, and managed as collections: aggregations ranging in size from several to several million individual items. This fact adds another complicating dimension to the "find" activity. Moreover, such collections frequently are not fixed in their content but rather grow over time as an organization adds to its corporate archives or a donor contributes additional materials to her personal papers in an archival institution. Such additions, and deletions due to weeding or transfer, may change the quantity of materials but the unit, a collection, fundamentally remains the same; this complicates the "identify" activity.

Archivists have developed sophisticated but often institutionally-specific descriptive systems to marry user needs and complex holdings. These include the familiar catalog and a class of access tools known as finding aids, typically referred to as registers or inventories based on models developed by the U.S. National Archives (NARA) and the Library of Congress Manuscripts Division. Whereas catalogs provide summary descriptions, finding aids convey more detailed data about contents, sometimes even to the level of individual items. Librarians will recognize a parallel situation with access to serial publications where catalog records provide summary data about a title but the specifics of holdings and their contents are shared between the serials holdings/circulation systems of the local integrated library system and content analysis by abstracting and indexing services.

When EAD appeared in 1995, the form and content of archival catalogs were well on their way to standardization. More than ten years had passed since the appearance of the MARC Format for Archives and Manuscripts Control and the publication of *Archives, Personal Papers and Manuscripts,* the first widely accepted codification of archival descriptive practice in the U.S. The structure of finding aids was more uncertain and idiosyncratic, though research by the developers of EAD demonstrated a broad level of *de facto* acceptance of the models developed by NARA and LC. EAD was envisioned as a tool that might spur the regularization of practice in this area. Though some institutions had begun to leverage the commonality of data found in both catalogs and finding aids, there was neither a clearly articulated understanding of the relationships between these classes of access tools nor a method for integrating them. The appearance of links between catalog records and finding aids using MARC Field 856 has provided a means for physically linking the two electronic files but a conceptual integration of the two remains to be accomplished.

STANDARDS

Despite the different approaches to identification, the archival and bibliographic traditions share a common suite of standards that prescribe the various components of a surrogate description and specify how that information ought to be ordered, shared, and retrieved. Various taxonomies have developed to classify these standards. One organizes them into four categories: structural, content, data values, and communication standards.

Data structure standards define the elements of information that need to be recorded about a collection, work, or item. What do we want to say about it? What information is required to satisfy user needs? This category of standards defines not only required data elements but also the sequence of their presentation. Both EAD and ISAD(G) are commonly included in this group.

Data content standards prescribe the internal form of a particular data element. For example, Rule 1.1 in APPM prescribes how titles for archival collections are formed. Rule 22.5C5 in AACR2 dictates the prescribed form of name that will be used in a catalog entry for the name of a married woman whose surname consists of a surname before marriage and her husband's surname.

Data value standards, such as authority files and thesauri, contain lists of established forms for personal, corporate, and place names, topical subject headings, and the like, created on the basis of rules prescribed in content standards. For example, the Library of Congress name authority file specifies (incorrectly–the middle name is wrong) that the authorized form of name for the author of this article is Fox, Michael J. (Michael Joseph) so as to distinguish works by him from those by others with the name Michael J. Fox.

Data interchange or communication standards establish methods whereby descriptive data may be shared among (or within) institutions or at least among their computers. This compatibility is obviously essential for resource sharing and user discovery. MARC and EAD clearly fall into this category.

These are conceptual functions that standards perform. Individual protocols do not line themselves up so neatly into four distinct categories. Many perform overlapping functions and the groupings themselves are not unambiguous. Everyone would agree, for example, that the USMARC Format for Bibliographic Data is principally a data storage and interchange protocol. However, in some respects it also exhibits the characteristics of a content standard through its inclusion of many coded values in the leader and fixed fields areas that permit machine processing, organization, and presentation of data useful for resource discovery. Perhaps EAD may be best understood by comparing and contrasting it to other standards. This may be particularly helpful given the overlap between our theoretical, functional model of standards and the mixed purpose of many real-life protocols.

ISAD(G)

The International Council on Archives' Ad Hoc Commission on Descriptive Standards adopted ISAD(G) in 1993. Four stated purposes were given for the standard: "ensure the creation of consistent, appropriate, and self-explanatory descriptions; facilitate the retrieval and exchange of information about archival material; enable the sharing of authority data; and make possible the integration of descriptions from different repositories into a unified information system." The document is now in the midst of a five-year review by the ICA's Committee on Descriptive Standards, the successor body to the original Ad Hoc Commission. The results of that review will be promulgated in conjunction with the ICA's Fourteenth International Congress to be held in Seville, Spain in 2000. The Committee has received and reviewed literally hundreds of suggestions for changes and enhancements from national archives and archival associations. Though some modifications will be made in response to those recommendations, it is clear from the committee's reported deliberations that neither the goals, the structure, nor the basic rules of ISAD(G) will change in any fundamental way. One can therefore assume that the following analysis will continue to be valid for the near future. Comments that follow reflect the current, original text.

The introduction lays out the scope of the document. "As general rules, these are intended to be broadly applicable to descriptions of archives regardless of the nature or extent of the unit of description. The rules guide the formulation of information in each of twenty-six (26) elements that may be combined to constitute the description of an archival entity." There are two salient points made in this statement. These are general rules; they were not intended to capture the descriptive requirements of every type of media. For example, little if any guidance is given on the particular documentary needs of archival map or photograph collections or for the description of electronic records. The Commission envisioned that successive committees would formulate separate sets of media-centric rules when it wrote, "Further specific rules should be formulated to guide the description of special categories of materials (such as cartographic materials, motion pictures, electronic files, or charters, notarial deeds, property titles)." In this way it was to parallel the International Standard Bibliographic Description (ISBD) in which one general code is supplemented by additional, separate codes for various types of physical carriers such as books or electronic records. This pattern is familiar to librarians at least as the structure of Part 1 of the Anglo-American Cataloguing Rules and to archivists in the format of RAD in which a chapter of general rules is supplemented by additional chapters that convey specialized rules for particular media. The concept that these rules apply to any unit of archival material regardless of its extent is equally significant and will become more apparent later when we consider multilevel description.

The body of the document is divided into twenty-six rules that are organized further into six functional areas: identity statement, context, content and structure, condition of access and use, allied materials, and notes. Again, in the concept of areas of description, ISAD(G) resembles its ISBD counterparts, though obviously there is no strong correlation in content between the area groupings in each.

The identity area encompasses five elements of description: reference codes that identify the repository and the materials; title statement; dates of creation; level of description, i.e., the archival category of materials documented, such as fọnds, series, file, or item; and the physical extent (quantity) of the records. The document identifies a common thread among these elements. They are "essential information" needed to "identify the unit of description." They are said to be "essential for international exchange of descriptive information." Such identification is both physical, through identifiers that uniquely denote an archival collection, and descriptive, through the inclusion of the title which is an essential ingredient in citation. These will literally, though perhaps not fully, satisfy the "identification" function. The notion that there is a group of basic elements needed to identify a body of records is very much a part of EAD as well, where it is represented by the concept of the Descriptive Identification or <did> element.

The context area consists of elements that convey information about the "origin and custody of the unit." These include the name of the creator, an administrative or biographical history, dates of accumulation, custodial history, and the immediate source of acquisition.

The third grouping of elements is the content and structure area which contains data elements that document the "subject matter and arrangement" of the documents being described. This includes the scope and content statement, appraisal, destruction and scheduling information, accruals (the expected addition of materials to the collection), and the system of the internal arrangement of documents within the unit.

The conditions of use and access area is broadly defined to capture all the factors that might limit the researcher who wishes to examine the materials. These include elements that capture legal status, access conditions either in the form of physical limitations or restrictions that might arise from law or pursuant to terms imposed by an individual donor, conditions that govern the use or reproduction of materials such as copyright, the language of materials, physical characteristics of the records such as their fragility or the necessity of specialized equipment to examine them, and the availability of finding aids that might facilitate the identification of appropriate items.

Users are often interested in related materials that might enhance their understanding of documents being described. One may record information about five different types of associated data in the allied materials area. This includes the location of original versions of the documents as well as copies; related materials with a "direct and significant connection," associated materials in other repositories, and information about publications based on the use, study, or analysis of the records. The last area of the standard, notes, provides a familiar catch-all element for data that cannot be accommodated elsewhere.

These twenty-six data elements are only half of the descriptive framework that ISAD(G) defines. The other is the concept of multilevel description. It is a generally accepted tenet of archival theory that all documents are created and many persist in the context of a larger body of historical documentation. The collections of papers of individuals and the records of organizations and governments are aggregations of materials that are or can be organized into a hierarchical sequence. Items are gathered together in files; files are organized by form or content into groups of materials called series. If the records are hierarchical, it seems obvious that their documentation similarly ought to be structured in multiple layers. ISAD(G) prescribes a documentation system that consists of multiple descriptions–one for each individual item, for each file, for each series, and for the record group or fond as a whole–all linked together to reflect the inherent hierarchy. It offers four principles for applying multilevel description: proceed from the general to the specific, link information about related components of the collection or fond being documented, limit the description of each component to information specific to it, and avoid repetition of data from parent to child component. The first two of these are inherent in EAD as well and the last two reflect common practice in the construction of finding aids.

So where does ISAD(G) fit into our standards model? Most would categorize it as a data structure standard. It provides the twenty-six elements previously described for recording many, though hardly all, of the basic data one might capture about a body of archival materials and a structure for organizing and combining that information into a hierarchically ordered documentation.

While sometimes described as such, it clearly is not a data content standard. The semantics that define each element are deliberately general, with just enough detail to identify the nature of its content. For example, one could hardly use ISAD(G) for practical, detailed guidance on how to construct a narrative describing the scope and contents of a body of materials. Rule 3.3.1, Scope and Content, briefly states: "Give a brief summary of the subject content (including time period) of the unit of description." Like the text in MARC 21 that describes the analogous Field 520, the Summary, and so on. Note, this brief explanation is more for identification than instruction. Other standards like APPM and RAD will have to provide more specific directions to the cataloger. There is another interesting aspect to ISAD(G). Whereas APPM and MARC are specifically directed toward catalog records and EAD at the construction of finding aids, ISAD(G) is not specific to any output format.

In 1996, the ICA Ad Hoc Commission published a companion standard to ISAD(G), the International Standard Archival Authority Record for Corporate, Personal, and Family Names known as ISAAR(CPF).[6] ISAAR(CPF) was born out of a desire not to replace existing authority file mechanisms, but to expand their scope. Information about the creating entity is central to the documentation of archival collections, vital in the "find" and "identify" functions. Archival documentation responds to that need by supplying information about the individual or corporate body responsible for the records at a level of detail that a librarian would consider inappropriate in a bibliographic description. Since a single creator, especially corporate bodies, may be responsible for many units of archival materials, it is more efficient to maintain such data in a single, linked location rather than duplicating it in multiple descriptions. This is the concept behind ISAAR(CPR)–documentation, separately maintained but fully integrated, that goes beyond the basic need for headings management found in bibliographic authority files. ISAAR(CPF) does this by providing a data structure that focuses on two elements: the name and the historical data associated with it. ISAAR(CPR) and ISAD(G) are intended to work together but fully integrated implementations are in their infancy.

How then does ISAD relate to EAD? From other articles in this issue, it should be clear that EAD is also a structural standard. In fact, ISAD and EAD share five very important characteristics.

Both prescribe fundamental descriptive elements, though EAD obviously has a more detailed data structure. They not only define these informational buckets but also place them in a hierarchical structure that conveys the whole-part relationships of the materials described. They create multilevel description. There is an underlying premise that the same elements of description apply to all levels of the hierarchy. Of course, in actual practice limited resources usually mean that description becomes less detailed as one documents smaller or more homogeneous units. For example, one may assign subject headings to a fond as a whole or even to individual series of records, but few institutions have the time or resources to assign specific subject headings to every item or to create a detailed description of its contents.

Both standards assume that there is a set of descriptive elements that are key to "ensuring a good basic description of an archival unit or component" and are "essential for international interchange." ISAD(G) and EAD include basically the same elements in this group. The corresponding elements (with the ISAD(G) element followed by its EAD equivalent) are Reference code/unitid and repository, Title/unittitle, Dates/unitdate, and Extent/physical description. EAD includes the origination (creator) element; ISAD(G) adds the name of the creator if it "is not included in the title." ISAD(G) adds one additional element to the list, level of description, which EAD incorporates in the form of a mandatory attribute value.

Finally, both standards have in common a set of weak semantics to describe the elements. If one examines the EAD Tag Library, for example, it becomes clear that the descriptions of particular elements and explanations of how they are to be used do not provide specific guidance on how one might formulate their contents. As with ISAD(G), one could not turn to EAD for direction on what data might be included in a useful biographical history. Neither standard intends to fill that role. Some external data content standard is required. This consanguinity between EAD and ISAD(G) is deliberate. Compatibility with ISAD(G) was a stated goal of EAD from the beginning. The group that developed the initial alpha version of EAD included a member who had been active on the ICA Commission that developed ISAD(G). The final review process that lead to version 1.0 of EAD included several modifications needed to meet the goal of full compatibility between the two. Indeed, one might aptly consider them not to be rivals but rather see that EAD is actually a concrete implementation of the documentary principles of ISAD(G), which have been enhanced by adding the possibility of including additional descriptive elements within the common framework of core data elements and multilevel description.

The two do differ in some interesting ways as well. ISAD(G) is broader in scope, intended to apply to informational systems of all types, both manual and automated. EAD is clearly chartered to provide a format for the electronic encoding of "a particular type of document know as inventories and registers." Despite this very specific mission, one might imagine EAD evolving someday to become the basis for a more generalized information system that applies to multiple output formats. Although ISAD(G) provides a conceptual model for multilevel description and provides an element wherein one declares the level of material being described, e.g., fond, series, item, and so on, it does not provide any specific mechanism for knitting separate descriptions of each of these components together into a comprehensive whole. The mechanism for doing so is left to the "linkage and informational content" rules and processes of local systems. There are no built-in mechanisms for specifying the order in which a group of sibling series descriptions should be presented or how parent and child descriptions might be connected together–what in MARC is referred to as link and sequence. All of these relationships are clearly expressed in EAD. They are inherent in the hierarchical structure of components and captured in the nested structure of SGML. One significant aspect of EAD as a structure standard has yet to be identified, an aspect ISAD(G) eschews by being output format neutral. It will be required to facilitate the full and useful interchange and interoperability of multiple finding aids. It is one we take for granted with the library catalog. Archivists lack a community standard that defines what constitutes a useful finding aid sufficiently detailed to be useful for resource discovery, as well as agreement on the overall structure of finding aids such as the order of presentation of elements. Libraries have benefited from a tradition of the common structural presentation of the catalog record. While online catalogs have supplanted some of the look and feel of a card file with labeled displays, nevertheless the overall appearance has been consistent, which leads to user recognition and understanding. Various forces, including the input standards of the bibliographic utilities, dictate standards for core and full-level descriptions, while public access systems exhibit a general level of consistency in the data shown to the public. Titles are given, authors represented where appropriate, publication dates shown even if supplied or inferred, and topical subjects are added. For finding aids, there is no accepted body of practice with respect either as to which elements are required or how they might be represented for display. Significant variations may be found within institutions and certainly across repositories. This needs to be redressed.

Finally, EAD differs from ISAD(G) in that, in addition to being a data structure standard, it is also, as an SGML file, a communication format. Not all standards fit neatly into a single bucket after all. EAD currently is constructed and managed in an SGML/XML technology infrastructure, with SGML/XML authoring and publishing tools. However, this may change. Archives may find it useful to generate descriptions and to manage them internally in relational or object-oriented databases. This would be particularly attractive in institutional settings such as corporate and government archives where descriptive data is only part of the information needed in a comprehensive information management system that tracks documents through their entire life-cycle, from creation to archival maintenance. Indeed, some archival theorists emphasize that in organizational and government archives description is part of the life-cycle management of records and not an *ex post facto* activity of archivists.[7] Such systems may employ the EAD structure principally as a data modeling device and as an export mechanism for inter-system communication and exchange. This parallels the situation where integrated library systems store catalog data internally in optimized data formats and utilize MARC only as a communication tool, a syntax in which data is received and exported.

MARC

As a standard, EAD is also closely related to MARC. Many see MARC principally as a communication standard. This is undeniable. Its roots lie in transfer of cataloging data between libraries via magnetic tape. Even as data communication has evolved from batch mode physical transfer to real time electronic interchange via protocols like Z39.50 and FTP, the MARC standards still include specifications for this very real housekeeping business. But it is also possible to argue that MARC is a structural standard as well. We employ descriptive (e.g., AACR, APPM, RAD, or the Oral History Cataloging Manual[8]) and content analysis protocols (Cataloging Manual: Subject Headings) but none of these defines the totality of the descriptive records. Arguably, it is only the MARC Bibliographic Format (and in the input standards of the bibliographic utilities) that one finds a full specification of all the elements of the catalog record. One may also argue that, in some limited fashion, both are content standards in terms of the coded data in the MARC leader and fixed fields and in the metadata specification in the EAD header.

MARC and EAD have several other points of similarity. Both can function as the technical basis for a system for resource discovery and delivery. They can be accessed in Internet space. There is another major area of tangency that may help the many archival managers who are concerned about the relationship between their MARC catalog records and their EAD finding aids. There seems often to be a fair degree of overlap in the content of both. With the development of a MARC SGML Document Type Definition, both MARC catalog records and EAD-encoded finding aids may coexist in the same SGML information space. While this feature has not been exploited to date, it does open up a number of possibilities. One is the opportunity of more closely integrating the two within a common system for creating, managing, and providing access to descriptive resources. This may occur either by integrating separate files into a single document or by freely and readily exchanging data between catalog records and finding aids by taking advantage of compatible SGML/XML file formats. Currently available applications make it relatively simple to migrate data from the EAD DTD structure to the MARC DTD specification through programming scripts or the transformational capabilities of

Extensible Style Language (XSL) processors,[9] though EAD does not always capture data at the same level of granularity and encoding specificity that is found in MARC. For example, the EAD subject element does not include all the subfield structure found in MARC Field 650. There are no indicator values in EAD.

CONTENT STANDARDS

We have seen EAD as a structural standard with parallels to ISAD(G) and a communication format with similarities to MARC, but we still have not identified a content standard that will specify for archivists how to formulate the informational content of particular elements. It will not be ISAD(G). The ICA Committee on Descriptive Standards has ruled that out as a role for that standard. That leaves three possible approaches for content specifications for finding aids in North America. The professional could continue to rely on local practice. This would seriously cripple, of course, any hopes for interoperability. This is already evident in the experience of some early EAD consortial implementations where the nonstandard content and presentation of legacy finding aids continues to present a major, though not insurmountable challenge to interoperability. Another option would be to formalize the use either of APPM or RAD, coupled with the application of authorities files such as the Library of Congress Name and Subject Authority Files and the Art and Architecture Thesaurus for controlled access points. This would require revision to either code to some extent, at least to correlate the descriptive rules with the EAD data elements for encoding.

APPM is widely employed as the content standard for catalog description by archivists in the U.S. but was not created with specific provisions for multilevel description and certainly does not consider itself to be a source of rules for finding aids. It has undergone one major revision in its second edition that more closely aligned its structure with that of MARC. RAD, developed later, reflects a Canadian descriptive model that strongly emphasizes the European tradition of multilevel description and begins by explicitly articulating such rules. The extent to which Canadian archivists currently apply the multilevel descriptive rules codified in RAD below the series level into the more detailed portions of the finding aid is not clear. But whatever the level of formal adoption of APPM and RAD for inventories and registers currently might be, both codes have influenced indirectly the content of finding aids as well as catalog entries in many repositories. This is hardly surprising. Archivists long have been aware of the relationship between the data in their two principle forms of access tools–a fact that was demonstrated clearly in the pioneering data modeling done by the National Information Systems Task Force. The relationship of the data between catalogs and finding aids, and therefore implicitly between EAD and APPM/RAD, is frequently questioned at archival meetings, workshops and on discussion lists. It does seem reasonable that the information in an effective scope and content description is not fundamentally different whether presented in a catalog or in a finding aid except in the level of detail and therefore in length. This correlation is demonstrated by various "crosswalks" that map the association between data elements in EAD and in these content standards.

Several meetings have been held by archivists in Canada and the U.S. working toward the goals of integrating into a single unified set of practice the descriptive practices now codified in RAD and APPM. Wendy Duff and Kent Haworth have reported on discussions that have suggested that a revised code ought to be output neutral–that is, not focused on catalogs or finding aids but rather emphasizing integrated description.[10] This is a reform for which many undoubtedly yearn. But until that time comes, archivists will have to draw on other sources for guidance on the content of EAD-encoded finding aids: local practice, interpolation from RAD, APPM, the EAD Tag Library,[11] and the EAD Application Guidelines.[12]

On the other hand, the structural underpinnings for archival finding aids are well in place, with ISAD(G) providing an internationally recognized, standards-based framework upon which EAD-encoded documentation may be created. It formalizes the important but often unstated premise that standardization is an essential factor in information sharing. It establishes and validates three critical tenets of archival description at the core of EAD: that there are standard data elements which are basic to any full and useful documentation, a core group of which are essential; that in its most detailed form, archival documentation must reflect the internal, usually hierarchical, nature of the underlying materials; and that these descriptive components are applicable in every form and at every level of description. Consistent application of these principles can only help to support the purposes of description set forth at the beginning of this article.

NOTES

1. Bureau of Canadian Archivists, Planning Committee on Descriptive Standards, *Rules for Archival Description* (Ottawa: The Bureau, 1990).

2. International Council on Archives, Ad Hoc Commission on Descriptive Standards, *ISAD(G): General International Standard Archival Description* (Ottawa: The Commission, 1994).

3. Steven L. Hensen, *Archives, Personal Papers, and Manuscripts,* 2nd Edition (Chicago: Society of American Archivists, 1989).

4. IFLA Study Group on the Functional Requirements for Bibliographic Records, *Functional Requirements for Bibliographic Records* (Frankfurt am Main: Deutche Bibliothek, 1997).

5. For a more detailed description of the nature and purposes of archival description, see Michael J. Fox and Peter L. Wilkerson, *Introduction to Archival Organization and Description* (Los Angeles: Getty Information Institute, 1998).

6. International Council on Archives, Ad Hoc Commission on Descriptive Standards, *ISAAR(CPF): International Standard Archival Authority Record for Corporate Bodies, Persons, and Families* (Ottawa: The Secretariat of the ICA Ad Hoc Commission on Descriptive Standards, 1996).

7. Chris Hurley, "The Making and Keeping of Records: (1) What are Finding Aids For," *Archives and Manuscripts* 26, no. 1: 58-77.

8. Marion E. Matters, *Oral History Cataloging Manual* (Chicago: Society of American Archivists, 1995).

9. For information about XSL, see *Extensible Style Language (XSL) Version 1.0,* available at <http://www.w3.org/TR/WD-xsl-19981216>.

10. Wendy M. Duff and Kent M. Haworth, "Advancing Archival Description: A Model for Rationalising North American Descriptive Standards," *Archives and Manuscripts* 25, no. 2 (Nov. 1997): 218-241.

11. *Encoded Archival Description Tag Library, Version 1.0* (Chicago: Society of American Archivists, 1998).

12. *Encoded Archival Description Application Guidelines, Version 1.0* (Chicago: Society of American Archivists, 1999).

Archival Cataloging and the Internet: The Implications and Impact of EAD

Steven L. Hensen

SUMMARY. Although the emergence of Encoded Archival Description might seem to obviate the necessity of creating MARC cataloging records for archival materials, it is becoming increasingly clear that the traditionally hierarchical models of archival description are well suited to the hyperlinked environment of the Internet. Thus, a fully-realized resource discovery mechanism for archival materials should move seamlessly from the very general (e.g., topical headings in catalogs) to the very specific (e.g., item-level descriptions in finding aids or even digital surrogates of items). In such a descriptive apparatus, MARC cataloging serves to provide important mid-level metadata. At the same time, the underlying specifics of these records will need to be reexamined in light of their evolving relationship with encoded finding aids. *[Article copies available for a fee from The Haworth Document Delivery Service: 1-800-342-9678. E-mail address: <getinfo@haworthpressinc.com> Website: <http://www.HaworthPress.com> © 2001 by The Haworth Press, Inc. All rights reserved.]*

KEYWORDS. APPM, archival cataloging, archival description, archival descriptive standards, archival metadata, Encoded Archival Description, EAD, finding aids, MARC AMC, RAD, USMARC

Steven L. Hensen is Director of Planning and Project Development in the Rare Book, Manuscript, and Special Collections Library, Duke University, Box 90185, Durham, NC 27708-0185 (E-mail: hensen@duke.edu).

[Haworth co-indexing entry note]: "Archival Cataloging and the Internet: The Implications and Impact of EAD." Hensen, Steven L. Co-published simultaneously in *Journal of Internet Cataloging* (The Haworth Information Press, an imprint of The Haworth Press, Inc.) Vol. 4, No. 3/4, 2001, pp. 75-95; and: *Encoded Archival Description on the Internet* (ed: Daniel V. Pitti, and Wendy M. Duff) The Haworth Information Press, an imprint of The Haworth Press, Inc., 2001, pp. 75-95. Single or multiple copies of this article are available for a fee from The Haworth Document Delivery Service [1-800-342-9678, 9:00 a.m. - 5:00 p.m. (EST). E-mail address: getinfo@haworthpressinc.com].

INTRODUCTION

In April 1995, the library at the University of California, Berkeley, and the Commission on Preservation and Access sponsored the Berkeley Finding Aid Conference. The purpose of this conference was to evaluate the work and results of a two-year project that had been underway at the library to develop a Standard Generalized Markup Language (SGML) Document Type Definition (DTD) for encoding archival finding aids. This encoding structure was designed to make the information in these finding aids more widely accessible and searchable via the Internet. As we now know, this conference, along with an ensuing Bentley Fellowship[1] and a considerable amount of effort by a number of individuals and institutions, has ultimately resulted in Encoded Archival Description (EAD), which was released in its full version 1.0 in the summer of 1998.

One of the first questions that emerged at the 1995 Finding Aid Conference following the prepared addresses was related to cataloging. If the detailed content of archival finding aids would soon be accessible via the Internet, was it still necessary to prepare catalog records for those archival resources–especially since most of the cataloging (assuming it was done correctly) was simply summary information derived from the finding aid? The immediate assumption then was that it probably *was* necessary–though nobody was able to articulate exactly *why* this might be so. Subsequent work on further development of EAD has left little time for a more considered response to this question. The issue, however, is persistent and it now deserves more thoughtful examination. The purpose of this paper will be to study this question in more detail and to ask two related questions: (1) If it is necessary to continue archival cataloging in tandem with EAD, what is the impact of EAD on that cataloging; and (2) Are there lessons to be drawn for the larger world of bibliographic control from the descriptive hierarchy represented by archival MARC records linked to an EAD instance?

EAD AND THE ORIGINS OF ARCHIVAL CATALOGING

Although EAD itself has been widely discussed and written about elsewhere,[2] it will be useful to examine briefly its basic origins by way of attempting to answer the questions posed above. In 1977 the Society of American Archivists received a grant from the National Endowment for the Humanities towards exploring issues surrounding the electronic sharing of archival information. The resulting National Information Systems Task Force [3] spent several years initially exploring the basics of archival information through the development of a data dictionary.[4] After this they engaged in a painstaking examination of potential archival information architectures and scenarios. In the end, the group concluded that "the superstructure used by the library community (the MARC format) could easily be adapted to archival purposes. The result was the USMARC Format for Archival and Manuscript Control (MARC AMC)."[5]

With the preparation of MARC cataloging for archival and manuscript materials now a routine part of the technical services for hundreds of libraries and archives, it may be difficult to conceive that the decisions behind the origins of this standard were (and, in some quarters, remain[6]) controversial. The reality, however, is that this conclusion was only reached after considerable reflection and debate. Much of this controversy revolved around the fact that MARC was a *library*-based standard designed specifically for the cataloging of published materials. Given that archivists then regarded themselves as somewhat apart (if not distinct) from the work and rituals of libraries and librarians, they rarely indulged in activity that could be specifically labeled as *cataloging*. Furthermore, given that their holdings were, almost by definition, unpublished and unique, there was considerable suspicion about whether MARC could have any applicability in a setting that seemed to cry out for a more specialized–dare I say *unique*–approach.

To be sure, although there was (and remains) nothing magical about the MARC format per se (it is, after all, a thirty-year-old database structure which was intended originally to facilitate the mass printing and sharing of catalog cards, the general forms of which themselves date back to the mid-nineteenth century), it had gradually become clear to the members of NISTF that there were more important issues at stake than designing an idealized "National Archival Information System" in the abstract. For such a system to be a success it needed to be reasonably accessible and understandable for the average archivist or manuscripts librarian. Furthermore, such a system could not depend on special software, systems, or programming that were beyond the limited financial resources of most archival repositories; in short, it needed to be something that could actually be implemented and that could *work*.

In these respects the MARC format easily met the requirements. Moreover, since many archival and manuscript repositories were already part of libraries that were involved in creating MARC cataloging records for other materials, many of the necessary infrastructures were already in place (the then nearly complete lack of understanding and rapport between cataloging departments and archives notwithstanding). All that was required was an adaptation of the MARC format that met the descriptive needs of archival and manuscript repositories. The subsequent successful mapping of the elements of archival description against the MARC format by Elaine Engst in the aforementioned data dictionary accomplished that fairly neatly. The concomitant (though nearly coincidental) publication of an AACR2-compatible data content standard, *Archives, Personal Papers, and Manuscripts* (APPM)[7] laid the groundwork for archivists to begin the process of sharing information about their holdings via existing bibliographic networks.

Several important grant-funded projects followed which were aimed at testing this new standard and creating a critical mass of archival cataloging records.[8] By any measure, these projects were a resounding success: various minor technical problems surrounding MARC-AMC implementation were identified and satisfactorily resolved; previously inaccessible information concerning a large and representative group of archival materials was now available through both RLIN and OCLC and, increasingly, through local online catalogs; and it became quickly and abundantly clear that this format could be used for a wide variety of archival materials and for a generally more "archival" approach to the description and management of an assortment of "non-archival" materials.[9]

Most important, however, and most directly relevant to the thesis here were the unanticipated benefits of integrating archival material with the rest of the bibliographic universe. These were "unanticipated" because neither the archival nor library communities were initially enthusiastic about the use of heretofore strictly bibliographic systems for archival description. As noted earlier, the archival community had historically had some reservations with respect to allying themselves too closely to the library world. It was perhaps understandable for them to regard systems that originally had been designed for the sharing of cataloging data for published materials to be either unsuitable or irrelevant for the description of material that was unique and for which the very idea of "sharing" cataloging data was preposterous.

Many in the library world, on the other hand, regarded with suspicion the insinuation of these so-called archival "bibliographic" records into their systems. By existing library standards, archival cataloging records were seen as anarchic and anomalous–and certainly far too lengthy! Many library catalogers and those involved with the bibliographic utilities frankly considered them to be an annoying and bumptious intrusion into an orderly world circumscribed by traditions and standards that had been more than a century in the making.

As archivists and manuscript librarians came to realize the importance of communicating information about their holdings via these MARC records, and began to integrate this work into their routines–either through participation in grant-funded projects or through collaboration with local cataloging departments–something interesting started to emerge. As the so-called "bibliographic utilities" became increasingly "littered" with cataloging records for archival and unpublished materials, the very purpose and focus of these systems started to evolve. No longer were the databases simply cataloging utilities, i.e., a system by which libraries could spread and share the burden of preparing cataloging for new publications. Instead, they were evolving into true information systems or "cultural resources databases," as the Research Libraries Group described them.

Through the juxtaposition and collocation of bibliographic descriptions of a variety of information resources, however unintentional originally, it was becoming clear that there were natural associations and connections among the materials that went quite beyond the demands of bibliographic control. Moreover, it was also obvious that the increasingly interdisciplinary nature of much research required information systems to deliver *all* relevant materials on a subject, not just the standard monographs and serials. Finally, it was discovered that this integration had the power to bring together and unite archival collections that had long been separated by the exigencies of circumstance and history.

Fully-integrated bibliographic systems or online catalogs functioning as true information resources (as opposed to simple cataloging utilities) are so prevalent today that it is sometimes difficult to recall that this phenomenon is less than ten years old. The more recent emergence of Web-based catalogs, with their ability to create hyperlinks through the MARC 856 field, has only intensified this phenomenon. No longer are catalogs simply devices designed to tell potential users *what* a library holds and *where* it might be located; instead, they exist as an essential component in a complex hierarchy of metadata, all of which is designed to inform users about the content and nature of information resources and their relationship to other resources–regardless of the physical format or location of those resources.

In this context then, it is almost inconceivable that archival resources would not continue to be cataloged into the same systems that provide description and navigation for all the other wide variety of information resources. As the Council on Library and Information Resources recently pointed out in a report which highlighted improved access to manuscript and archival resources as one of the key issues in libraries today, "The most significant impediment to greater access to manuscript materials is the lack of adequate finding aids, in easily located sites. The highest priority, therefore is to continue to create machine-readable records of manuscript holdings and make those records easily accessible on the Web or on a bibliographic utility."[10] Implicit in this observation is the importance of providing access to these materials in relation to other materials and the underlying assumption of the existence of a seamless web of cultural information resources.

Also of particular interest to this discussion is the apparent interchangeability in the above quotation of the terminology of "finding aids" and "machine-readable records . . . on a bibliographic utility." The implication herein reflects the fundamental reality of archival description: all archival work is essentially description, with the differences existing only in the purposes and the place in the descriptive hierarchy served by that purpose. As the Working Group on Standards for Archival Description put it in 1994, "Archival description is the process of capturing, collating, analyzing, and organizing any information that serves to identify, manage, locate, and interpret the holdings of archival institutions and explain the contexts and records systems from which those holdings were selected." [11] Such a definition recognizes the essential multiplicity of descriptive tools; it also implicitly underlines the interrelatedness of those tools. Furthermore, *Archives, Personal Papers, and Manuscripts* codifies this principle when it declares: "Archival catalogs may be only one part of a more complex institutional descriptive system, which may include several other types of *finding aids* (e.g., registers, inventories, calendars, indexes, and shelf and container lists). In such a system, a catalog record created according to these rules is usually a summary or abstract of information contained in other finding aids, which in turn contain summaries, abstracts, or lists based on information found in the archival materials themselves." [12] More specifically, it also points out that "The chief source of information for [the cataloging of] archival materials is the finding aid prepared for those materials."[13]

Thus, in the context of a correctly configured archival descriptive system, all the components of that system are equally important. Moreover, the relative dynamism of these components in a digital context should not raise questions regarding the continuing utility or efficacy of any single element. Rather, looking at the system as a whole, these digital enhancements create a kind of synergy in which the whole becomes greater than the sum of its parts.

MARC RECORDS AS NAVIGATIONAL METADATA

Web-accessible MARC cataloging records for manuscript and archival materials for which EAD-encoded finding aids also exist, become then a critical component of the electronic descriptive hierarchy, enabling better understanding of the described materials at whatever level they are approached, as well as facilitating navigation between the descriptive components and among related resources. Thus, in such a system, a user launches a subject or name search in an online catalog. The search returns MARC records for relevant materials–which also includes archival materials. These MARC records should clarify the context or relevance of the search term to the described materials. Following links from the MARC record (via field 856) the user then may be led to relevant EAD-encoded finding aids. The top or entry level for these finding aids normally contains summary information (in biographical and scope and contents notes) that is more detailed than that in the MARC record. These notes lead in turn to detailed descriptions of the organizational components (or series) of the collection. Finally the user is led to very specific folder- or item-level descriptions. The entire process then is one of moving from a very generalized topical or name heading through increasingly detailed layers of metadata–a kind of "hierarchy of surrogacy,"[14] if you will–to a very specific entry for a relevant item or group of items. Furthermore, with the potential built into EAD to embed digital surrogates of collection material, the user could be led beyond mere descriptive metadata and eventually to images or transcriptions of the actual relevant items themselves.

While it is possible in this system to bypass any particular level–and indeed, more sophisticated and knowledgeable users may not require this sort of systematic unfolding of context and explanation–the absence of any of the descriptive components thwarts both fuller understanding of the material as well as effective navigation of those components on the Internet.

What is particularly interesting about the relationship between archival cataloging and EAD is that the descriptive systems described above which encompass archival description predate any sort of electronic or digital environment:

> In the United States, for example, some repositories have prepared published summaries of their holdings, and during the economic depression of the 1930s, the government funded a major historical records survey as a work relief project. In the late 1950s, more systematic efforts were initiated to assemble summary descriptions of resources nationwide. The commencement in 1959 of the multi-volume *National Union Catalog of Manuscript Collections,*[15] followed by the 1961 publication of Hamer's path-breaking *Guide to Archives and Manuscripts in the United States,*[16] helped identify the location and general scope of the manuscript collections within participating repositories.[17]

Helpful as these paper-based projects were, however, it was not until the advent of the MARC AMC format in the late 1970s that U.S. institutions gained the ability to disseminate information about their holdings more widely via national bibliographic systems. MARC AMC provided a *data structure standard* for sharing information about archival and manuscript holdings, enabling their integration with library bibliographic data

> in online catalogs. The first edition of APPM, published at roughly the same time in 1983, provided a companion *data content standard* for that same information. The assignment of controlled access points to the resulting catalog records enabled archival holdings to be searched with the same flexibility and precision as published materials. MARC records can accommodate only summary information about holdings, however, and so have played the role of pointers to the existence of detailed paper-based finding aids.[18]

The emergence of EAD has completed this process and has now made possible a fully dynamic descriptive apparatus. The pieces of the apparatus have always been there; MARC-AMC, EAD, and the Internet have made them fully vigorous and functional.

At the same time, it must be remembered that the use of MARC-based archival cataloging is an almost exclusively American phenomenon. The reasons for this have much to do with the fact that MARC-based bibliographic systems (such as RLIN and OCLC) have been almost non-existent in Europe and, more understandably perhaps, in the rest of the world.

EAD AND THE FUTURE OF ARCHIVAL DESCRIPTIVE STANDARDS

Turning away for the moment from the overall question of whether we should continue to create MARC records in an EAD environment, there are still issues about the nature of that cataloging that are legitimate areas of inquiry. These have to do, first of all, with the relationship between the text of the catalog record and the finding aid from which it was derived. Consider that in an EAD environment it is now possible to conduct not only full-text searches on archival finding aids, but also fully *contextualized* searches–that is, searches focused on the internal context, both physical and intellectual, of the information as reflected in the EAD encoding.[19] Unfortunately, this type of searching has not been fully explored or researched; this is in part because of the lack of an as-yet critical mass of encoded finding aids and in part due to little understanding on the part of researchers with respect to the structural significance of these finding aids. It is hoped that further experience and research will clarify the procedural and concomitant economic implications of the depth of encoding detail that may be needed to fully support such searching. While it is possible in most online catalogs to focus searches based on specific MARC tags, there is nothing within MARC, or the various systems that have been built upon it, that can provide for nearly the level of specificity that is possible in a deeply encoded EAD instance. Furthermore, these EAD searches can theoretically be conducted across multiple finding aids from a variety of repositories,[20] creating, at the very least, the potential for navigational confusion–returning search results from a variety of finding aids from many different institutions and systems and, most important, from a variety of finding aid *levels*. Future user interfaces for union finding aid databases will need to provide better navigational clues than they currently do.

In traditional archival cataloging, the cataloging is based directly on the finding aid–or, in terms more traditional library catalogers can understand and appreciate, the finding aid *is* the touchstone of cataloging: the "Chief Source of Information."[21] Thus, the substance of that cataloging (i.e., the notes) consists of an informed and intelligent summary or abstract of information found in the finding aid–along with the concomitant access points generated therefrom. It would seem that, with the entirety of that finding aid now accessible and searchable, the nature and content of the summary ought to change–especially since one of the main purposes of the catalog record has always been to guide a potential user to the finding aid as quickly as possible. While there is little hard experience yet to support this contention, we may certainly speculate on what the impact might be.

Currently, archival cataloging rules give only general guidance on the content of the notes;[22] the exceptions are the Scope and Content note and the Biographical/Historical note, both of which constitute the essential nucleus of the "bibliographic" record. In the case of both notes, APPM is quite specific. For the Biographical/Historical note, the rules instruct the cataloger: "Record *briefly* [emphasis supplied] any significant information on the creator/author of the archival materials required to make its nature or scope clear."[23] It then suggests the types of information that would be appropriate here and offers a final caution in a "bold note"[24] that "Elaborate biographical or historical essays are usually not appropriate for a catalog record . . . "[25] With the Scope and Content note, the instructions are to "Give information relating to the general contents, nature, and scope of the described materials,"[26] with more specific guidance on what kinds of information to include and the preferred order of that data. What is important to observe here is that these cataloging notes almost always have their direct–and *fuller*–equivalent in the finding aid. To repeat: archival cataloging is an intelligent and informed summary of information recorded in the finding aid. The cataloging rules discussed above can easily be applied more expansively to their equivalents in finding aids.

Given that these rules were formulated in a pre-EAD environment, it might reasonably be supposed that a new cataloging paradigm is emerging and that the very substance of the relationship between archival finding aids and archival cataloging has been forever altered. I would argue that this is *not* the case–at least not at this stage in the evolution of EAD.

The strength of EAD and the basis of its almost instantaneous broad appeal to the archival community has been that it was based on and developed from longstanding practice in and principles of archival description. The Berkeley Finding Aid Project recognized from the beginning that "to be successful, an encoding standard for finding aids must reflect and further the shared interests of the archival community and of the agencies and institutions that support it."[27] Towards that end, the original document type definition (DTD), which was called "FindAid," was based on a thorough examination of archival descriptive practice and finding aids from a wide variety of repositories. The subsequent revision of that DTD into what has become EAD was no less scrupulous with respect to existing descriptive practice and standards and, in fact, went considerably beyond the original DTD by incorporating the principles laid down in the General International Standard Archival Description (ISAD(G)).[28]

Furthermore, within the traditional structures of archival description was an almost perfect marriage with SGML. Archival materials, by their very nature, are highly hierarchical; the control and description of these materials reflects those hierarchies and are manifested not only in tools that are internally hierarchical, but are also hierarchical in their relationship to other tools. Within the essentially recursive [29] structure of SGML exist all the tools necessary to accurately and efficiently manage and reflect those requirements. As Daniel Pitti has pointed out, "SGML models text on a hierarchical model: a document, for processing purposes, is reduced to a tree, with elements as nodes. A collection, when broken down into its components can also be modeled as a tree."[30] Thus the essentially hierarchical nature of archival materials and description match nearly perfectly with the essentially hierarchical nature of SGML.

The point here is that EAD has been carefully crafted to reflect and accommodate the past as well as (it is hoped) the future of archival description. While it is certainly possible that new approaches to archival control and description may emerge in the rapidly evolving digital environment, the present reality is that traditional archival description as embodied in an EAD-encoded finding aid and its companion, a linked USMARC record, have, through the application of cutting-edge technology, suddenly emerged as the very model of metadata management for Web-based information resources. In fact, I have argued elsewhere[31] that libraries in general would do well to look at the archival model of description and control that depends on hierarchically layered metadata, rather than the labor-intensive and potentially irrelevant approach currently employed wherein detailed item-level description is lavished indiscriminately on all library materials (and worse, with the focus still on increasingly ambiguous or meaningless physical details of the "item in hand").

This is not to say that archival description in all its particulars currently exists in a state of perfect harmony. There must certainly be approaches to optimizing not only the overall descriptive apparatus, but also the specific relationship between the cataloging and the finding aid. For example, although a number of repositories are already doing this, the addition of the summary Biographical/Historical and Scope and Contents notes to the finding aid seems to offer both navigational and informational advantages. A user moving from the catalog record to the finding aid could be led (directly, perhaps?) to its exact equivalent in the appropriate context of the fuller information from which it was derived, thereby enabling immediate and more direct drilling into those more deeply nested hierarchical levels that may be more relevant to his or her inquiry.

Another "optimization" can be found in the practice (again, already followed in some institutions) of providing in the finding aid the exact access points that are already present in the cataloging. Although there is nothing in the cataloging rules absolutely requiring this, it has long been recommended practice to provide in the notes firm anchors for all access points provided in the cataloging record (6XX and 7XX fields). In the past, when the navigation of the descriptive apparatus was entirely manual, it was very important to provide contextual clues at every point in the process by way of confirming the relevance of the retrieved material. In today's more dynamic digital environment it is possible to create virtual relevance hyperlinks between and among the various forms of description. Thus, a subject search leads to a series of catalog records, each of which should explain the importance of the search term in the context of the described material. The presence in the finding aid of those same terms–especially since these access points are generally constructed under authority control–facilitates uniform searching of cataloging and finding aids, in addition to reaffirming context.

Happily, both of these enhancements may be easily achieved with EAD. All of the elements in EAD that have direct equivalents in USMARC have an "encoding analog" attribute.[32] Although part of the rationale for these attributes is to ensure conformity between EAD and other data structure standards, their presence should also allow for eventual "harvesting" of MARC records directly from the finding aids. This will allow archival repositories to focus most of their descriptive effort on the creation of full and consistent finding aids with the catalog record then provided as a byproduct of that effort. Another advantage to this is that it mirrors current practice in using the finding aid as the "chief source of information" for the cataloging. While the process is presently entirely manual, using encoding analogs for the purposes of creating MARC records automates it, while also further synchronizing the essential and inevitable relationship between the finding aid and the catalog record.[33]

A final area of concern is that of data content standards (sometimes known as "cataloging codes"). It was perhaps fortuitous that coincident with the development and release of the MARC-AMC format, *Archives, Personal Papers, and Manuscripts* (APPM) was also released. Although most archivists did not immediately understand it in these terms at the time, MARC represented a "data structure standard" for the communication of bibliographic information. The library world already had its "data content standard" in AACR.[34] This provided rules and instructions for formulating and formatting the actual information in the various cataloging areas, which would then be converted into MARC format. It was hoped that, with the publication of AACR2, there might be something useful for manuscript and archival catalogers. Unfortunately, this was not the case. AACR2 presented archival catalogers with problems and inconsistencies with existing archival theory and practice that were not only far beyond those in AACR, but were essentially irresolvable.[35]

Today, with EAD emerging as an internationally-based "data structure standard" for archival finding aids and description there is a clear need for a companion content standard. While existing archival descriptive standards[36] are adequate to a point, none of them were designed with the specific structure and requirements of either archival finding aids or, more particularly, EAD in mind. Accordingly, there is currently movement towards reconciling APPM, ISAD(G), and RAD into a single North American standard, which, it is hoped, will provide a useful foundation for similar work to proceed on a more international scale–particularly since EAD implementations are already well underway in a number of European countries and in Australia.

Towards this end, there have been a number of activities. In the summer of 1996 a group of archival description experts convened at the Bentley Historical Library at the University of Michigan, under the auspices of the Library's Fellowship Program for the Study of Modern Archives.[37] This group concluded that a fully articulated reconciliation of the existing content standards that was attuned to the needs of all forms of archival description would meet the growing demand for greater integration of access to primary resources by providing a content standard for EAD encoded finding aids as well as cataloging and other description. A summary of the findings of this work was published by Wendy Duff and Kent Haworth under the title of "Advancing Archival Description: A Model for Rationalising North American Descriptive Standards."[38]

In addition, a conference convened in Toronto in October 1997[39] to discuss the future direction of the *Anglo-American Cataloging Rules*. It was hoped by the archivists in attendance[40] that the conferees (consisting largely of the leading cataloging theorists and library administrators from around the world) would agree that the progress of the Internet-based information age had been such to justify a substantial overhaul of existing cataloging rules (which, I am obliged once again to point out, are rooted in principles going back to the middle of the nineteenth century). And further, that such an overhaul might well look to the hierarchical metadata structure of archival description for a model. Unfortunately, this was not to be the case. The inertia inherent in existing catalogs of millions upon millions of bibliographic records is sufficient to discourage most library bureaucrats and administrators from undertaking massive and systemic changes–particularly in an environment that is itself so volatile as to defy reasonable calculation.

The archival community has thus concluded that it must proceed on its own. While the library world may yet move more decisively, it is clear that it will not do so in time for archivists to draw any benefit with respect to problems that are immediate and crucial. With the assistance of the Gladys Kriebel Delmas Foundation, a group[41] assembled for a planning meeting in Toronto in March of 1999 to discuss the particularities of how the development of a North American standard for archival description might emerge. One of the results of that meeting was a document entitled "Toronto Accord on Descriptive Standards." The following principles were articulated in this document:

1. American and Canadian archivists are both committed to the use of descriptive standards in archival work.
2. We recognize that users of archives benefit greatly when archives follow common descriptive practices. A common North American descriptive standard would be of great benefit to users both in the United States and Canada.
3. For archivists, a common descriptive standard would be more cost-effective. North American archivists would only have to develop and maintain one set of standards, not two.
4. Canadian and American archivists share many principles in common, making a united North American standard feasible. Among them are:
    - a common descriptive practice and a commitment to the principle of provenance (*respect des fonds*) as the basis for archival organization and description;
    - a willingness to accept and use flexible structures;
    - a recognition that we have both already learned much from each other;
    - an openness to the possibility of merging our mutual standards;
    - a respect for differences and diversity within our respective cultures;
    - a willingness to work together.

5. Given the utility and feasibility of a common set of archival descriptive standards, both American and Canadian archivists are committed to further cooperation and collaboration in the development and maintenance of shared North American archival descriptive standards. This may extend to the creation of a common development and maintenance infrastructure and approval process for archival descriptive standards.[42]

While the precise details of how this work will proceed is not yet clear (much will depend on securing adequate funding support), there is a already a firm commitment to examining EAD and the *Rules for Archival Description* with respect to determining their potential for synchronization as companion data content and data structure standards. It is expected that subsequent work will move toward developing new rules or revising existing rules for archival cataloging to be consistent with whatever results from the EAD/RAD harmonization. While this work is driven by a clear need for a content standard for encoded finding aids, it will be important that whatever resulting changes that are suggested for the EAD DTD will be submitted through normal EAD Working Group [43] channels to a rigorous review process that will take into consideration the full international impact of these changes. At the same time, as archival descriptive standards evolve (the Canadian and U.S. archival communities are currently contemplating a North American-based amalgamation of APPM and RAD towards developing a foundation for rules for multilevel description), EAD must be nimble enough to accommodate new approaches.

Unfortunately, the use of MARC for cataloging archival materials is not widely applied or appreciated outside the U.S. The reasons for this may well be based on the historic sense of separation between the archival and library communities throughout much of Europe, [44] but the fact remains that the integrated online descriptive systems now in place in the U.S. are not likely to be replicated in a European environment any time soon. This is unfortunate.

While the broad applicability and robustness of EAD make it tempting to use as a stand-alone database, its real power is fully realized when used in conjunction with MARC cataloging. MARC summary level descriptions are valuable because they integrate archival collections with bibliographic collections, and in a very real sense, provide a broader context for them than is possible in the finding aid as a stand-alone description. An archival collection, when discovered in a bibliographic catalog, is discovered in and among related published materials. Further, if other "non-book" resources are also in the "bibliographic" catalog, you have a broad cultural resource context within which the archival and manuscript materials are established. Although this may go beyond what more traditional archivists regard as their descriptive responsibility, I would argue that the broader cultural contextualizing of their holdings is increasingly important and ought to be added to their responsibilities.

ITEM-LEVEL CONTROL, CATALOGING, AND EAD

Another area in the archival descriptive apparatus deserving further study is the potentially anomalous relationship emerging between traditional collection-level archival cataloging and the increasingly dense item-level descriptions found in deeply encoded EAD instances. This is particularly true where that instance serves as a platform for the presentation of digitized collection materials. In one sense, this shouldn't surprise us since the development of rules for archival cataloging was a direct response to the then-widespread practice of cataloging manuscripts and archival collections item-by-item.[45] Previous library cataloging rules failed to acknowledge the importance of provenance and context in archival description and instead tended to treat collections and fonds as little more than casual accumulations of variously interesting items–a much more antiquarian approach, if you will. Thus, both RAD and APPM strongly emphasize the importance of collection- (or fonds- , in the case of RAD) level description as a way of preserving the provenance and authenticity of the original material with respect to the vital relationships between the component items. As APPM points out, "The significance of the whole derives from interrelationships among its components. Emphasis on individual components may tend to obscure the importance of the whole."[46]

In this model, as noted earlier, the cataloging carries summary information and the finding aid is designed to fill in the details. From a cataloger's perspective (to say nothing of that of the manager), such an approach is significantly more efficient than preparing individual cataloging records for every item in a collection–especially when that collection may contain tens of thousands of items. Thus, the emergence of the archival cataloging record in tandem with the traditional finding aid was welcomed as a more cost-effective and less time-intensive way to provide access to manuscripts and archives. EAD has certainly made this mechanism even more efficient (notwithstanding the encoding overhead) by providing a fully dynamic articulation of this principle. Unfortunately, the efficiencies are not as thoroughgoing as one might expect.

Institutions that are using EAD as a platform for digital collection presentation (my own, most particularly[47]) have concluded that traditional folder or item captions from finding aids are usually insufficient for searching, description, and identification of the digital items. While it is a cliché that "a picture is worth a thousand words," it is becoming increasingly clear that it often takes at least that many to convey adequately the context, meaning, significance, and technical details of digital images of archival materials–whether those materials be images of text or images of pictures.

The result is that the descriptive metadata for digitized collection material has evolved into elaborate database records that fully describe the contents of each item and greatly facilitate complex searching both within and across collections. For example, in the Duke "Ad*Access" project, advertisements which formerly may have been grouped together in a folder under a general heading, such as "Ford Motor Company newspaper ads, 1941-1943" now have a record containing forty-three database fields (some of which are repeatable) for each digitized item in that folder. While a few of these fields contain management data, most of them are designed to provide enhanced access to the digital collection and include such critical information as "Headline," "Product," "Famous Name" (i.e., celebrity used as part of the ad), several fields regarding the type of illustration used and the artist's name, presence of specific ethnic minorities in the ad, and so on.

While most would agree that indexing archival material to this level of specificity is certainly advantageous for users, it seems equally clear that many might regard this as "descriptive overkill" of a kind perhaps approaching the excesses of the item-level manuscript cataloging of years past. There are, however, some important differences.

First, this is usually only done for items that have been digitized and presented *in situ* within the finding aid. Experience has shown that the presentation of digital collection material (whether archival or printed) on the Internet generally carries a higher metadata overhead. Images (either textual or pictorial) with no concomitant descriptive text are essentially lost on the internet. The data bytes that constitute the image are binary "textual" gibberish that are beyond the reach of even the most sophisticated search engines. Is it thus easy to understand why "metadata" has become such a buzzword with respect to Internet-based information. This metadata is all the more important with the sort of complex information-laden digital objects that library and archival materials represent on the Web. If access to the content of such materials is to be optimized consistent with the potential of the Internet, they must carry a richly detailed jacket of descriptive metadata. A simple caption description will suffice for an item or items that are not digitized; however, as soon as they become digital their descriptive requirements increase significantly.

Second, the digitization process is such that it lends itself easily to routinized metadata capture. Much of the actual data entry can be automated through the use of data templates, databases, perl scripts, and other methods. In addition, the actual image capture and scanning process is often sufficiently time-consuming for the scanning technician to manage most of the metadata management while the image is being scanned and processed.

Finally, what distinguishes the detailed description under discussion here from the item-level cataloging of the past is the focus on *access*. Item-level manuscript cataloging as it is prescribed in AACR2 chapter four, and as it was practiced by many in the past (and still is in some quarters) drew heavily on some of the traditions of rare book cataloging and had its focus almost entirely upon the physical and artifactual characteristics of the item. Thus there are elaborate foliation formulae, binding and watermark analyses, comments on the ink, and the general physical condition of the item and almost nothing that would lead one to the content beyond author and title statements and the usual limited and perfunctory subject headings. The item detail associated with digitized archival and manuscript materials is almost always focused on enhancing and elaborating on access to the intellectual content of the item–with the exception of some minimal technical information on image capture and compression format (most of which can usually be generated automatically through the scanning software).

The difficulty here is that there is currently very little guidance in descriptive standards or cataloging codes on the nature and structure of this information. It will be necessary for future revisions of these codes and standards to address these issues and to do so in a way that will be consistent with archival principles, descriptive traditions, and EAD. In addition, such projects as the "Making of America" [48] are very much engaged in developing metadata standards for these sort of digital objects. Their work (particularly in developing the MOA DTD[49]) should prove compatible with current EAD implementations, but will also help inform the process of incorporating such functionality in future revisions of EAD.

CONCLUSION

In the final analysis, it must be remembered that however much cataloging functions as a tool of library administration and management, it is primarily one of access. It is (to very loosely paraphrase the so-called "Paris Principles"[50]) the only way that potential users of library materials can discover *what* materials might be related to their needs and *where* those materials might be located. On the Internet, both the *what* and the *where* are now both problematic and volatile. Archival description and, more specifically, archival cataloging linked to EAD-encoded finding aids, offer an approach in which a carefully articulated descriptive apparatus serves as a dynamic mechanism for resource discovery at any level in either the descriptive or materials hierarchy. Lynn Howarth, Dean of the Faculty of Information Studies at the University of Toronto, has recommended that AACR be revised to provide the "essential framework for a 'front-end' tool, a kind of meta-surrogate that could serve as a gateway to discrete parts of an item . . . In a sense I envision a kind of *Rules for Archival Description* that provides for an increasingly detailed and hierarchically structured series of records all linked successively."[51]

Archival cataloging and EAD co-exist as parts of an essential metadata structure for management and resource discovery of manuscript and archival materials. While there will be inevitable adjustments in their relationship to each other, they currently stand as a digital articulation of basic archival descriptive principles, while also offering a model for the larger world of digital information management.

NOTES

1. The University of Michigan's Bentley Historical Library, in cooperation with the Mellon Foundation and the National Endowment for the Humanities, sponsored an annual Bentley Library Research Fellowship Program. In the Summer of 1995, they funded an application by Daniel Pitti to convene a group to examine the DTD that had been developed at Berkeley. The team included Pitti, Steven DeRose (Electronic Book Technologies), Jackie Dooley (University of California, Irvine), Michael J. Fox (Minnesota Historical Society), Steven Hensen (Duke University), Kris Kiesling (University of Texas), Janice Ruth (Library of Congress), Sharon Gibbs Thibodeau (National Archives and Records Administration), and Helena Zinkham (Library of Congress).

2. See particularly the special issues of the *American Archivist* devoted to EAD: volume 60, nos. 3-4; the *EAD Tag Library* (Chicago: Society of American Archivists, 1998); and the forthcoming *EAD Application Guidelines* (scheduled for publication by the SAA in the Summer of 1999).

3. The membership of NISTF consisted of Richard Lytle, chair, and David Bearman, project director, (both of the Smithsonian Institution), Maynard Brichford (University of Illinois), John Daly (Illinois State Archives), Charles Dollar (National Archives and Records Administration), Larry Dowler (Yale University), Max Evans (State Historical Society of Wisconsin), Steven Hensen (Manuscript Division, Library of Congress), Tom Hickerson (Cornell University), Charles Palm (Stanford University), and Nancy Sahli (National Historical Publications and Records Commission). For a detailed summary of the work of NISTF, see Richard Lytle, "An Analysis of the Work of the National Information Systems Task Force," *American Archivis*t 47, no. 4 (Fall, 1984): 357-365.

4. Elaine Engst, "Standard Elements for the Description of Archives and Manuscript Collections," unpublished report delivered to the National Information Systems Task Force, 1979.

5. Steven Hensen, " 'NISTF II' and EAD: The Evolution of Archival Description," *American Archivist* 60 (Summer 1997): 287.

6. See, for example, Chris Hurley, "The Making and the Keeping of Records: (1) What Are Finding Aids For?" *Archives and Manuscripts* 26: 58-77.

7. Steven L. Hensen, *Archives, Personal Papers and Manuscripts: A Cataloging Manual for Archival Repositories, Historical Societies, and Manuscript Libraries* (Washington, DC, 1983). For a fuller account of the emergence of APPM relative to

MARC-AMC, see Steven L. Hensen, "The Use of Standards in the Application of the AMC Format," *American Archivist* 49 (Winter, 1986) (from paper delivered at SAA Annual Meeting, Washington, D.C., 1984) (also reprinted in: Steven M Spivak and Keith A. Winsell, editors, *A Sourcebook on Standards Information: Education, Access, and Development* [Boston, 1991]), and Steven L. Hensen, "Squaring the Circle: The Reformation of Archival Description in AACR2," *Library Trends* 36 (Winter 1988).

8. Most of these projects came out of and were sponsored by the Research Libraries Group, which initiated a thorough and robust implementation of MARC AMC in its Research Libraries Information Network (RLIN).

9. It has always been a source of irritation among many archivists that the library world in the past separated categories of library materials by "book" and "non-book." While such a taxonomy may be understandable, given the focus of most libraries in the past, there has always been the whiff of something mildly distasteful in the term "non-book." The cataloging rules have reinforced this perception by treating "non-book" material as if it were a defective book.

10. Council on Library and Information Resources, *Scholarship, Instruction, and Libraries at the Turn of the Century*. (Washington, DC: CLIR, 1999), 15.

11. Society of American Archivists, *Standards for Archival Description: A Handbook* (Chicago: Society of American Archivists, 1994). Out of print; web version available at: http://www.archivists.org/publications/stds99/index.html.

12. Steven L. Hensen, *Archives, Personal Papers, and Manuscripts: A Cataloging Manual for Archival Repositories, Historical Societies, and Manuscript Libraries,* 2nd Edition. (Chicago, Society of American Archivists, 1989) rule 0.7, p. 3-4. Hereafter cited as "APPM."

13. APPM, rule 1.0B1, p. 9.

14. I have always been grateful to Richard Saunders for coining this particularly apt and euphonious phrase.

15. Library of Congress. Descriptive Cataloging Division. Manuscripts Section, *National Union Catalog of Manuscript Collections* (Washington, DC: Library of Congress, 1959-1993).

16. Philip Hamer, *Guide to Archives and Manuscripts in the United States* (New Haven: Yale University Press, 1961).

17. Important union lists were published in other countries as well. For example, the most comprehensive such publication in Canada was: Public Archives of Canada, *Union List of Manuscripts in Canadian Repositories = Catalogue collectif des manuscrits archives canadiennes.* W.K. Lamb, Director, and Robert S. Gordon, Editor. (Ottawa: Public Archives of Canada, 1968).

18. *EAD Application Guidelines* draft (5/13/99) (Chicago: Society of American Archivists, Summer 1999), 3-5.

19. For example, specifying personal names only in container lists and not as part of the text of other notes, or dates in biographical notes, but not in container lists.

20. Although the only practical way to do this at the present is to use a union database, such as the American Heritage Virtual Archives Project (http://sunsite.berkeley.edu/amher/) or the RLG Archival Resources site (http://www.rlg.org/arrhome.html), it is anticipated that the emergence of XML on the World Wide Web will greatly facilitate cross-institutional searching of EAD-encoded finding aids.

21. APPM, rule 1.0B1, p. 9.

22. It is assumed that the "hard data" areas of cataloging, such as main entry, title, and physical description should be relatively unaffected by the emergence of EAD.

23. APPM, rule 1.7B1, p. 24.

24. "Bold notes" are employed throughout APPM to provide information regarding specific archival application of certain rules or to provide commentary or orientation (p. viii).

25. APPM, rule 1.7B1, p. 25.

26. APPM, rule 1.7B2, p. 25.

27. Daniel Pitti, "Development of an Encoding Standard for Archival Finding Aids," *American Archivist* 60 (Summer 1997): 279.

28. International Council on Archives. *ISAD(G): General International Standard Archival Description, adopted by the Ad Hoc Commission on Descriptive Standards,* Stockholm, Sweden, 21-23 January 1993 (Ottawa, Ont.: International Council on Archives, 1994). (http://www.archives.ca/ica/isad.html).

29. Recursion refers to a feature in SGML wherein elements may contain one or more instances of themselves while also being nested within other elements.

30. Daniel Pitti in an e-mail message to the author, April 15, 1999.

31. Steven L. Hensen, "Archival Description and New Paradigms of Bibliographic Control and Access in the Networked Digital Environment," in *The Future of the Descriptive Cataloging Rules,* Brian E. C. Schottlaender, editor. ALCTS Papers on Library Technical Services and Collections, no. 6 (Chicago and London: American Library Association, 1998).

32. "Encoding analogs are attributes on EAD elements that correspond in type and function to fields or subfields found within other data structure standards such as MARC. Encoding analogs have been included in EAD to permit the exchange of finding aid data in systems that conform to relevant national and international data structure standards." *EAD Application Guidelines* (draft) (Chicago: Society of American Archivists, 1999), 39.

33. It must be pointed out that the "automatic" generation of MARC records from an EAD instance is currently only a theoretical possibility; no one has actually done it yet. Further research and possible changes in EAD may be necessary to realize MARC record generation fully.

34. Although the Library of Congress disingenuously insisted for years that there was no formal relationship between AACR and MARC.

35. For a fuller discussion of these issues, see the references noted in footnote 7 above.

36. These consist of the afore-mentioned APPM and ISAD(G) and also include: Bureau of Canadian Archivists. Planning Committee on Descriptive Standards. *Rules for Archival Description* (Ottawa: Bureau of Canadian Archivists, 1990). Usually referred to as "RAD."

37. This group consisted of Wendy Duff, Michael J. Fox, Kent Haworth, Steven L. Hensen, Kris Kiesling, and Kathleen Roe.

38. Wendy Duff and Kent Haworth, "Advancing Archival Description: A Model for Rationalising North American Descriptive Standards," *Archives and Manuscripts* 25: 194-217.

39. Joint Steering Committee for the Revision of AACR. *International Conference on the Principles and Future Direction of AACR,* Toronto, Ontario, Oct. 23-25, 1997.

40. Wendy Duff (Faculty of Information Studies, University of Toronto), Kent Haworth (York University), and Steven L. Hensen (Duke University).

41. The Canadian representative at this meeting included Wendy Duff, Kent Haworth, Bob Krawczyk, Mireille Miniggio, Margaret Stewart, and Hugo Stibbe. The US representatives include Michael J. Fox, Steven L. Hensen, Peter Hirtle, Kris Kiesling, Lisa Weber, and Martha Yee.

42. "Toronto Accord on Descriptive Standards." Final draft edited by Peter Hirtle and distributed via e-mail on April 13, 1999.

43. The EAD Working Group, a group formed by the Society of American Archivists' Standards Committee and Technical Subcommittee on Descriptive Standards, maintains formal responsibility for the ongoing maintenance of EAD in collaboration with the Library of Congress.

44. This supposition is based largely on anecdotal evidence and from scanning the archival literature from the U.K. and Australia. This separation existed to almost the same degree in the U.S. before the advent of MARC-AMC; the successes of archival cataloging and now EAD may be attributed largely to the degree that archives, libraries, museums, and so on, increasingly understand their respective interrelatedness in the larger arena of cultural resources.

45. Chapter 4 of AACR2 represents a substantially item-level approach to cataloging manuscripts, with little attention given to matters of provenance or context. APPM was developed in reaction to the limitations of this chapter.

46. APPM, rule 0.10, p. 5.

47. See especially the Library of Congress/Ameritech-sponsored "Historic American Sheet Music" project (http://scriptorium.lib.duke.edu/sheetmusic), the "Ad*Access" project (http://scriptorium.lib.duke.edu/adaccess) the IMLS-sponsored project (as of this writing, incomplete) on the writing and photographs of documentary photographer William Gale Gedney (http://scriptorium.lib.duke.edu/gedney)

48. http://www.umdl.umich.edu/moa/

49. http://sunsite.berkeley.edu/MOA2/papers/DTD.html

50. "Statement of Principles, International Conference on Cataloging Principles, Paris, October 1961" in Michael Carpenter and Elaine Svenonius, eds. *Foundations of Cataloging: A Sourcebook* (Littleton, CO.: Libraries Unlimited, 1985), 179.

51. Lynn C. Howarth, "Key Lessons of History: Revisiting the Foundations of AACR," in *The Future of the Descriptive Cataloging Rules,* Brian E. C. Schottlaender, editor. *ALCTS Papers on Library Technical Services and Collections,* no. 6 (Chicago and London: American Library Association, 1998)

The Online Archive of California: A Consortial Approach to Encoded Archival Description

Charlotte B. Brown
Brian E. C. Schottlaender

SUMMARY. The provision of universal union access to archival and manuscript resources is one reason to utilize Encoded Archival Description (EAD) for finding aids. A consortial approach to the encoding of archival finding aids offers efficiencies of scale, expertise, infrastructure, and funding. In addition, the consortial approach facilitates the formation of a union database of finding aids. The Online Archive of California (OAC) is a consortium of special collections repositories whose finding aids are integrated into a single, searchable database which describes the contents of primary source collections throughout California. Formed in September 1995, the OAC's initial goals are: (1) to create machine-readable versions of all existing finding aids; (2) to encode all existing finding aids according to EAD; and (3) to create the OAC union database of finding aids: *<http://www.oac.cdlib.org/cgi-bin/oac>. [Article copies available for a fee from The Haworth Document Delivery Service: 1-800-342-9678. E-mail address: <getinfo@haworthpressinc.com> Website: <http://www.HaworthPress.com> © 2001 by The Haworth Press, Inc. All rights reserved.]*

Charlotte B. Brown is Assistant Head for the Department of Special Collections and the UCLA University Archivist, UCLA Library, Box 951575, Los Angeles, CA 90095-1575 (E-mail: cbbrown@library.ucla.edu).

Brian E. C. Schottlaender is University Librarian, University of California, San Diego, 9500 Gilman Drive 0175G, La Jolla, CA 92093-0175 (E-mail: becs@ucsd.edu).

[Haworth co-indexing entry note]: "The Online Archive of California: A Consortial Approach to Encoded Archival Description." Brown, Charlotte, B., and Brian E. C. Schottlaender. Co-published simultaneously in *Journal of Internet Cataloging* (The Haworth Information Press, an imprint of The Haworth Press, Inc.) Vol. 4, No. 3/4, 2001, pp. 97-112; and: *Encoded Archival Description on the Internet* (ed: Daniel V. Pitti, and Wendy M. Duff) The Haworth Information Press, an imprint of The Haworth Press, Inc., 2001, pp. 97-112. Single or multiple copies of this article are available for a fee from The Haworth Document Delivery Service [1-800-342-9678, 9:00 a.m. - 5:00 p.m. (EST). E-mail address: getinfo@haworthpressinc.com].

KEYWORDS. Archival description, archival consortia, Encoded Archival Description, EAD, finding aids, Online Archive of California, OAC, project administration, retrospective conversion

INTRODUCTION

"Does the information exist, and if so, where?" These are two of the primary questions asked by those who try to locate information within archival records or manuscript collections. The questions reference the process of identifying information and obtaining access to it, a process which is constant, irrespective of the research interest or type of user. Unfortunately, the user often takes a serendipitous route, consulting an inconsistent variety of descriptive tools, in an attempt to identify relevant information. As a result, success is dependent upon the user's persistence and a measure of luck. The odds, however, are improving.

The Encoded Archival Description (EAD) standard enables archivists and manuscript librarians to provide users with finding aids that identify and describe archival and manuscript resources in a consistent fashion.[1] Implementation of the EAD by multiple repositories can provide universal union access to resources, such as that offered by the Online Archive of California (OAC).

The creation of the OAC union database is a focused, statewide strategy to provide the people of California universal access to archival and manuscript resources located throughout the state. The OAC contains thousands of archival and manuscript finding aids, encoded according to EAD and representing collections held by dozens of California repositories.[2] The beneficiaries of the OAC are both the residents of California and users worldwide.

The notion of a union database of finding aids representing collections held in California repositories was proposed in 1995.[3] In the initial discussions, it was clear to potential OAC participants that: (1) the EAD standard was a key development in U.S. archival practice; (2) archival and manuscript repositories should begin testing and implementing the EAD standard with the goal of forming a California union database of finding aids; and (3) forming a consortium of California repositories was preferable to having each repository undertake a unilateral approach to the encoding of its finding aids.

ADVANTAGES OF THE CONSORTIAL APPROACH

Though the impact of the OAC within the state of California and nationwide has yet to be fully realized, the benefits of taking a consortial approach to the implementation of the EAD are already apparent. Most importantly, the consortial approach ameliorates the challenges inherent in the establishment of an EAD standard and in the establishment of a union database of finding aids by centralizing many of the time-dependent and technically difficult functions. This allows participants to focus their efforts upon the site-specific aspects of EAD implementation. Also, the consortial approach fosters consistent implementation of standards and best practices, both within and outside the EAD construct. Finally, the consortial approach facilitates financial and operational economies of scale.

Centralized Functions

The centralized functions of the OAC fall into two general categories: (1) functions related to EAD implementation and (2) functions related to establishing the OAC union database. Examples of centralized functions relating to EAD implementation are:

- obtaining funds through the preparation and submission of grant proposals
- designing and presenting workshops to orient and train participants
- establishing centralized encoding units to encode participant's machine-readable finding aids
- developing template(s) for the re-keying and encoding of non-machine readable finding aids
- developing toolkits (including templates, conversion guidelines, and style sheets)
- monitoring to ensure consistency of EAD encoding across all OAC finding aids according to the OAC's *EAD Retrospective Conversion Guidelines*
- developing finding aid conversion macros
- providing ongoing "Help Desk" assistance to OAC participants.

Centralized functions relating to the creation and maintenance of the OAC union database include:

- customizing database software
- establishing and maintaining a Persistent Uniform Resource Locator (PURL)
- developing criteria and procedures for addition of members to the OAC
- developing finding aid submission routines and a tracking system for publishing encoded finding aids
- composing OAC homepage text and tutorials
- maintaining database statistics and user logs.

OAC members realize other benefits from the consortial approach besides those mentioned above. Primary amongst these is the general development and promotion of standards throughout the membership, including:

- finding aid content standards
- standards for collection-level MARC bibliographic records derived from encoded finding aids
- standard thesauri to be applied to specific types of finding aids
- metadata standards
- subject taxonomies.

The growing sense of community amongst the OAC repositories can also be viewed as a benefit. OAC participation is demonstrated evidence of a repository's membership within the community of state-wide archival and manuscript repositories. Every opportunity to consult the OAC reminds the repository's staff and administration of their relationship to the whole, and of the value of their contributions to fostering access to California resources.

From a collection management perspective, the OAC union database significantly broadens a repository's ability to conduct collection analyses, document specific collection content, and monitor repository use. Repositories are now able to review and refine their collection policies based upon the collection documentation available on the OAC. Existing cooperative collection management arrangements are strengthened, and opportunities to create new cooperative arrangements are becoming evident.

Also of interest to collection curators is the OAC's ability to intellectually re-integrate physically dispersed collections and to clarify or enhance documentation related to a collection's provenance. An analysis of consortial-level holdings benefits preservation programs, at the repository level and regionally. OAC documentation supports cooperative conservation treatment proposals, as well as the review of local and regional salvage priorities. By the same token, the uniqueness of a collection may be further documented by consulting the OAC, allowing a repository to more appropriately prioritize the collection within the repository's overall preservation program.

Consortial Approach: The Users

For many archivists and special collections librarians, the overwhelming reason to implement the EAD is to offer users substantial improvements in the identification of and access to primary source materials. Both the OAC and the

Research Libraries Group's Archival Resources Service promote collection identification and access on a large scale, a scale only a consortial approach can provide. Both databases utilize what Fred Miller has described as an "integrated descriptive program": the online bibliographic record–contained in the Melvyl®, OCLC, or RLIN databases–is linked to the encoded finding aid which is in turn linked to selected digitized collection surrogates.[4] Though the evidence is thus far anecdotal, OAC members have yet to encounter a researcher who is not delighted to have a single online access point more than 5,000 finding aids, all of which are linked from online bibliographic records.

A large finding aid database is advantageous to the user only if it offers seamless navigation and an effective, easily understood search engine. In truth, the OAC has not yet arrived at this ideal state, although navigating the OAC is not difficult once the hierarchical presentation of the finding aids and the database is understood. OAC members and users have noted that the symbols used in several of the database icons are not intuitive and the current search commands are only serviceable. As the database continues to grow and new repositories are added, the consortium's members have assigned high priority to improving the OAC's navigation and search functions.[5]

Though OAC members have yet to fully utilize the monthly OAC transaction logs as a public services tool and source of collection information, it is worth noting that the OAC's logs are organized by: query terms/hits, query terms/no hits, and IP addresses. A recent analysis of the query term/no hits data by UC-Berkeley resulted in changes to the content of selected UC-Berkeley finding aids, with the object of improving database retrieval by keyword or phrase.[6] Expanded to the more than 5,000 OAC finding aids, an analysis of the OAC transaction logs might uncover heretofore unknown search patterns or methodologies, indiscernible in a smaller-scale data set.

Consortial Approach: Funding

Once a repository decides to implement EAD, staffing and training usually require an infusion of temporary funding. Obtaining these kinds of funds from within the institution itself is often problematic; frequently outside funding is needed. Since many regional and national granting agencies prefer proposals that include multiple institutions, the consortial approach to funding EAD implementation has proven singularly effective in obtaining extramural funding.

Consortial Approach: Leveraging Resources

For two-thirds of the OAC repositories, applying the EAD standard to finding aids can be viewed as one of the final stages of bibliographic retrospective conversion–an undertaking most libraries have been pursuing for upwards of twenty years. As with any recon project, implementing EAD requires an investment in staff, training, and overhead for a *finite* amount of work. Budget officers and administrators inevitably weigh the cost of EAD recon, which targets primary source collections, against earlier recon efforts aimed at the circulating and reference collections. "Is it worth the expense and effort?" they ask. The consortial approach provides an acceptable answer.

As with any automation project, the retention of trained staff is of ongoing concern. Since the OAC consortium has centralized encoding, workflow is consistent enough to offer flexible schedules, both full-time and part-time. Centralizing encoding also fosters consistent training, allows the OAC to monitor closely encoding standards, and encourages the development of expertise amongst the encoders. This, in turn, has positive consequences for the content of the OAC database.

HISTORY OF THE OAC

In 1993, the concept of providing "nonproprietary encoding standards for machine-readable finding aids" was being formulated by Daniel Pitti at the University of California Berkeley Library.[7] Shortly after Pitti's April 1995 Berkeley Finding Aid Project (BFAP) presentation on the development of the EAD, Kathy Donahue and Charlotte B. Brown met with Brian Schottlaender to propose the implementation of the EAD by the special collections units of the University of California's (UC) nine campus system.[8] Schottlaender supported the proposal and began polling the other UC campuses regarding their participation on a consortial basis.[9]

At Schottlaender's invitation, thirty-nine representatives from the UC special collections units, the Getty Research Institute for the History of Art & the Humanities, the Huntington Library, Stanford University, and the University of Southern California, assembled in September 1995 to discuss the potential for a collaborative EAD effort. A consensus was reached: the scope of the encoding effort would be determined, and an EAD funding proposal would be submitted to the University of California Digital Library Executive Working Group. The Online Archive of California (OAC) consortium was formed[10] [see Appendix I: OAC Timeline, 1995-1999].

In truth, implementing a consortial approach to the EAD was the working assumption throughout the discussions of the September 1995 planning meeting. The scope of such an effort had not yet been precisely determined[11] and few of the attending manuscript librarians or archivists appreciated the intellectual, administrative, and financial impact EAD implementation would have on day-to-day archival and manuscript functions. Nevertheless, attendees at that September meeting already clearly understood and appreciated the enormous benefits to be derived from online access to all UC finding aids and, consequently, advocated the formation of the consortium to their respective administrators.

ADMINISTRATION OF THE OAC

Schottlaender was an early supporter of Pitti's EAD efforts.[12] Upon initial funding of the OAC by the University of California Office of the President's Digital Library Executive Working Group, the following administrative organization was established in the Fall 1996:

- Brian Schottlaender, Project Administrator
- Charlotte B. Brown, Project Coordinator
- Daniel Pitti, Database Designer
- Alvin Pollock, Finding Aid Conversion Specialist

In 1997, Pitti departed for the University of Virginia, and Tim Hoyer, Project Manager of the OAC in Berkeley–where the bulk of the OAC's EAD markup was centralized–began working closely with Alvin Pollock on database formation and overall project design. This administrative organization carried the OAC through its subsequent evolutionary phases, including its integration into the California Digital Library.

California Digital Library (July 1998)

A second OAC administrative tier was formed with the July 1998 integration of the OAC database into the California Digital Library (CDL). Primary among the goals associated with this formal integration was incorporating the OAC's finding aids into the breadth of resources accessible via the CDL, an objective achieved in time for the CDL Web site's public debut in January 1999 (<http://www.cdlib.org>). An equally high priority was porting the OAC database, originally hosted at UC Berkeley, to a CDL server. The database now receives the full benefit of the resources of the CDL Technologies Division, including 24-7 system support.

Additional CDL goals for the OAC include:

- Converting as many extant finding aids as possible–machine-readable and legacy[13]–for inclusion in the OAC database.

- Creating as many MARC collection-level records as possible in the Melvyl® union catalog to complement OAC finding aids.
- Creating digitized content in at least one identified thematic (subject) area.
- Integrating both EAD and MARC processing routines into mainstream archival processing activities by, among other things, assisting participants with encoding self-sufficiency.
- Reevaluating and revising the design of the OAC interface.
- Evaluating the pros and cons of the Dynaweb software platform currently used on the OAC site.

CDL integration initiated the formation of two new OAC advisory structures: the OAC Advisory Working Group and the OAC Metadata Standards Working Group. At the same time, Schottlaender's role as OAC Project Administrator was formally integrated into the CDL administrative structure with his appointment (.25 FTE) as Senior Associate to the CDL Executive Director. His responsibilities extended to primary content development, especially in the context of the OAC. With the OAC now tightly stitched into the CDL, the consortium began to develop a far more coherent and robust structure.

All along, one of the major challenges facing the crafters of the OAC had been to scale it up–politically and otherwise–from the Berkeley Finding Aid Project in the first instance and the University of California EAD (or UCEAD) Project in the second. The Working Groups and the breadth of input they afforded OAC administrators were critical in making the OAC a true consortial effort. The groups were charged as follows:

OAC Advisory Working Group

- Develop a clear description of the OAC and its boundaries.
- Develop guidelines as to who can participate in the OAC and what the requirements for, and responsibilities of, such participation are.
- Develop a strategy for ensuring the representation of extant UC Library archival finding aids in the OAC database no later than December 1999.
- Develop a strategy for ensuring the inclusion of corollary MARC collection-level cataloging in the Melvyl® database no later than December 1999.
- Identify approaches to "mainstreaming" OAC-based processing into ongoing UC Library archival processing routines, and costs associated with that mainstreaming.
- Develop a strategy for incorporating museum content into the OAC database.

- Develop a strategy for identifying thematic areas in which to begin populating the OAC with digitized primary content.
- Prepare recommendations for mechanisms to foster inter-institutional collaboration for digitization.
- Identify strategies for funding OAC work over the long term.
- Identify issues associated with licensing OAC content and external (i.e., non-OAC) access to that content.

OAC Metadata Standards Working Group

- Oversee accurate, standardized usage of EAD elements. This will include monitoring use of the OAC Project Guidelines in addition to studying the use of other EAD elements with a goal of determining "best practice" within the OAC union database (e.g., use of <controlaccess>).
- Oversee issues relevant to the interaction between EAD-encoded finding aids and USMARC-encoded collection-level records (e.g., use of the 856 field).
- Communicate standards-related issues and recommendations to the OAC Project Administrator and participant membership, as necessary and appropriate.
- Keep the CDL and OAC participant membership apprised of national EAD development and implementation issues and communicate OAC input to the EAD Working Group of the Society of American Archivists.

Funding of the OAC (1996-1999)

Based upon the discussions held during the September 1995 planning meeting, the startup phase of the OAC was projected to take two years at an estimated cost of $1,105,000 ($595,000 in funds requested and $510,000 in cost sharing). The University of California Office of the President agreed to provide half of the funding with the understanding that OAC project managers would obtain matching funds from non-UC sources. Matching funds were initially secured in the form of a grant of $330,000 from the California State Library under the auspices of the Library Services & Technology Act (LSTA), covering OAC operations from October 1996 through September 1998. The consortium then obtained a second LSTA grant of $355,000 for the period October 1998 through September 1999.

Centralized OAC Units

Grant funding for the OAC consortium offered all OAC participants two EAD options: (1) to encode finding aids onsite with training paid by the OAC, or (2) to submit finding aids to centralized locations for encoding and mounting onto the OAC database. Six OAC repositories chose to encode onsite: Stanford University, UC-Berkeley, UCLA, UC-San Diego, UC-Davis, and the University of the Pacific. The remaining OAC participants submitted their finding aids to an OAC centralized encoding unit, for markup by the consortium's encoding staff.

Among the nine UC campuses, the UC-Berkeley Bancroft Library has the largest number of archival and manuscript collection finding aids. UCLA has the second largest number dispersed among its five special collections units. Of the total number of finding aids, a considerable number are legacy finding aids that require conversion to a machine-readable format. Again, a substantial proportion of the OAC's legacy finding aids were held at the UC-Berkeley Bancroft Library and at UCLA.[14] It seemed practical, therefore, to establish encoding units at both UC-Berkeley and at UCLA.

PROFILE OF OAC MEMBERSHIP

All California repositories that utilize finding aids to access their collections–libraries, historical societies, museums–are potential sources of OAC content. As of December 1999, forty-four repositories were represented in the OAC. Currently twenty-five of the repositories are archival and/or manuscript units administered by an academic institution. As the OAC database grows, the diversity of repository types will no doubt increase, as will that of the constituencies served by those repositories. Currently the OAC includes finding aids from the following types of institutions:

- art museums
- historical museums
- historical societies
- independent archives
- private colleges and universities
- public libraries
- state universities

The California State Library and the California State Archives are also members of the OAC.

OAC Affiliates

One of the hallmarks of the OAC, from its inception, has been the participation of non-University of California "affiliate" institutions. Participation by these institutions is essential to achieving the objective of universal union access to California resources. As eager as affiliate institutions are to facilitate greater access to their collections, many still require assistance in the conversion of their finding aids and in training their staffs to create new finding aids following the EAD standard. At this point, the OAC, with its unique aggregation of expert staff and technical infrastructure, offers the most economical means for capturing valuable archival information and for assisting understaffed repositories in becoming self-sustaining participants in the future. To that end, the OAC has developed the following Statement of Participant Benefits and Obligations:

Benefits

- Digital publication of one's finding aids and their delivery via the Internet.
- Access to OAC training, documentation, and productivity tools.
- Access to knowledgeable OAC staff and colleagues.
- Enhanced discovery potential for one's clientele due to the integration of one's holdings into the greater OAC whole.
- Ability to get statistical reports of collection use (which, in turn, facilitates collection appraisal).
- Expanded grants opportunities, due to:
  - ability to participate in consortial grant applications.
  - ability to reference OAC participation in individual grant applications.

Obligations

- Agreement to follow OAC metadata standards when creating finding aids for inclusion in the union database.
- Agreement to follow OAC digitization standards when creating digital surrogates for inclusion in the union database.
- Agreement to adhere to minimum OAC automation infrastructure specifications.
- Agreement to create MARC record corollaries to EAD instances, and to link the two (via the 856) from within the University of California's Melvyl® union catalog (required for UC participants; desirable for others).

CONCLUSION

Much has been accomplished in the four years since OAC development began. The primary initial objective of the consortium has, by and large, been achieved: that is, the creation of broad-based and integrated access to finding aids for archival and manuscript collections geographically dispersed throughout the state of California. The consortial approach to this effort has allowed OAC participants to leverage their collective staff, knowledge, and financial resources–resources which would have been individually inadequate to the task. It has had a number of additional benefits as well. It has facilitated both the rapid establishment of a broad membership base and the rapid deployment of a critical mass of database content. Perhaps most importantly, it has made available to the end user the discovery benefit that accrues to integrating individual finding aids and the finding aids of individual institutions into the larger whole of the OAC.

This benefit has been further leveraged by the fact that the OAC has also made considerable progress with one of its other significant strategic objectives: providing users with access to digital content from its collections in the context of the union database of finding aids. While the finding aid conversion project was proceeding, OAC members began to make a substantial amount of digital content available to their users. In the California Heritage Digital Collection, the Ishigo Collection, the Eastman Collection, the Free Speech Movement Archive, the Honeyman Collection, the Roberts Collection, and collections from the Berkeley Art Museum/Pacific Film Archive and UCLA's Fowler Museum, OAC users gained access to rich collections of digital facsimiles from important museum and research collections. The OAC has also recently launched a number of ambitious projects that will bring an even greater amount of high quality digital content to its users. With funding from LSTA, LC/Ameritech, IMLS, and the federal government through the auspices of the Library of Congress, OAC partners are beginning projects that will bring OAC users large digital collections. These include major museum collections, the collections of cased photographs at the Bancroft and State Libraries, the collections documenting Japanese-American relocation held by various OAC consortium members, the collections documenting Chinese in California 1850-1920 held by the California Historical Society and the Bancroft Library, and a major group of collections documenting California's ethnic heritage held by yet other OAC consortium members.

NOTES

1. Encoded Archival Description as maintained by the Encoded Archival Description Working Group of the Society of American Archivists and the Network Development and MARC Standards Office of the Library of Congress.

2. In most cases, collections represented by finding aids submitted to the OAC must meet two conditions: the collection must be located in a California repository and

be accessible to users. OAC repositories are encouraged to submit finding aids for all collections, not just those relating to the history of California.

3. The idea of creating a union database of finding aids from the nine campuses of the University of California, the Getty Institute for the History of Art & the Humanities, the Huntington Library, Stanford University, and the University of Southern California was informally discussed in May 1995 by the authors and Katherine Donahue, Head of the History and Special Collections Division of the UCLA Louise Darling Biomedical Library. The first OAC planning conference was held in September 1995 [see Appendix I: *OAC Timeline (1995-1999)*].

4. For an excellent overview of the concept of an integrated descriptive program, see Frederic Miller, "Archival Description" in *Reference Services for Archives and Manuscripts, The Reference Librarian* 56 (1997): 62-63. Providing users with digitized collection surrogates from primary source materials has been underway for many years. The intellectual linking of surrogates to the container lists included in machine-readable finding aids and to the MARC 856 field within machine-readable online bibliographic records is a more recent development.

5. Attendees at the February 1999 OAC FAST workshop discussed several instructional options: in-service training guidelines for the OAC, revision of OAC online tutorials, and the creation of an OAC Users Group. OAC tutorials will be revised as of the January 2000 release of the California Digital Library (CDL).

6. February 27, 1999 observation by Alvin Pollock, OAC Finding Aid Conversion Specialist, during the Society of American Archivists FAST workshop, UC-Berkeley.

7. "Choosing an Encoding Standard" in *Development of the Encoded Archival Description Document Type Definition. Encoded Archival Description.* Library of Congress <http://www.loc.gov/ead/eadback.html>

8. Schottlaender was formerly Associate University Librarian for Collections & Technical Services at UCLA. The UCLA Department of Special Collections reported to him until his departure for UC-San Diego in September 1999. The nine campuses of the University of California system are: UC-Berkeley (UCB), UC-Davis (UCD), UC-Irvine (UCI), UCLA (Los Angeles), UC-Riverside (UCR), UC-San Diego (UCSD), UC-San Francisco (UCSF), UC-Santa Barbara (UCSB), and UC-Santa Cruz (UCSC).

9. The following UC special collections librarians and archivists participated in the discussions that lead to the establishment of the OAC: Sid Berger/UCR, Rita Bottoms/UCSC, Charlotte B. Brown/UCLA, Anne Caiger/UCLA, Robin Chandler/UCSF, Lynda Claassen/UCSD, Stephen Davison/UCLA, Deborah Day/UCSD, Katherine Donahue/ UCLA, Jackie Dooley/UCI, Peter Hanff/UCB, Brigitte Kueppers/UCLA, Richard Lindemann/UCSD, William Roberts/UCB, John Skarstad/UCD, David C. Tambo/UCSB, Bradley Westbrook/UCSD, and David Zeidberg/UCLA.

10. When formed in September 1995, the consortium was named the University of California-EAD (UCEAD). However, from the outset the UC representatives envisioned consortial participation to include all interested California-based repositories. In January 1997, the UCEAD was renamed the Online Archive of California (OAC) to more accurately reflect the eligibility and participation of all California repositories.

11. It was only two months later that a survey of UC special collections units indicated that over 3,680 finding aids (92,000+ pages) were eligible for encoding.

12. Schottlaender was in regular communication with Pitti during the conceptual stages of the BFAP, ca. 1992, prior to the formation of the OAC in 1995.

13. Legacy finding aids are defined as un-encoded finding aids created before implementation of the EAD; they an be either in machine-readable form or typed/handwritten. Typed/handwritten legacy finding aids require re-keying into a machine-readable file prior to encoding.

14. As of the formation of the OAC in 1995, all of the finding aids held by the UC-San Diego Department of Special Collections were in machine-readable format. UC-San Diego was the first OAC member to encode and publish all of its finding aids in the OAC union database.

APPENDIX I. OAC Timeline 1995-1999

The following timeline presents the sequence of OAC accomplishments and indicates benchmarks for the population of the OAC database during its first year of LSTA funding.

1995	Apr.	Berkeley Finding Aid Project EAD conference.
	Sept.	Formation of Online Archive of California (OAC)–initially called the UC-EAD–during the first University of California EAD planning conference.
1996	Sept.	Initial funding received from UC Office of the President.
	Oct.	Second UC planning conference for OAC.
1997	Jan.	OAC workshop: • Research Libraries Group FAST training. • OAC calendar and benchmarks established. • Finding aid (f.a.) content determined. • OAC action list developed.
	Jan.	UCLA Electronics Publication Assistant (1 FTE) hired to encode UCLA finding aids.

Mar. UC-San Diego is first UC campus to encode all finding aid.

Spring OAC database configuration and administration established.

Workflow designed for submitting finding aids from six UC campuses (UC-Davis, UC-Irvine, UC-Riverside, UC-San Francisco, UC-Santa Barbara, UC-Santa Cruz) to UC-Berkeley; UCLA and UC-San Diego will do their own encoding.

April UCLA Electronic Publications Assistant is trained and UCLA workflow is established.

Summer OAC Toolkit developed: boiler plates, conversion guidelines, style sheets. Potential OAC Affiliates (California repositories) contacted; Affiliate finding aids mounted on the OAC.

Negotiations with Apex Data Services on re-keying and encoding non-machine-readable legacy finding aids.

Sept. Funding of OAC: awarding of 1997-98 LSTA funds, $330,000

*****Oct. 1997Benchmark - 30,000 encoded pages*****

[Benchmark achieved in early Summer 1997]

1998 Jan. OAC evaluation conducted by Anne Gilliland-Swetland/ UCLA Department of Library and Information Services: survey and interviews of 1996-97 OAC participants.

July California Digital Library (CDL) assumes administration of OAC.

Sept. Funding of OAC: awarding of 1998-99 LSTA funds, $355,000.

OAC conference: to review progress, determine next OAC phase.

OAC Advisory Working Group formed; OAC Metadata Standards Working Group formed.

***** Sept. 1998-2,420 finding aids (59,431 encoded pages)*****

Dec. Test: broad subjects assigned to selected OAC finding aids from CDL Broad Subject list; subject coding embedded into finding aid metadata to facilitate subject searching via CDL search engine.

1999 Jan. Final report of OAC survey and evaluation submitted by Anne Gilliland-Swetland.

California Digital Library (CDL) opens publicly available website, including OAC database.

Feb. Society of American Archivists (SAA) FAST workshop offered to seventeen OAC affiliates.

First batch of re-keyed legacy f.a.'s returned from vendor; re-keying workflow established and administered by UC-Berkeley encoding unit.

May Development of subject taxonomy for University of California finding aids published on the OAC.

Sept. Funding of OAC: conclusion of 1998-99 LSTA grant.

Consortial Approaches to the Implementation of Encoded Archival Description (EAD): The American Heritage Virtual Archive Project and the Online Archive of California (OAC)

Timothy P. Hoyer
Stephen Miller
Alvin Pollock

SUMMARY. The libraries at the University of California, Berkeley and Duke University have favored the "consortial approach" to implementing Encoded Archival Description (EAD) by concentrating on "retrospective conversion" of "legacy" finding aids and their integration into union databases. This paper will add to the work that appeared in The American Archivist (v. 60: 3-4) by describing the experiences of two of the earliest EAD implementers with a special focus on the importance of the develop-

---

Timothy Hoyer is the retired Head of the Bancroft Library Technical Services and Director of Digital Archives Development, The Bancroft Library, University of California, Berkeley, CA 94720-6000 (E-mail: thoyer@library.berkeley.edu).

Stephen Miller is Director of the Digital Library of Georgia, University of Georgia Libraries, Main Library 4th Floor, Athens, GA 30602 (E-mail: sdmiller@uga.edu).

Alvin Pollock is Lead Programmer for the California Digital Library's Online Archive of California and the University of California, Berkeley, Library's Electronic Text Unit, 250 Moffitt Library, UC Berkeley, Berkeley, CA 94720-6000 (E-mail: apollock@library.berkeley.edu).

[Haworth co-indexing entry note]: "Consortial Approaches to the Implementation of Encoded Archival Description (EAD): The American Heritage Virtual Archive Project and the Online Archive of California (OAC)." Hoyer, Timothy, P., Stephen Miller, and Alvin Pollock. Co-published simultaneously in *Journal of Internet Cataloging* (The Haworth Information Press, an imprint of The Haworth Press, Inc.) Vol. 4, No. 3/4, 2001, pp. 113-136; and: *Encoded Archival Description on the Internet* (ed: Daniel V. Pitti, and Wendy M. Duff) The Haworth Information Press, an imprint of The Haworth Press, Inc., 2001, pp. 113-136. Single or multiple copies of this article are available for a fee from The Haworth Document Delivery Service [1-800-342-9678, 9:00 a.m. - 5:00 p.m. (EST). E-mail address: getinfo@haworthpressinc.com].

ment "an acceptable range of uniform practices" both in consortial union databases and in the continuing community effort to establish EAD "best practice." It will also suggest that a mixed EAD implementation strategy offers the best chance of long-term success (i.e., the development of separate guidelines for the retrospective conversion of legacy finding aids and for the creation of new finding aids).

KEYWORDS. American Heritage Virtual Archive Project, archival consortia, Encoded Archival Description, EAD, finding aids, Online Archive of California, OAC, retrospective conversion

INTRODUCTION

From the beginning of their participation in the development of Encoded Archival Description (EAD), the Library at the University of California, Berkeley, and the Special Collections Library at Duke University have favored what Michael Fox has referred to as the "consortial approach" to implementing EAD.[1] They have concentrated on retrospective conversion of legacy finding aids and their integration in union databases. Both libraries participated together in the original Berkeley Finding Aid Project (BFAP) that lead to the development of EAD, and both were partners (with Stanford and Virginia) in the first EAD union database project, the NEH-funded American Heritage Virtual Archive Project. Berkeley, continuing along the same path, helped bring the findings of the American Heritage Project directly into the University of California's EAD union database project (UCEAD), which began with the participation of the archives and special collections of its nine campuses and has since grown, as the California Digital Library's (CDL) Online Archive of California (OAC), to encompass repositories throughout the state.

The principle established in these projects–that community agreement on acceptable encoding practices is an essential part of the continued development and implementation of EAD–has formed the bedrock of the EAD experience of Berkeley and Duke, and their partners. This paper will add to the work that appeared in the Summer and Fall 1997 issues of the *American Archivist*[2] by describing the experiences of two of the earliest EAD implementers with a special focus on the importance of the development of "an acceptable range of uniform practices" both in a consortial union database and in the continuing community effort to establish EAD "best practice."

EAD AND "BEST PRACTICE"

The EAD Document Type Definition (DTD), while specifying the structure and syntax of a finding aid, was not designed to be prescriptive. EAD mandates very few required elements, rarely dictates the order or frequency in which elements may occur, and does not describe the form or nature of the content of any of those elements. While the Society of American Archivists' (SAA) EAD Workshop, *EAD Tag Library,* and upcoming *EAD Application Guidelines* go a long way toward standardizing encoding within the EAD community, much is still left open to interpretation and, thus, to variation in the practice of individual repositories that employ it. This means that even within the confines of SAA-recommended practice, the same types of information can be legitimately encoded a number of different ways.

Recognizing that the consistency of the data within a union database is the key to its success, partners in the NEH-funded American Heritage Virtual Archive Project (Berkeley, Duke, Stanford, and Virginia) made it their first order of business to agree on "an acceptable range of uniform practices" for the conversion of finding aids into EAD. The encoding practices agreed upon by the American Heritage partners were documented by Daniel Pitti in *The Encoded Archival Description Retrospective Conversion Guidelines: A Supplement to the EAD Tag Library and EAD Guidelines*. By beginning the project with a common understanding of how EAD was to be applied, the American Heritage partners, including Duke and Berkeley, created a model for consortial EAD conversion projects and laid the ground work for the larger community enterprise of developing EAD "best practices." *The EAD Retrospective Conversion Guidelines* were almost immediately employed, with relatively few changes, by the archivists and special collections librarians of the University of California when they met in January of 1997 to begin the University's Encoded Archival Description (UCEAD) Project. Because of its acceptance of the *Guidelines* originally developed in the American Heritage Project, UCEAD was able to expand during the course of its first year to include repositories throughout California. Now known as the Online Archive of California (OAC) (http://sunsite2.berkeley.edu/oac/), this EAD union database includes over 3,300 finding aids (72,000 pages) from forty-five repositories, and continues to grow.

The complete *EAD Retrospective Conversion Guidelines* used by Duke, Berkeley and their partners are available via the World Wide Web (http://sunsite.berkeley.edu/amher/upguide.html). They outline a set of rules–some mandatory, some suggested–or encoding legacy finding aids in a consistent manner. In some cases, the *Guidelines* also set rules governing content.

Here is a brief outline of some of the more important decisions documented in the *Guidelines,* including a description of the rationale used to arrive at them:

1. The *Guidelines* recommend a common form of unique identifier for archival collections. The identifier should not only be unique within the confines of the individual repository, or within a union database like the OAC or the American Heritage union database, but also should uniquely identify the collection worldwide. The framers of the *Guidelines* rejected the widespread practice of using a local accession number, call number, or record number from either a local Online Public Access Catalog (OPAC) or a bibliographic utility, in favor of the more general and standards-based approach of assigning a Formal Public Identifier (ISO/IEC 9070:1991) used within the framework of the SGML Open Catalog format. In addition to being unique, these identifiers prove useful in linking between finding aids no matter where they are located since they can be used verbatim within SGML Open catalog files. The Formal Public Identifier for a collection is encoded within the <eadid> element. It consists of a formal owner/identifier for the repository holding the collection (derived from the Library of Congress name/authority record for that repository or constructed according to principles outlined in the *Anglo-American Cataloging Rules, 2d edition, revised (AACR2),* the USMARC repository code for the institution, the accession number or call number of the collection, and the title of the collection.
Example:

```
<eadid type="SGML catalog">PUBLIC "-//University of California
Berkeley::Bancroft Library//TEXT (US::CU-BANC::BANC MSS
92/894 c::The Arequipa Sanatorium Records)//EN"
"arequipa.sgm"</eadid>
```

Due to the hierarchical nature of Formal Public Identifiers, individual objects within a collection (such as a digitized photograph or scanned images of a selection of pages) can be identified and linked using a standard form.

```
PUBLIC "-//University of California, Berkeley::Bancroft
Library//TEXT (US::CU-BANC::BANC MSS 92/894 c::The Arequipa
Sanatorium Records::Letter, 1965)//EN"
```

Such a linkage is persistent and always resolves correctly even when the URL of a finding aid or an individual object within the finding aid changes.

Besides allowing hyperlinks between finding aids and digital objects, the identifiers allow links to MARC collection-level records by using a separate catalog file where each catalog entry resolves to a local catalog number or bibliographic utility number.

2. The *Guidelines* stipulate that finding aid titles should be constructed so that users will know that the resource they are retrieving is a *guide* to the collection, not a digital representation of the collection itself. Typically this involves prepending a phrase such as "Guide to the," "Inventory of the," or "Register of the" to the formal name of the collection within the <titleproper> element. The formal name of the collection would be retained within the top-level <unittitle>.
Example:

```
<titleproper>Inventory of The Arequipa Sanatorium Records,
<date>1911-1958</date></titleproper>
```

3. The *Guidelines* make certain elements which are optional in the EAD DTD mandatory or "mandatory when applicable." The top-level <did> of the finding aid requires a title (<unittitle>), the name of the repository (<repository>), a physical description of the collection consisting minimally of a size (<physdesc>), and the collector or creator of the collection (<origination>) when applicable. Additionally the creator or collector, and the repository name must be in the form used in the Library of Congress Name Authority File or must be constructed according to principles described in AACR2.
Example:

```
<did>
 <head>Descriptive Summary</head>
 <unittitle label="Title">Robert E. Badham Papers,
 <unitdate type="inclusive">1929-</unitdate></unittitle>
 <unitid label="Collection number">E872.B33 1962</unitid>
 <origination label="Creator">Badham, Robert E.</origination>
 <physdesc label="Extent"><extent>117 boxes</extent></physdesc>
 <repository label="Repository">
 <corpname>University of California, Irvine. Library.
   Dept. of Special Collections.</corpname>
 . . . etc.
</did>
```

ENCODING

Berkeley

Under the *EAD Retrospective Conversion Guidelines,* many encoding-related policy decisions remain the responsibility of the individual repository. The level of detail in the markup (i.e., "granularity") varies among American Heritage and OAC partners. Many encode each personal, corporate, or geographic name wherever it appears within the text of the finding aid. Some encode it when it occurs within the Scope and Content for the collection. Others, such as the Bancroft Library, encode it only within an explicit <controlaccess> element or within the top-level <did>, ignoring it elsewhere in the finding aid. Such a decision was made in recognition of the fact that resources vary from institution to institution. The total number of finding aids which need to be encoded for a particular repository is also a factor.

As a result of this variation in the granularity of the data created in the EAD union database projects, a lowest common denominator approach was adopted for the search interface developed for those databases. Interface designers felt that providing an option to limit searches by personal, corporate, or geographic name might mislead users, who might reasonably expect a complete set of search results when what this option would actually retrieve would represent only a relatively small subset of finding aids. Although anecdotal evidence suggests a free text search for a personal name, when carefully constructed, retrieves virtually identical results as a search limited to <persname> elements, the decision not to encode down to this level precludes such useful manipulation of the data as the construction of analytical indexes of personal, corporate, and geographic names and topical subjects. In recognition of this problem, the OAC is now considering a plan to enrich its finding aid database by retrospectively encoding these terms.

It must be stressed that, despite the length and detailed nature of the *EAD Retrospective Conversion Guidelines,* most policy decisions involving encoding are left to the individual repository. In both the American Heritage and OAC databases, Berkeley's Bancroft Library, for instance, has used its own internal set of extremely detailed markup instructions to augment the *EAD Retrospective Conversion Guidelines*. These were the product of regular weekly meetings in which encoders discussed examples of encoding problems and arrived at a consensus on how they should be marked up. In the face of uncertainty about the "right way" to solve an encoding problem, consistency was considered to be of the highest importance. As the encoding team marked more finding aids and learned more about EAD, archival practices, and the nature of finding aids, team members naturally reexamined past encoding practices and decided that some of the early decisions had either produced undesirable results or were entirely incorrect. Fortunately, the consistency imposed by the team decision-making process very often made it possible, in light of these discoveries, to globally correct or enhance the finding aid database by program.

As the local, Bancroft-specific guidelines evolved, they tended toward greater simplicity. As mentioned above, in the early stages of the American Heritage Project Bancroft encoders marked up personal, corporate, and geographic names wherever they occurred within the finding aid. Each weekly meeting, however, turned up examples and problems relating to this decision. Unnormalized forms of these names, initials, forenames or surnames used in isolation, and other irregularities in the original finding aids, created various problems relating to markup at this level of detail. Encoders were spending far more time than necessary thinking and making decisions about matters of minor importance. The decision was made to cease encoding down to this detail within the container list, but to continue the practice within the scope and content note of the finding aid. Eventually this decision too was dropped.

By the same process, Bancroft encoders also discontinued the practice of creating explicit hypertext links between "see" and "see also" references within the container list. Creating such links was found to be *very* time-consuming and no satisfactory programmatic solution was found to automate or partially automate the process. Another problem encountered by the encoding team was caused by the common early practice of Bancroft archivists of mixing several types of information, such as scope and content, arrangement, organization, and biographical information, in a single prose section consisting of one or more paragraphs. Although the encoders recognized that separating these pieces of information into their correct EAD elements, <scopecontent>, <arrangement>, <organization>, <bioghist>, and so on, would be useful and desirable, accomplishing the task would involve teasing apart grammatically linked sentences and phrases, grouping like information together, and substantially changing wording and punctuation. Not only would this prove time-consuming, but, more importantly, archivists advising the project team were uncomfortable with the idea of encoders with relatively little archival experience or training making such extensive modifications in the content of the finding aids. The decision was made to "encode it as it lies," and such hybrid prose sections were left unchanged and marked as <odd>.

In retrospect, the decision to "encode it as it lies" may have been unwise, especially when applied to the container list. As any programmer who has dealt with EAD-encoded finding aids in any fashion discovers, nowhere is consistency more important than within the container list. As the most complex piece of a finding aid, the consistency of the <dsc> is the key to being able to manipulate and format it in a variety of ways. Bancroft encoders preserved the order of container list elements, essentially duplicating the layout of the original page. This decision was made not in recognition of the fact that the original layout on paper was intellectually important, but purely as a time-saving measure. Had a decision been made to devote the additional resources necessary to encode each container list in a single, common format, rearranging elements into a common order, and making minor changes to wording and punctuation as necessary, much more could be done with the data today. This bears out the experience of archivists at the Minnesota Historical Society (MHS) when they began to consider using EAD for their finding aids.[3] In Berkeley, because of the complexity of the range of different finding aids confronting them, the encoders and archivists who participated in the weekly meetings could not take as radical an approach to redesigning finding aids as was taken at MHS. As it is, it is not inconceivable to imagine someday programmatically overlaying a common format and order of elements in the container lists of recon finding aids in the OAC database, but as yet, no decisions have been made to actually do so. It might be worth noting here that the evolving Technical Specifications for the *Museums in the Online Archive of California (MOAC) Project* mandate a large degree of consistency within the container list as "best practice" for the museum implementation of EAD within the OAC. Various experiments with the finding aids encoded to these Technical Specifications to date illustrate dramatically the value of this approach to encoding container lists because of the flexibility it allows for the manipulation of the data.

Unlike the American Heritage Project, where all partners did their own encoding, much of the OAC's markup is done in a centralized support unit at Berkeley by staff from the Library's Electronic Text Unit (ETU) and the Bancroft Library (UCLA also maintains a markup unit and a number of other OAC members do their own markup as well). OAC partners send their finding aids–as ASCII text files, word-processing documents, or relational database files–via FTP to a centralized directory on a server. These finding aids are then prioritized and assigned to encoders. Even within finding aids authored in the Bancroft Library, as we have seen above, there are differences in layout and file format among individual finding aids. Add to this the complexity of the finding aids submitted by the numerous OAC partners, and the total data set is as varied as one can imagine. As a result, no single tool can be used to convert all finding aids into EAD.

At this point a word on SGML editing tools may be in order. Most encoding institutions discover over the course of their projects that the role of SGML editing tools is an evolving one. At the outset of a project, an SGML editor is critical (e.g., SoftQuad's Author/Editor or ArborText's AdeptEditor). It is an indispensable tool for learning SGML, becoming familiar with EAD, and validating EAD-encoded finding aids. As encoders become familiar with EAD tags and rules they realize that while an SGML editor remains useful as an *authoring* tool for archivists creating new finding aids, its utility as a *conversion* tool is extremely limited. After encoders have learned new, efficient techniques for quickly converting text documents into EAD, the SGML editor is relegated to the role of reference tool. In this context it is useful primarily for determining which elements are available in which contexts, and which attributes and attribute values are available for each element. SGML editors are critical in the initial stages of a project, after which their usefulness drops off dramatically. Developing other tools and techniques for the purposes of conversion will increase markup speed and efficiency by orders of magnitude.

Most encoders discover the benefits of word processing macros very quickly. As noted below in the description of Duke's encoding system, the container list is always encoded in a process separate from the rest of the finding aid. Constructing a single word processing macro to encode the preliminary material in a finding aid is not feasible because its format and layout vary so widely among finding aids and from institution to institution. In a project like UCEAD/OAC, finding aids also arrive for encoding in a variety of file formats. Most have been delivered in MS Word, WordPerfect, plain ASCII text, or occasionally in HTML. So any macro created to encode preliminary material frequently needs to be developed in parallel in MS Word and WordPerfect (conversion between these two formats has proven to be impossible in most cases). Even within a specific word processing format, layout and formatting can vary so extensively that creating a single macro proves impossible. The solution to this problem developed by Berkeley's lead programmer for both the American Heritage Project and the OAC, has been the creation of a Web-accessible *template* program. Encoders connecting to the OAC project Web site (http://sunsite.berkeley.edu/FindingAids/uc-ead/tools.html) are presented with a template containing series of labeled boxes which, when filled in with text copied from an electronic finding aid, generates a complete, fully encoded EAD instance for the preliminary material. The program performs much of the low-level encoding automatically, detecting blank lines within prose sections and splitting them into <p> elements, encoding complex chronological lists into valid <date>/<event> pairs, and so on. In most cases the instance is complete, requiring no further editing for the preliminary material. Like traditional templates, "boilerplate" text, such as the name and address of the encoding repository, can be supplied automatically, but, unlike traditional templates, when minor changes are made, new versions do not need to be distributed to all encoders. While not as efficient as Duke's encoding macros, this approach proves to be fast and flexible for dealing with the wide variety of finding aids received by Berkeley's OAC encoding team.

The online Web template method, however, is not an appropriate approach for encoding container lists, which must be done as a completely separate step. At Berkeley, finding aids which are created using a database program are imported into Microsoft Access–a program with which the Library has some expertise–and the EAD encoding is generated as a report. The great majority of the finding aids received from OAC partners are authored using a word processor and are encoded using one of two methods. The most efficient method is to use perl, a text manipulation programming language. All Berkeley encoders learned perl by enrolling in a five week perl course through the University Extension program. Most finding aids converted to EAD using perl are completed by utilizing a technique called "stepwise refinement." Encoders key in a series of perl commands, each customized for the specific formatting and layout characteristics within the finding aid. Each perl command overlays more and more detailed "layers" of markup, using the results of the previous commands to create the subsequent command. Generally when the container list is encoded to a particular level it will then be opened in an SGML or ASCII editing tool for further correction and markup. Occasionally partners submit batches of finding aids that are so consistent in formatting and layout that it is considered worthwhile to invest the time to create a more complex perl program to encode the entire container list with a single command. Because of their consistency, these types of finding aids can be encoded in a remarkably short period of time. The number of finding aids to be encoded and their relative consistency in layout and formatting are the keys to deciding whether it is worth the several days of effort required to create the more complex, customized perl program to handle them.

Perl works best with ASCII text files, however. Word processing files have to be converted first to ASCII text before conversion with perl can begin. In addition, certain formatting codes in the word processing file are lost when converted to ASCII (bold, italics, and so on). Although such pure formatting characteristics are often not retained within an EAD-encoded finding aid, more often than not they may represent critical intellectual information. An italicized word or phrase can represent a title or the name of a ship, for example. These formatting codes have to be converted to their appropriate EAD tags, either using macros or a mildly complicated search and replace, before the files are converted to ASCII text. A more frequent problem arises because many word processing formats do not convert well to ASCII text. Most commonly, all indentation within a hierarchical container list may be lost. The hierarchical layout is critical to correctly encoding the various nesting <c>s. In such cases, using macros for the entire conversion process makes the most sense. After a three-day intensive macro workshop held in the Library, and with a detailed macro manual available, OAC encoders quickly became adept at using macros to encode container lists. Like the perl method, most macros are small and created very quickly. Several small macros will be used to encode various parts of the container list, or if the body of material is deemed large enough and consistent enough, a larger, more complex macro will be created to encode the entire container list with a single click of a button.

Since all three methods of conversion–database conversion, perl, and word processing macros–bypass the normal checks imposed by a true SGML editor, checking the encoded file with a validating SGML parser is a critical final step in the process. When conversion of the container list is complete, it is joined to the preliminary material created using the online Web template and is validated using James Clark's NSGMLS.

In a union database project like the one producing the OAC, ownership of the finding aid data and the archiving of the SGML finding aid files are issues of considerable importance. Once the encoding has been completed, who is responsible for the content of the finding aid and how will changes in it be communicated? In the OAC, the institution holding the collection is responsible for their SGML files and is expected to archive them. The procedure for revising encoded finding aids established at the outset of the project is for the "owner" of the finding aid to make changes to the archival SGML file and to send a copy of the revised SGML file to the union database's center for republication. Version control procedures for SGML files need to be worked out carefully.

Duke

As previously mentioned, many policy decisions regarding encoding were left to the individual repositories participating in the American Heritage and OAC projects. Staff at Duke University's Rare Book, Manuscript, and Special Collections Library made many such local policy decisions when beginning work on the American Heritage project. One of the major decisions was to create a richly tagged collection of finding aids by providing subject tagging throughout container lists using elements such as <persname>, <corpname>, <geogname>, and so on. Although time-consuming, it was felt that the high granularity and additional options provided by such tagging would prove beneficial in the long term.

Some decisions were false starts which were later corrected. When the Duke finding aids were initially encoded, a <controlaccess> section containing standardized subject terms was not included. Due to the importance and added value of the inclusion of such terms, they were later derived from the MARC records for the collections when available and added retrospectively to the previously encoded finding aids. The majority of the Duke finding aids were produced within the last fifteen years, and thus had a fairly regular structure and conformed to conventions of modern archival description. While a few had a tabular layout featuring columns of information, most could be formatted during encoding in a non-tabular fashion. At the beginning of the project, the tabular structures of EAD were employed, but this process was quickly found to add greatly to the overhead of tagging with little benefit. Thus the decision was made to produce only non-tabular finding aids, changing the layout from the original if necessary.

Staff at Duke developed their own routines for encoding finding aids while working closely with Berkeley and other American Heritage Project consortial partners in order to gain the benefits of shared tools and expertise. In order to successfully encode a significant number of Duke's finding aids, it was necessary to devise a flexible encoding system that met several criteria. First, it had to accommodate finding aids produced in different electronic formats (e.g., word processed using different versions of Microsoft Word software, plain-text formats, or scanned and processed with Optical Character Recognition (OCR) software). Second, it had to be flexible enough to deal with different finding aid layouts and with a variety of container lists. Third, it needed to allow for quality markup in a short amount of time, by providing as much automation as possible.

After working with several sample finding aids, Duke's project manager soon discovered that a fully automated method of quickly and accurately encoding the container lists would be very difficult to achieve given the variations in existing container lists. On the other hand, he also found that the regularity of the <eadheader>, <frontmatter>, <did>, and <admininfo> sections, as well as text elements with predictable patterns such as dates, tend to lend themselves to more automated processing.

As the first step in creating an encoding system, the project manager devised a template, in the form of a "dummy" document instance, based on the *EAD Retrospective Conversion Guidelines*. Next, since most of Duke's finding aids were created using Microsoft Word, tools were devised for encoding based on the WordBasic macro language used in MS Word version 6. It was found that the WordBasic macro language was both powerful and relatively easy to learn and use. Due to the complexities involved in encoding, these tools were designed to be used as one step in a complex process rather than as a single automated encoding system.

While the macros developed in WordBasic for Word 6 worked well for the duration of the American Heritage project, serious flaws with that approach have become evident over time. Microsoft shifted away from the WordBasic macro language found in Word 6 and implemented Visual Basic for Word as the new macro language for Word 97. It became quickly apparent that the code written in Word 6 would not automatically update correctly to the new format.

Moreover, even if it had updated correctly, artifacts of the conversion would render the code hard to edit and update. This created a situation in which the older version of Word must be maintained specifically for the encoding process as a stopgap measure while a new encoding system is devised. Such a situation makes clear the need to base primary encoding tools on more reliable software packages such as perl, and to use only simple, easily-written macros when needed for certain tasks.

The encoding process begins with an evaluation of the finding aid to determine the level of regularity and consistency with which it is formatted and to look for any irregularities which may need special attention. A high degree of consistency in the finding aid allows the encoder to use macros to automatically mark up a number of elements. For instance, a macro searches the MS Word document for styles such as italics which should be encoded within the <title> element, and cleans some of the formatting elements such as headers and footers which, while important to the printed document, are extraneous to the encoding process. Next, the encoder splits the MS Word file into two files, one containing the title page, administrative information, biographical note, scope and content note, and controlled access terms (derived from the MARC record for the collection), and another containing the container list.

To encode the first file, the encoder first arranges data such as the title of the collection, the name of the creator of the finding aid, the inclusive dates of the collection, the name of the encoder, date of encoding, the copyright and provenance notes, and so on, so that it may be processed. Upon processing this structured data is captured as variables which are then placed into a template to create the header section of the encoded finding aid through the end of <admininfo>. The <bioghist>, <scopecontent>, and <controlaccess> sections also lend themselves to similar automation. After arranging the components of these sections in the necessary order, the markup is quickly completed by macro.

The container list is often the most complex and time-consuming part of the retrospective conversion process. By allowing for single key access to common elements and strings of elements, for example "<c01 level="series"><did><unittile>," as well as automated processing of similarly formatted sections of the container list, the tools developed in Microsoft Word allow the encoder the ability to quickly provide the basic markup for container lists. Similar to Berkeley's process of "stepwise refinement" using perl, this process first generates a basic skeletal markup to which layers will be added later. The skeletal markup is then processed through a number of macros that locate and mark dates and extent statements such as "(2 folders)" and clean and regularize the resulting markup.

When the markup of the container list is complete, the full finding aid is assembled from the separate files and is validated against the EAD DTD using James Clark's NSGMLS. At the beginning of the American Heritage Project, SoftQuad's Author/Editor was used for the same process and evaluated; however it was found to be unwieldy for large-scale conversion when compared to plain-text markup using Microsoft Word and validation using NSGMLS. As discovered by Berkeley, such SGML authoring and editing tools are helpful for learning and the creation of new finding aids, but are not as helpful in the conversion process.

While most of Duke's finding aids were already in either Microsoft Word or plain-text format, there were a number of older finding aids which existed on paper only. These were scanned using OmniPage Optical Character Recognition (OCR) software with good results. A Hewlett Packard ScanJet 4c scanner with document feeder was purchased for this purpose. It was found that the best results were obtained when the original typescript was available. Copies, depending upon their clarity, tended to yield acceptable results, however all text generated by OCR needed proofreading and correction. The only text which was completely inadequate had been printed by a dot matrix printer. For finding aids such as these, which were still important enough to be included in the project, re-keying was the only solution. While this conversion was appropriate for a small number of finding aids, repositories with a large number of paper-only finding aids would want to consider outsourcing this conversion, as Berkeley did for the OAC project.

Because of Duke's involvement in the proto-EAD development project, the Berkeley Finding Aid Project (BFAP), a number of Duke finding aids had been encoded with BFAP's FindAid DTD, the predecessor of EAD. With the assistance of American Heritage Project staff at Berkeley, these finding aids were converted to EAD using perl scripts and then manually revised to ensure that they conformed to the standards set out by the project guidelines.

FINDING AID "PUBLICATION" AND USER WEB INTERFACE

When Berkeley and Duke began working together in the American Heritage Project, there were few choices when it came to publishing databases of SGML finding aids on the World Wide Web. We opted for the INSO Corporation's DynaWeb software and our experience with it is amply documented below. Nevertheless, we recognize that even at the time there were other options which offered attractive alternatives to DynaWeb. American Heritage partner, the University of Virginia's Special Collections Department, taking advantage of the Electronic Text Center's expertise with SGML, employed the OpenText search engine in conjunction with locally written interface forms and HTML filtering programs to produce local online access to its EAD finding aid database.[4] Michael Fox has described a number of other methods of publishing EAD finding aids in an article in the *American Archivist*.[5] Recently several new entrants into this field, Dual Prism and SIM, have offered new products that are extremely promising. Although it might be useful to review these products and fully discuss the options available at this time, the following description will stick to our experience of publishing EAD finding aids to date. It should not be read as an apologia for a single method of delivery but rather as a report on where we are now.

Berkeley

The American Heritage Virtual Archive and the Online Archive of California (OAC) both use INSO Corporation's DynaWeb to publish their finding aids on the Web. DynaWeb–and its associated publication tools–was provided free to the Berkeley Library and the CDL under INSO's academic grant program. Under this program the software is free but participating institutions are obligated to take a week-long training program in Rhode Island for about $2,000. Additionally, institutions must pay for the yearly maintenance contract, about $3,000. DynaWeb uses a stylesheet to convert EAD-encoded documents into HTML "on the fly" (stylesheets for both American Heritage and OAC were developed at Berkeley). A common misconception about both the American Heritage and OAC databases is that the finding aids are either encoded in HTML, or that DynaWeb somehow "dumbs down" the content by virtue of its conversion into HTML. In fact HTML is simply the delivery format. It is used by Web browsers to render the documents on the screen, but in fact DynaWeb is a fully SGML-compliant engine "under the hood." The DynaWeb search engine allows users to perform sophisticated queries across all finding aids in the entire database. In addition to keyword, wildcard, proximity, and Boolean searching, DynaWeb contains thesauri for several different languages. Searches can return exact phrase matches or can consult the thesauri and return synonyms. Search stemming allows retrieval of grammatical variants: a search for "buy" will return "buying" and "bought." Finally, users can limit their searches to specific SGML elements, including access to all attribute values, and limit element-specific searches to a particular context (i.e., make use of a specific element's "ancestry"). Users are not expected to understand the underlying SGML encoding and syntax of the finding aids they are querying. Context-sensitive searches are made available through simple search forms which effectively hide the underlying SGML from users. DynaWeb is fully XML-compliant, so OAC partners may create and submit their EAD-encoded finding aids in whichever syntax they prefer, either SGML or XML. Finally, DynaWeb utilizes HTML as its display format so that users are required neither to access the American Heritage or OAC Web site with a particular brand of Web browser nor to purchase a browser plugin such as Panorama or MultiDoc Pro.

At the time DynaWeb was chosen as the publication mechanism for the American Heritage Project's finding aid database, there were no other commercial products available which delivered SGML content over the Web. Several years later there are more options available, both for delivery of SGML and XML, and recently the OAC conducted a survey of available commercial products, weighing their respective strengths and weaknesses as compared to DynaWeb. The OAC compiled a list of DynaWeb features, many considered critical, others highly desirable. DynaWeb excels in the following areas:

1. Fully SGML and XML compliant. DynaWeb provides access to all attribute values, handles recursive elements seamlessly, and contains a complete entity-management system–important features often lacking in other SGML and XML Web delivery software.
2. A powerful stylesheet language. The DynaWeb/Dynatext stylesheet language is the most powerful and flexible in use within the industry. The capabilities of other publication software, Panorama for example, lag far behind in functionality.
3. Dynamic, expandable/collapsible table of contents. DynaWeb automatically generates a dynamic table of contents, always visible in a frame on the left-hand side of the document. Any section of the table of contents can be expanded or collapsed with the click of the mouse.
4. Fully customizable interface. Such user interface objects, such as the button bar, table of contents, search forms, and other navigation features are controlled by editable configuration files. Almost any feature of the DynaWeb interface can be customized using a powerful adaptation of the TCL scripting language.
5. Handles huge documents seamlessly. The single most important feature of the DynaWeb system is its ability to handle huge SGML documents as easily as it does small ones. Many of the EAD documents in the finding aid database are in the order of 10 Mb in size and the OAC expects finding aids in the order of 100 Mb in the near future. Any future replacement software must be able to handle documents of this size.

DynaWeb is not without its weaknesses. Cross-collection searches can be very slow, particularly when searches are limited to specific SGML elements. DynaWeb combines a search engine with a collection management system and an HTML conversion system, all in one package. This tight integration of diverse features often makes customization of certain specific aspects of the software very difficult or at times impossible, despite its powerful customization mechanism. One of the options which is being explored at Berkeley is to bypass DynaWeb's slow cross-collection searching component with a separate search engine such as OpenText or Verity, and to hand search results off to DynaWeb for display and rendering of individual finding aids. This would allow the OAC to leverage DynaWeb's strengths, such as its ability to handle large documents and its powerful stylesheet language, and bypass its weaknesses, such as its slow cross-collection searching function and its difficult-to-customize collection management system.

Duke

During the first experimentation with the FindAid DTD, a site at Duke was set up which made use of the Panorama SGML browser for viewing native SGML, and a custom application of OCLC's FRED application for providing HTML versions of the encoded finding aids.[6] This approach had several drawbacks that made it necessary to seek a long-term solution to providing access to the encoded finding aid collection. First, both Panorama and the HTML conversion system lacked the ability to search across all of the finding aids. Second, users were required to download and install the Panorama helper application which, while fine for demonstration purposes, was a significant hindrance to the average user. Finally, the person who originally set up the HTML conversion system had since left the institution, making it difficult to maintain and upgrade.

Although DynaWeb was being used for the American Heritage union database, Duke applied for and received its own grant of software from the INSO prior to the start of the American Heritage Project. This allowed the library to take advantage of the strengths of the DynaWeb discussed above, and also implement other SGML-based projects. A primary concern was the fact that the online finding aids database would constitute mission-critical information for the library. Several factors such as the speed of DynaWeb itself and the speed of the network connection between North Carolina and California made it apparent that this information should be stored locally to provide quick access to on-site and campus users. Like the University of Virginia, another participant in the American Heritage Project, Duke decided to both locally maintain their finding aids and contribute them to the American Heritage database.[7]

FINDING AID INVENTORY AND THE PROJECT TRACKING DATABASE

Although encoding and publication are unquestionably the core activities in any EAD implementation, there are a number of other activities, as Michael

Fox has pointed out, that are important to successfully implementing EAD.[8] In the case of both Berkeley and Duke, gaining control of their collections of finding aids and selecting finding aids for conversion have been key activities. A complete inventory of all collections to be represented in an EAD finding aid database (union or otherwise) should be completed as soon as possible at the outset of an EAD conversion project. In the experience of EAD conversion staff at both Duke and Berkeley, the tracking database is the indispensable tool for the management of EAD workflow. Information to collect in a tracking database includes:

- Is there a finding aid for the collection?
- Is the finding aid in machine-readable form?
- Does the finding aid need to be scanned or re-keyed?
- Is the collection cataloged?

There is other critical information that needs to be recorded during the process of finding aid conversion. Here is a brief account of how this was done at Duke and Berkeley.

Duke

The process of gaining intellectual control over the finding aids of the Rare Book, Manuscript, and Special Collections Library at Duke University was the first and one of the most important tasks that was undertaken when embarking on the EAD retrospective conversion process. Whereas finding aids are typically considered a means to an end, EAD and the retrospective conversion process challenges us to consider the finding aids themselves as important documents–the byproduct of the human activity of archiving. While visitors to the research room typically use printed and bound finding aids, there may also be collection control files which may contain important descriptive information, as well as an archive of electronic files used to generate the print versions. Much like the appraising and processing of an archival collection, bringing order and arrangement to the body of finding aids is the first step to gaining a full understanding of what materials are available for the retrospective encoding process.

A number of questions needed to be addressed by the project manager as a preliminary step to gaining a broad view of the finding aids collection:

- What are the primary points of access to the archival collections?
- Where are the finding aids and other forms of access located?
- How are finding aids created within the institution?

- What formats, both modern and historical, of finding aids are used?
- How has archival description changed during the institution's lifetime?

By first relying on information gained from those who created and used finding aids–technical and research services staff–and then by a process of listing and evaluating the finding aids available in a variety of forms, an overall view of the finding aids collection was formed. Information gained from the technical services and research services staff was helpful not only in determining where and in what forms finding aids may be located, but also in determining which collections had the highest demand and research value. This information proved useful later when prioritizing the finding aids for encoding.

The next step in gaining intellectual control over the finding aid collection was to create a listing of the hard copy finding aids available to researchers. At Duke, the reading room contains six vertical file drawers of folders which contain copies of finding aids for collections open to the public. Sometimes other information related to the collection such as newspaper clippings or biographical information is included. The folders are arranged alphabetically by title of collection. A Microsoft Access database was created to serve as a method for arranging information about the finding aids and for tracking the encoding process.

As a first step in adding information to the database, the titles of the reading room folders were listed along with their contents. The contents were indicated as follows:

Full finding aid:	A complete modern finding aid including cover pages, administrative information, biographical note, scope and content note, and container list
Description/index:	A finding aid reflecting past archival practice which often consisted of a narrative collection description incorporating both biographical and collection information, and possibly an index of names of correspondents contained within the collection
Box list only:	A collection for which only a container list was created
Information only:	A folder which only contained information about the collection, often published articles or clippings, rather than finding aids (having been identified, these could be ignored in favor of those containing actual finding aid materials)

The next step in organizing knowledge about the finding aid collection was a survey of the electronic files stored in shared directories on the library's fileserver. Although Duke follows standard guidelines for creating finding aids, there were numerous inconsistencies in the naming and forms of the files because these directories were largely a byproduct of that activity and had been created by numerous people over a period of years. Surveying the files, often by opening them to determine their contents, allowed them to be linked with the collection list generated from the printed finding aids. The filenames, a maximum of eight characters in length, were by convention created after the last name of the creator of the collection described in the finding aid, (e.g., "allen.doc"). However, many inconsistencies, such as finding aids created as multiple Word documents, misnamed files, or similarly named collections, made the process of determining which files went to which collection a tricky one. This information was added to the database along with the following additional information describing the makeup of the finding aid files:

Microsoft Word files:	Finding aids completely in MS Word format, whether made up of single or multiple files
Text files:	Finding aids in text format only
FindAid DTD:	SGML finding aids encoded with the FindAid DTD, the predecessor to EAD
Paper only:	Legacy finding aids which existed only in paper form or more recent finding aids for which the electronic files had been misplaced

In addition to this information, notes were made as to the approximate number of pages of the finding aid, and whether it appeared to be in a regular and consistent format. Fields to track the progress and completion of the encoding process were also added, as well as indication as to whether or not a finding aid belonged to the Hartman Center for Sales, Advertising, and Marketing History, a center within the library whose finding aids would require slightly different treatment. The list of fields thus included:

Collection Name	Title of the Collection
Contents	Contents of Reading Room Folders: Full|description|boxlist|info
Type	Word|text|findaid|paper
Hartman	Y|N
Files	Name(s) of Word or text files
Scanned	Y|N (for OCR scanned items)
Proofed	Y|N (for OCR scanned items)
Encoded	Y|N|in progress
Valid	Y|N
Notes	NOTES

Berkeley's Electronic Text Unit has created a greatly expanded database format for multi-institution projects, described below.

Once the finding aid survey was complete, the resulting database provided a good overview of the nature of the conversion project. The next step was to prioritize the finding aids for encoding. The information gained from library staff about which collections were either the most important or the most heavily used was considered of the first importance. Ease of conversion was considered the next most important factor–the finding aids were evaluated by their file type and by the regularity and consistency of their formatting and description.

For test purposes, a number of short Microsoft Word finding aids with consistent formatting and description were chosen first. Once the encoding system had been developed enough to be considered reliable, the other finding aids were processed, including longer and less regular finding aids, in relative order of importance. Paper-only finding aids were dealt with last, using scanning and Optical Character Recognition (OCR) technology to generate text which was proofread, edited, and then encoded.

Berkeley

Staff in Berkeley's Electronic Text Unit (ETU) set up Microsoft Access databases in all Berkeley finding aid conversion projects (BFAP, American Heritage, and OAC) to track the course of finding aids through the conversion process. These databases were also used to gather statistics (e.g., number of finding aids converted, number of pages converted, average time to convert a finding aid, and so on). At an early stage of finding aid conversion Berkeley experimented with outsourcing paper finding aids for scanning and OCR. Relevant information about the state of the finding aids in this workflow was recorded in the database. For the OAC, paper finding aids belonging to many of the partners are being outsourced to Apex Data Services, Inc. for re-keying and preliminary markup. A special Web-accessible database has been created to track this workflow. Ideally, the tracking database in a union database project should be interfaced with the Web so that staff from the collaborating institutions themselves can input and edit the database via a standard Web browser such as Netscape. The database should be organized such that each institution has its own table within the database and each table is password-protected so that collaborators may only edit their own data. Drawing together its different experiences of creating tracking databases for several conversion projects, ETU staff has recently developed a list of suggested fields for such a Web-accessible, multi-institution tracking database:

<table>
<tr><td>CallNo</td><td>An identifying number for the collection</td></tr>
<tr><td>Title</td><td>Title of the collection</td></tr>
<tr><td>Institution</td><td>The institution</td></tr>
<tr><td>Repository</td><td>The repository within the institution</td></tr>
<tr><td>Subject</td><td>A broad subject category for the collection</td></tr>
<tr><td>FindingAidExists</td><td>Yes|no|in progress|paper only</td></tr>
<tr><td>ScanQuality</td><td>Good|medium|poor</td></tr>
<tr><td>Scan</td><td>Yes|no|in progress|re-key</td></tr>
<tr><td>ScanNotes</td><td>Any notes associated with scanning or re-keying of paper copies</td></tr>
<tr><td>Cataloged</td><td>Yes|no</td></tr>
<tr><td>OriginalFilename</td><td>Filename of the document sent for conversion</td></tr>
<tr><td>Format</td><td>Format of the submitted file (e.g., ASCII, MS Word)</td></tr>
<tr><td>NoOfPages</td><td>Total number of pages for the submitted file</td></tr>
<tr><td>SGMLFilename</td><td>Filename of the completed SGML file</td></tr>
<tr><td>DateSubmitted</td><td>Date the file was FTP'd to central institution</td></tr>
<tr><td>DateEncoded</td><td>Date the file was converted to EAD</td></tr>
<tr><td>DatePublished</td><td>Date the file was made public on the Web</td></tr>
<tr><td>Revisions</td><td>Date and nature of any revisions made after the file was published</td></tr>
<tr><td>Encoder</td><td>Initials of the individual who encoded the file</td></tr>
<tr><td>DateCheckedOut</td><td>Date the encoder checked out the file for encoding</td></tr>
<tr><td>NoOfHours</td><td>The number of hours required to encode the file</td></tr>
<tr><td>Difficulty</td><td>Easy|medium|hard</td></tr>
<tr><td>Project</td><td>Any grant-funded project</td></tr>
<tr><td>GenericNotes</td><td>Any generic notes</td></tr>
<tr><td>MarkupNotes</td><td>Any notes associated with how the finding was marked up.</td></tr>
</table>

The careful analysis of the workflow of a finding aid conversion project is essential to the creation of such a database. Recording information about the key aspects of each of the processing steps is also critical and, although Berkeley has yet to do so, maintaining the database to record future revisions along with the conversion history of each finding aid, particularly if such information can be exported to the <revisiondesc> in the <eadheader>, will offer a repository long-term control over its finding aid collection.

CONCLUSION

For the libraries at Duke and Berkeley, the process of implementing EAD has begun with the conversion of legacy finding aids. Staff at both institutions viewed this as a community-based process requiring a necessary regularization of finding aids so that they could co-exist together in a union database. This closely paralleled the way EAD itself was developed, beginning with Daniel Pitti's efforts in BFAP to create a data model for finding aids based on examples of existing finding aids he gathered from the community. It has been important in the Duke and Berkeley experience to demonstrate that it is possible to capture what archivists have traditionally done. But there were practical considerations behind this decision too. Our experience with retrospective conversion of catalog records has shown us that we rarely have the luxury of redoing past work.

Nevertheless, as early as the Berkeley Finding Aid Conference in April 1995, members of the community have been calling for a complete rethinking of what a finding aid ought to be in the world of digital access. As EAD has begun to be implemented, this position has not been the sole preserve of archival "visionaries" who make finding aid redesign a prerequisite for beginning a finding aid conversion project. Dennis Meissner of the Minnesota Historical Society (MHS) has convincingly made the case that the individual repository considering the implementation of EAD ought to take the time to "re-engineer" its finding aids before it begins.[9] Seriously rethinking the structure and presentation of electronic finding aids is undeniably important to the overall development of EAD as a standard and to its successful implementation. As the previous pages testify, Berkeley's experience in the American Heritage and UC-EAD/OAC consortial union database projects has shown that there are many pitfalls in the process of harnessing EAD to retrospective conversion. "Encode it as it lies" does indeed produce mixed results. But Berkeley's experience with consortial partners has also shown that a lack of resources and a fear of the effort involved in re-engineering older finding aids can create a formidable barrier to doing anything at all.

The conflict between the new and the old in the case of EAD implementation seems to pose a problem to the community at large when it comes to determining what "best practices" should be. The gulf between legacy and new finding aids makes applying the same principles to encoding them very difficult. For those who wish to provide the widest access to their collections,[10] perhaps a mixed EAD implementation strategy offers the best chance of long-term success. Such a strategy might develop distinct guidelines for retrospective conversion and for the creation of new finding aids.

As if in recognition of this, the OAC's Metadata Standards Group, which oversees the development of "best practices" for the union database, is about to review a draft document by member Bill Landis, entitled *Online Archive of California Best Practice Guidelines: Encoding NEW Finding Aids Using EAD*. These *Best Practice Guidelines* go beyond the rudimentary rules set out in *EAD Retrospective Conversion Guidelines* by defining archival description for new OAC finding aids based on the rules for multilevel archival description found in *General International Standard Archival Description (ISAD (G).* Should some version of the *Best Practice Guidelines* be adopted, the OAC Metadata Standards Group will undoubtedly address itself to what programmatic changes can be made in the OAC's "recon" finding aids to make them reside more comfortably in the same union database with finding aids created under the new dispensation. Here the consistency striven for during retrospective conversion should once again prove useful.

Regardless of where one comes down on the question of new versus old however, the principle that EAD implementation and further development are most fruitfully done in the context of a wider community is hard to deny. All those who are beginning an EAD project or are contemplating one ought to look closely at what has been done by RLG, Harvard, and Yale and in projects like American Heritage and UCEAD/OAC. They should review and criticize the documentation that such implementations have created, while, at the same time, paying close attention to what the Library of Congress and the Society of American Archivists (SAA) are doing to help define EAD "best practices." We can only hope that in the not-too-distant future the SAA EAD Working Group will review the work of major EAD projects, and begin work on a new EAD technical document, *EAD Best Practice Guidelines*. For this important work it is crucial that they draw upon the relatively coherent pools of existing community experience with EAD.

NOTES

1. Michael J. Fox, "Implementing Encoded Archival Description: An Overview of Administrative and Technical Considerations," *American Archivist* 60 (Summer 1997): 330-344.
2. *American Archivist* 60, nos. 3-4 (Summer, Fall 1997).
3. See Dennis Meissner, "First Things First: Reengineering Finding Aids for Implementation of EAD," *American Archivist* 60 (Fall 1997): 372-387.
4. See David Seaman, "Multi-institutional EAD: The University of Virginia's Role in the American Heritage Project," *American Archivist* 60 (Fall 1997): 436-444.
5. Fox, *American Archivist* 60 (Summer 1997): 339-342.
6. See http://www.oclc.org/fred/
7. Seaman, *American Archivist* 60 (Fall 1997): 436-444.
8. Fox, *American Archivist* 60 (Summer 1997): 330-344.
9. Meissner, *American Archivist* 60 (Fall 1997): 372-387.
10. But, as Michael Fox suggests, this might not necessarily conform to the goals and missions of all repositories. Fox, *American Archivist* 60 (Summer 1997): 330-344.

Providing Unified Access to International Primary Research Resources in the Humanities: The Research Libraries Group

Anne Van Camp

SUMMARY. Gaining access to primary research materials is critical to the support of research and learning. The Research Libraries Group, an international consortium of research institutions devoted to making such resources available, is engaged in several initiatives to make archival materials, museum records and objects, and cultural heritage information available to researchers in an electronic environment. With a well-established history of commitment to enhancing access to unique or rare materials, RLG is now exploring the technical possibilities of achieving international, integrated access to textual and visual materials. That seamless web of resources so desired by researchers is increasingly becoming a reality. This article summarizes the history, current accomplishments, and new RLG initiatives to bring an invaluable array of primary research resources to the desktop in a useful and meaningful way. *[Article copies available for a fee from The Haworth Document Delivery Service: 1-800-342-9678. E-mail address: <getinfo@haworthpressinc.com> Website: <http://www.HaworthPress.com> © 2001 by The Haworth Press, Inc. All rights reserved.]*

Anne Van Camp is Manager of Member Initiatives for the Research Libraries Group, Inc., 1200 Villa Street, Mountain View, CA 94941 (E-mail: Anne_Van_Camp@ notes.rlg.org).

[Haworth co-indexing entry note]: "Providing Unified Access to International Primary Research Resources in the Humanities: The Research Libraries Group." Van Camp, Anne. Co-published simultaneously in *Journal of Internet Cataloging* (The Haworth Information Press, an imprint of The Haworth Press, Inc.) Vol. 4, No. 3/4, 2001, pp. 137-145; and: *Encoded Archival Description on the Internet* (ed: Daniel V. Pitti, and Wendy M. Duff) The Haworth Information Press, an imprint of The Haworth Press, Inc., 2001, pp. 137-145. Single or multiple copies of this article are available for a fee from The Haworth Document Delivery Service [1-800-342-9678, 9:00 a.m. - 5:00 p.m. (EST). E-mail address: getinfo@haworthpressinc.com].

KEYWORDS. Access to primary resources, archival description, Encoded Archival Description, EAD, finding aids, Research Libraries Group, RLG

WHAT IS RLG?

Since its inception in 1975, The Research Libraries Group (RLG) has had the mission of enhancing access to information that supports research and learning. The four major research institutions that initially came together to pursue this goal are now part of an international non-profit corporation of 160 institutions. The purpose of the organization remains the same–to develop cooperative solutions to the problems that research institutions face in the acquisition, delivery, and preservation of information.

The membership of RLG includes universities and colleges, public libraries, national libraries, archives, historical societies, museums, and independent research institutions. In addition to providing the technical infrastructure and support for the delivery of electronic information, RLG coordinates member participation in collaborative initiatives in functional and content-related areas. These include the development of standards for description and preservation, the sharing of resources, and the pooling of expertise in collection-related areas such as art and architecture, archives and primary resources, East Asian studies, Jewish and Middle Eastern studies, and law.

In serving the cooperative activities of its members, RLG has developed computerized services that can also be used by other libraries and research institutions anywhere in the world. Besides the RLIN® bibliographic database for library and archival collections access and management, RLG offers CitaDel®, a citations access service of over a dozen databases; Marcadia®, an automated copy cataloging service; and Ariel®, an Internet-based document transmission system clearer and cheaper than faxing.

In addition to the RLIN library support system, interfaces to RLG's data resources include Zephyr®, a Z39.50 server that lets users of other online systems search through the commands and record displays of their own systems; Eureka®, a user-friendly interface designed for campuswide access by students and faculty; and now Eureka® on the Web, for searching RLG's data resources via World Wide Web browsers.

SUPPORT OF THE PRIMARY SOURCES COMMUNITY

The Archival Experience

RLG has had a long and abiding interest in supporting not only mainstream library and print collections but in finding ways of integrating access to the primary source materials critical to advanced research in all areas of the humanities and social sciences. Archives, manuscript collections, visual materials, and objects are examples of the resources that scholars seek when conducting their research. They have traditionally been the most difficult sources to find and use.

In the early 1980s, RLG pioneered the implementation of a bibliographic standard that would allow archival collections to be described and presented in electronic form along with other more traditional library resources. The MARC-AMC (Archival and Mixed Collections) format was designed to accommodate the description of collections of primary source materials. The MARC record proved to be an excellent way of describing, at the collection level, the variety of archives, personal papers, and manuscripts that were available in widely dispersed repositories. With the implementation of the RLIN-AMC file, for the first time scholars could find descriptions of archival collections integrated with books, journals, and other secondary sources in one bibliographic database.

Initially, the archival community seriously questioned the use of the format. There were also those who, unaccustomed to thinking about description at the collection level, believed that because the materials being described were unique, there was little hope for finding a standard way of describing them. Nonetheless, the benefits of the compromise of extending a bibliographic standard proved to far outweigh the arguments against its adoption and use. Today there are nearly 500,000 RLIN-AMC records representing collections in hundreds of institutions.

With the advent of the World Wide Web and the ability to provide much more detailed information about an institution's holdings, the compromises of earlier times were re-evaluated. Experimentation with mounting and displaying full texts of archival finding aids (the more detailed guides that explain both the context and the contents of large collections) led to the development of the new archival descriptive standard, the EAD (Encoded Archival Description).

Daniel Pitti, then at the University of California at Berkeley, initially conceived the idea to use Standard Generalized Markup Language (SGML) and develop a document type definition (DTD) to impose some consistent markup and presentation of finding aids in the electronic environment. If successfully developed and applied, it would enable the presentation of the highly complex, hierarchical nature of archival finding aids and would enhance access to archival collections by making the full text of the guides searchable. The results of the early work done at Berkeley were presented to the archival community at a conference in March 1995. Following that meeting, a group of archivists with the expertise to interpret and refine the work done by Pitti, took on that responsibility and ultimately released the Encoded Archival Description (EAD) document type definition. The history of this development is well documented in two separate issues of *The American Archivist,* the journal of the Society of American Archivists.[1]

The enthusiasm for this standard and the archival community's rapid acceptance and adoption of it continue to be remarkable. Because this standard relates to the basic tools that archivists develop–finding aids–and the prior experience of applying standards to descriptive practice and realizing exceptional results, the community has been quick to understand its value and to take advantage of it.

The Research Libraries Group, encouraged by its member institutions, helped to promulgate the use of EAD by developing a training workshop that was offered throughout North America and in the U.K. and Australia. The workshops introduced hundreds of archivists to the use of EAD and gave some practical hands-on experience in creating and marking up finding aids using this new system of description. As more and more institutions began implementing EAD, both for new collection guides and for retrospective conversion of older printed guides, it was clear that this would certainly be a beneficial practice both for archivists and for the ultimate users of those tools. The workshop is now being offered through the Society of American Archivists and training is also available at the University of Virginia's Rare Book School.

PROVIDING UNION ACCESS TO EAD ENCODED FINDING AIDS

In addition to helping archivists learn about EAD, RLG released this year a service called Archival Resources that provides integrated searching and access to the RLIN-AMC file and to full-text EAD encoded finding aids that are on servers at remote institutions. The advantages this service offers include: powerful searching for content across collections wherever they exist, the union of related or complementary collections in a virtual manner, the preservation of both the context and hierarchy of information about collections, and the possibility of allowing the researcher access to rich detail included in the guides. This service already exhibits huge promise for greatly enhanced access to archival holdings throughout the world.

Just as the union catalog for AMC records provided an enormous boon to researchers finding primary sources along with secondary source materials, the idea of providing access to archival finding aids in an aggregated manner has similar benefits. Searching across guides, one can find complementary research materials from widely dispersed collections and in unexpected ways. One need not know ahead of time (or guess) that there are valuable resources related to a particular research topic located at Harvard, the University of Iowa, or the University of Liverpool.

The idea of one-stop shopping has tremendous appeal in the increasingly chaotic world of Web searching. An example of how this service works to the benefit of the researcher desiring quality control to information retrieval follows: Using the search topic, "The American Communist Party," in Archival Resources, the researcher can find out that there are more than fifty collections of papers represented in the Archival and Mixed Collections file (AMC) and can easily learn where those papers are located. In addition, there are several full-text finding aids to important collections from Yale University, from the Hoover Institution at Stanford University, and from other, less obvious institutions. A Web search on that same topic will get you a fairly large result of books available on that and related topics from Amazon.com and several personal home pages of members of the Party. While such results may be useful, there is certainly no comparison to the information contained in the finding aids to important archival resources.

Many individual institutions and a growing number of consortia are taking advantage of the Web to make information about their collections more widely available and in many cases mounting finding aids locally–usually in an HTML or other textual format. In each case, decisions are being made locally about which finding aids warrant this kind of treatment and what kind of markup and presentation is best for local use. Many institutions assume that if they make their finding aids available on their Web site, then anyone can and will find them.

Some consortial and cross-institutional projects have proven beneficial in helping establish some consistency in markup and presentation for more than a single repository, and this is a good thing. For example, the Online Archive of California (OAC) has established some particular tagging and presentation guidelines that are required of all participating institutions in the OAC. This is helpful to the researcher who is interrogating that data, since the search results will have a consistent look and feel about them and will be easy to navigate. One limitation to this kind of local aggregation is that collections in California repositories have broader connections to related information beyond California, and many researchers may not know that.

The desire to share this information even more broadly is gaining appeal as the demonstrated value of cross-institutional, integrated, international searching becomes more apparent. By aggregating this kind of information in a consistent, moderated, and well-maintained environment, the value to the researcher is unquestionable.

As researchers become more sophisticated in using the Web as a resource, they expect to have much less mediation when it comes to discovering relevant information. There will always be some kind of mediation, of course, imbedded in the creation of finding aids and the presentation decisions that institutions make about their collections. The goal of an integrated service like Archival Resources is to be intuitive and end-user-friendly so that the researcher need not guess where the information is coming from or how it is being maintained. The authenticity of the information is equally important, and providing a service through RLG, that expectation of high-quality authenticity will be met.

CHALLENGES AHEAD

Application Guidelines

In building the Archival Resources service, the contributors have been asked to follow some minimal guidelines so that a consistent presentation of finding aids can occur. Reaching agreement on those application guidelines is a negotiated process, since all contributors must be comfortable with the recommendations, which cannot be too burdensome or they will not be used.

The set of guidelines for the RLG service was developed by the RLG EAD Advisory Group during a meeting in Washington D.C. in March of 1998. The Advisory Group included representatives from several member institutions that are currently engaged in large-scale EAD implementation projects. Institutions represented included: Harvard University, Yale University, the University of California at Berkeley, Stanford University and the Library of Congress.

The objectives of the guidelines are to:

1. facilitate interoperability by imposing a basic degree of uniformity in the creation of a valid SGML document and to encourage the inclusion of elements most useful for retrieval in a union index and for display in an integrated, cross-institutional setting,
2. offer researchers the full benefits of SGML in retrieval and display by developing a set of core and fuller data elements to improve resource discovery.

The recommended application guidelines can be applied both in retrospective conversion of legacy finding aids as well as in the creation of new finding aids. The full set of recommendations can be found at the RLG Web site at <http://www.rlg.org/rlgead/too12.html>.

One example of one of the minimal requirements is the use of a repository tag that identifies the repository. When a single institution is presenting its own materials on its own Web site, there is usually no need to write the name of the institution on each guide. But if those guides are to be included in a larger universe, this is one of the most important items of information associated with the guide.

As the practice of encoding finding aids proliferates and more content is available, undoubtedly common practices will emerge, suggesting the most useful application of the standard. Some more difficult problems will be finding the best approaches to using controlled vocabularies or imposing some assisted searching techniques so that search results become more valuable. This will be especially true when searching guides that come from a variety of types of institutions where use of controlled vocabularies may vary and where content standards may be different.

Already there are several examples of using EAD to encode guides to other kinds of collections such as photographs or museum collections. These guides make use of the fundamental construct of a structured document, relating information about the whole collection to its various components. There are also excellent examples of embedding photographs or other visual documents in the guides, or at least providing links to the whole information objects. Searching and indexing across languages is already possible in other RLG resources, and the inclusion of non-English finding aids in Archival Resources is already anticipated.

Selection for Collaborative Projects

Local selection decisions about guides to be created in or converted to electronic form using EAD are driven by institutional imperatives and funding opportunities. Selection of finding aids for inclusion in collaborative projects is a topic of much discussion. There are few models for this kind of selection–particularly along content or subject matter. Aggregating resources around a theme is an excellent way of creating critical mass in a subject area and has been successfully used in other kinds of collaborative projects.

Another potentially powerful use of the virtual union of information is the reuniting of dispersed collections. For example, the records that document such things as the transfer of technology from the old world to the new, the movement of people from one continent to another, or the activities of a large, diversified, international corporation, are often located in archival repositories around the world. Bringing those collections together in a virtual environment is one of the most practical applications of this new descriptive technique.

The discussion of this kind of selection should continue and the benefits to be drawn from this kind of collaboration must be demonstrated. While the current available number of electronic finding aids is relatively small compared to the known universe of guides, the number will increase rapidly and the decisions for selection should be documented by institutions and shared with the community to better inform others as they face these kinds of decisions.

User Evaluation and Behavior

Because Archival Resources is a new service and a new way of presenting information for research use, it is important to monitor how it is being used and whether the indexing and presentation are useful. There are two different user groups that need to be consulted–first, the contributors to the service must be kept in mind as a user constituency, since they will be the group to help ensure the vitality and longevity of the service, interpreting it to their own institutions and users. And second, the researchers who actually take advantage of the content of the service need to be consulted about the value of their search experiences and results.

There are currently a few institutions that have taken user evaluation seriously; the results of their work will be useful to inform others wishing to carry this forward. In particular, it has been suggested that by making primary source materials more accessible in this fashion, there will be new audiences for the content. It will be important to document how those audiences are introduced to these resources and how they use them in order to make more informed decisions about the usefulness and practicality of EAD presentation.

More informed analysis of these issues will also be helpful at this stage of implementation of an integrated service, to help determine how to best present cross-community information and how to maintain the quality of the information to be gleaned from these resources.

LONG-TERM VISION

Several years ago, professional association meeting programs were rife with sessions on what resources were available in various repositories. Archivists would get together and tell each other what new collections they had or what subjects were being developed in their holdings. Historical association meetings held numerous sessions on the "discovery" of new research resources. Historians and other researchers complained endlessly about the serendipitous nature of conducting primary research. Funding agencies doled out grants to scholars to "visit collections." All were time-consuming, expensive and unpredictable ways of conducting research.

In trying to improve access to primary resources, the challenges that continue to face us include: developing the technology to make this discovery and delivery of information more seamless, building better, easier tools for local implementation, the maturation of content standards and application guidelines for EAD and related descriptive schemes, and obtaining the financial support at the institutional and the consortial level to enable massive production of many more electronic resources.

Future research scenarios might allow a scholar in Tokyo to produce a full-length documentary on Japanese-American internment camps during World War II without having to visit California or Hawaii or Arizona. Locating and using records of orphans sent from the U.K. to Australia for a better life might be the strategy a nineteenth century family historian in Michigan would use in writing a thesis. A researcher hoping to do a definitive study of the Arts and Crafts movement could find all the primary and secondary sources needed without ever leaving the office.

As research in the humanities becomes increasingly interdisciplinary, and as researchers become more and more sophisticated and excited about using primary resources in new ways, the dream of being able to provide a seamless access service for the discovery and delivery to the desktop of information about collections and actual surrogates of images, items, and documents will soon be a reality.

NOTE

1. *American Archivist* 60, nos. 3 and 4.

EAD and Government Archives

Meg Sweet
Matthew Hillyard
Derek Breeden
Bill Stockting

SUMMARY. At the beginning of 1996 the means of reference to the Public Record Office's 150km of records dating back to the 11th century were, as far as the user was concerned, all on paper and mainly available on a single site. This article traces the development since then of the Public Record Office's hierarchical Internet catalogue (PROCAT) and in particular the role that EAD has had in this process. Two major EAD projects are described with particular emphasis on how the developing EAD standard was utilized in the context of a large national archive. Aspects of EAD relating to data exchange, data preparation, standardization and publication are all discussed as are its relationship to emergent XML technologies. Finally a role for EAD within PROCAT is described even though it is in essence a traditional relational database. *[Article copies available for a fee from The Haworth Document Delivery Service: 1-800-342-9678. E-mail ad-*

Meg Sweet is PROCAT and Access to Archives Programme Manager at the Public Record Office, Kew, Richmond, Surrey TW9 4DU (E-mail: meg.sweet@pro.gov.uk).

Matthew Hillyard is SGML Editor at the Public Record Office, Ruskin Avenue, Kew, Richmond, Surrey, TW9 4DU, United Kingdom (E-mail: matthew.hillyard@pro.gov.uk).

Derek Breeden is IT Project Manager within the Information and Records Department at the Public Record Office, Kew, Richmond, Surrey, TW9 4DU (E-mail: derek.breeden@pro.gov.uk).

Bill Stockting is Senior Editor of the Access to Archives Programme A2A at the Public Record Office, Kew, Richmond, Surrey TW9 4DU, United Kingdom (E-mail: william.stockting@pro.gov.uk).

[Haworth co-indexing entry note]: "EAD and Government Archives." Sweet, Meg et al. Co-published simultaneously in *Journal of Internet Cataloging* (The Haworth Information Press, an imprint of The Haworth Press, Inc.) Vol. 4, No. 3/4, 2001, pp. 147-168; and: *Encoded Archival Description on the Internet* (ed: Daniel V. Pitti, and Wendy M. Duff) The Haworth Information Press, an imprint of The Haworth Press, Inc., 2001, pp. 147-168. Single or multiple copies of this article are available for a fee from The Haworth Document Delivery Service [1-800-342-9678, 9:00 a.m. - 5:00 p.m. (EST). E-mail address: getinfo@haworthpressinc.com].

dress: <getinfo@haworthpressinc.com> Website: <http://www.HaworthPress.com>

KEYWORDS. Archival information systems, archival description, Encoded Archival Description, EAD, finding aids, government archives, Public Record Office

THE STARTING POINT

As the National Archives of the United Kingdom, the Public Record Office holds something like 150 kilometers of records produced over the last nine hundred years by approximately three hundred government departments, agencies, and courts of law. The records themselves are principally paper-based, in files and volumes, but include parchment rolls, electronic records, and even a pair of inscribed wooden doors.

At the advent of EAD in the UK, we were wrestling with the problem of our existing means of reference to the records not quite meeting their original purpose. The *PRO Guide* was first introduced in the 1970s as the central means of reference to the PRO's holdings. It took as its starting point the 15,000 or so individual series, or classes, of records produced by the various departments and agencies, rather than the departments themselves. The core of the *Guide* was its class descriptions, incorporating highly structured data elements such as covering dates and site of production, as well as a large text block of "description" which might include such elements as scope and content, arrangement, or related material. Centering on the class rather than the fonds was an attempt to deal with the issue, particularly prevalent in twentieth-century government, of functions moving within, and between, departments. Not only do the functions shift with alarming frequency, but the record series documenting those functions sometimes move with them. During its lifetime a file series might have a range of genuine creators chronologically, possibly not all from within the same parent department. For this reason description began at the series rather than fonds level.

However, starting some way down the natural hierarchy brought with it its own issues to be resolved. The serial provenance of so many records raised the specter of heavily over-loaded administrative histories for each series. Not only that, but there would also be massive duplication across series with shared or partially shared provenance. To deal with these difficulties a whole section of the *Guide* was devoted to administrative histories of the record-creating departments and agencies. Each departmental history was broken down, as necessary, into subsections, covering the distinctive administrative units operating within the departments. Cross-references were made from the series descriptions to the relevant administrative history/histories and, from the other end, each administrative history (sub)section ended with a summary of the record series produced by the department/division being described.

Because of the technological constraints of the 1970s it had been felt necessary to organize the departmental administrative histories according to a broad numerical classification (e.g., 200s for finance, 900s for education). This never worked successfully in practice. Far too many departments, particularly of the last fifty years, straddle neatly classified divisions. The most recent Conservative administration here introduced a Department for Education *and* Employment; the present Labour government has a new Department of the Environment, Transport *and* the Regions. Neither of these fits neatly into a pre-determined classification; to incorporate them properly in the *Guide* would have involved a certain amount of duplication as well as cross-references within the administrative histories section, on top of all the cross-references between sections.

More fundamentally, the number of cross-references, more or less useful, from the series descriptions to the administrative histories, was proving unproductive. There could easily be four or five when a file series had been long-lived and peripatetic, but on occasion the number could extend to as many as fifteen. It took a very devoted user to trawl backwards and forwards through fifteen sets of cross-references to get a sense of the context(s) in which the particular records had been created. Users simply were not following through the cross-references, losing a part of the archival description that would aid their interpretation of the records; meanwhile a good deal of time and labor was going into producing the under-used administrative histories.

Under the old system a user selected the series of interest from the *Guide* and moved from there to the individual class, or series list. At orderable document level the lists have been traditionally fairly minimal (recording unique reference, former reference(s), covering dates, scope and content, and special access conditions, the last named usually arising from our particular obligations in relation to the Public Records Acts of 1958 and 1967). In recent years the lists have been preceded by introductory notes, rich in content, describing the whole series. The notes largely duplicated, but also expanded, the *Guide* class descriptions and made no attempt, other than through the use of headings, to demarcate between different kinds of data elements.

Things were ripe for change. Users were demanding remote access to descriptions of the records, if not the records themselves. The need to retro-convert the 300,000 or so pages of class lists into electronic form enabled us to rethink our overall provision of description of the records. We knew that we wanted to provide Web access to one seamless, hierarchical catalog (in the British sense of top-to-bottom finding aid) of our holdings. We identified seven levels of description, from government department at the top to smallest orderable unit (item) at the bottom. The PRO endorsed ISAD(G), the international standard for archival description; our catalog needed to follow ISAD(G)'s basic principles of multilevel description, proceeding from the broad to the narrow, avoiding redundancy of information, and so on, and also to include all the data elements identified by ISAD(G). Similarly we were in broad agreement with ISAAR(CPF), the international standard for archival authority records, and committed to following our own national Rules for the Construction of Personal, Corporate and Place Names. What was missing, at least for the transitional period between deciding to change and full adoption of the new online catalog (to be known as PROCAT), was a data structure standard.

EAD, then still in beta form, looked as though it might fit the bill. An essential prerequisite was conformity with ISAD(G). Mapping between the two was almost completely transparent. EAD was designed for multilevel archival description. We could start at the top, providing the appropriate degree of administrative history for each component level. Serial creators could all, where necessary, be named, without apparently privileging one over another. Authority control could be partially exercised. Large text "fields" could be managed. We had difficulties about the unavailability of certain elements, such as those covering separated or related material, at any other than the top level, but recognized that EAD was still in test form; we could experiment with it and, if it proved effective for our purposes in other ways, lobby for changes to its structure to be made before issue of the release version.

A small pilot project with a tiny microcosm of our catalog confirmed all our expectations of EAD. It also highlighted potential areas of difficulty, which will be covered in detail in the following pages. Was EAD sufficiently scalable? All previous experimenters with EAD had worked with comparatively small-scale finding aids; any one of our three hundred or so individual hierarchies might constitute thousands and thousands of individual components. What about our particular responsibilities in relation to the Public Records Acts, the definition of Public Records and legally binding closure periods? How about searching, effectively and speedily, within and across hierarchies? What of storage and upkeep of so many SGML files, most of which were dynamic in the sense of being added to and/or amended? What of global, or even bulk, editing?

THE CORE EXECUTIVE PROJECT AND EAD BETA

As part of the development of PROCAT we had defined an archival hierarchy of seven levels and the data elements available at each of these levels. In the first instance we did so with the needs of our business in mind, but we also made sure that the proposed structure conformed to ISAD(G). Although we were happy that we would be able to collect new data in this form, we needed a way of testing this structure to see if it would work with our legacy data. We also needed to test the process of data preparation and develop the local detailed rules that would editorially control data input into PROCAT. These rules, while based on ISAD(G) and national and international cataloging practice generally, reflect our position as a government archive.

As a way of testing our hierarchy and data elements, we developed a project known as the Core Executive, which began in April 1997. The idea was to produce a subset of the whole catalog that would be small enough to complete in an eighteen-month timeframe but would be of sufficient scale to produce the information we needed from it. The subset of the catalog chosen was that of the central policy making departments of British Government–hence Core Executive. The material dated from 1916 when the War Cabinet began formally producing records, which, with those of the Prime Minister's Office, form the heart of the Core Executive. The catalog entries for selected records of the Treasury, Foreign Office, and Ministry of Defense were also chosen along with two short-lived departments of the 1960s and 1970s: The Department of Economic Affairs and the Civil Service Department.

Having chosen the material we looked at how we would present it online. Here we were able to make use of our small EAD pilot project. The finding aids at all levels relating to a single small department (the Department of Economic Affairs) had been encoded in the beta version of EAD. The resulting electronic finding aid had been presented to groups of colleagues across the office and a consensus emerged that EAD was worthy of further testing. This pilot had, however, left us with major questions about EAD. First, it had left us with the impression that EAD as developed in the beta version was more at home with relatively small manuscript collections of the sort found in university archive departments than the larger record accumulations generated by government. Could EAD deal with the size and complexity of our "collections," which usually equate to the records of a government department? Second, if so, we wanted to see how we could make the resulting encoded finding aids available online. Could we use EAD to provide a functioning online finding aid for our users?

We first had to map our proposed data elements to beta EAD's elements. In doing so we found a basic concordance. In some significant areas we found no direct match, due mainly to the nature of our business as a government archive (see Table 1). This resulted in our proposing a number of changes to the beta version that were accepted for inclusion in version 1.0 by the EAD Working Group.

TABLE 1. Mapping of Core Executive to EAD Beta

Core Executive Data Element	***EAD Beta Data Element***
Access conditions	<accessrestrict>
Accruals	
Accumulation dates	
Administrative/biographical history	<bioghist>
Appraisal/destruction information	<appraisal>
Arrangement	<arrangement>
Closure status	
Copies information	<altformavail>
Creation dates	<unitdate>
Creator name(s)	<origination>
Custodial history	<custhist>
Existence of copies	<altformavail>
Former reference	<unitid>
Former reference (PRO)	<unitid>
Immediate source of acquisition	<acqinfo>
Index terms	<controlaccess>
Index terms: Corporate name	<controlaccess><corpname>
Index terms: Personal name	<controlaccess><persname>
Index terms: Place name	<controlaccess><geogname>
Index terms: Subject name	<controlaccess><subject>
Language(s)	<archdesc langmaterial =>
Legal status	<archdesc legalstatus = 'otherlegalstatus' otherlegalstatus = 'public records'>
Level	<archdesc level =>
Location of originals	
Note	<note>
Physical condition	<physfacet>
Physical description, extent	<physdesc><extent>
Physical description, form	<physdesc><genreform>
Place of deposit	<repository>
Publication note	<add><bibliography>
Reference	<unitid>
Related material	<add><relatedmaterial>
Restrictions on use	<userrestrict>
Scope and content	<scopecontent>
Separated material	<add><separatedmaterial>
Title	<unittitle>
Unpublished finding aids	

Like many other national archives, the PRO has a particular statutory framework in which it operates, in our case the Public Records Acts of 1958 and 1967. We found that EAD beta did not allow us fully to describe our records as the functions we have to administer under the act necessitate. We were, for example, even unsure how to express this legal status. The legal status attribute of the <archdesc> and <c> tags did have a "public" option, but we felt this was likely to be interpreted in a more general fashion than appropriate for our specific circumstance. For the Core Executive, therefore, we opted to use the "otherlegalstatus" value for the legalstatus attribute and in the otherlegalstatus attribute we inserted the value "public records." While version 1.0 has not added to the values available for the legalstatus attribute, the tag library does now allow us (and indeed any other government archives so bound) by example to use the "public" value.[1]

We also had an element for which there was no EAD match relating to the closure of government records for periods of thirty years (or longer) according to the Public Record Acts. While the information relating to the closure of the records themselves could be encoded by the <accessrestrict> tag, in some instances we are also obliged to close the description of closed records. Traditionally, in the paper inventory, this has occasioned a reference number with a blank entry and a note that the description is closed. We needed, therefore, an EAD tag to represent this Closure Status element and in the Core Executive, we decided to use the <odd> tag for this purpose, and this purpose alone.

The government archive environment, in common with that of the commercial sphere, is very dynamic. We at the PRO are at the end of the government records life-cycle and this also makes demands on our cataloging, which have been reflected in EAD encoding in the Core Executive.

We had to make use of EAD beta elements more than once to represent all the data elements we needed. Government departments, for example, often wish to call back files and do so using their own reference rather than the one we use to identify a file. This former reference is, therefore, a necessary element for us to encode and we have had to use the <unitid> tag for this as well as our own reference. Indeed, the fact that the PRO represents a continuum of curatorial care for government records for more than nine hundred years means that we have occasionally changed our reference for a particular document. This has also been recorded and we thus have a second Former Reference element and a third use for the <unitid> tag. In this case, of course, the problem can be overcome by the appropriate use of the label or type attributes. This, however, was not the case in the beta version for the <altformavail> tag, which we not only wished to use to encode information about copies but also information about originals when we held the copies.

Some of our data elements that reflect the dynamic nature of our environment also had no match in EAD beta. Many of the file series that we accession are not closed and records will continue to accrue to a series. This fact, as well as information regarding when and at what rate such accruals happen, is of course very useful to our users and in the Core Executive we made use, rather unsatisfactorily, of the <processinfo> tag to encode it. The inclusion of the Accruals (<accruals>) element in version 1.0 has resolved this particular issue.

This last example underlines a significant area of difference between government archive collections and manuscript ones: the central position of the record series. It was this difference that was at the root of the major problem for us with the structure of EAD beta.

In describing government archives one is also describing the movement of functions over time as they become the responsibility of different government agencies. In order to find records related to a particular function, a reader will need to move from record series to record series, and logically this is achieved by the Related Material and Separated Material elements. In our context, therefore, these elements take on a specific role at this level. We need to use the Related Material element to refer users to series of records documenting the same (or similar) functions, which may precede or follow that series chronologically. It follows that related material references should always be reciprocal. The Separated Material element takes on an even more specific role. As the structure of government changes and functions are passed on from one agency to another, parts of record series relating to a particular function are commonly re-registered in a new record series. As these re-registered records are "associated by provenance . . . but physically separated" we wish to encode this information as separated material from the originating series with a reference to the series into which the records had been re-registered. A reciprocal reference was then made in the Scope Content element of the latter series.

The problem was, of course, that in EAD beta these elements were only available as sub-elements of the <add> tag, which was only available within <findaid>. In our context this meant that we could only encode these elements in relation to our top, department, level rather than the lower levels, particularly series, where we needed it. Furthermore, <add> appeared at the end of the finding aid, which meant even data encoded at this level was to a certain extent lost from a user's view. These problems were further compounded by the fact that we also needed a Publication Note element at all levels, which was not possible as it equates to the <bibliography> tag, which is also only available in <add> in EAD beta. We, finally, also had a need for an Other Finding Aid element in which to encode references, again particularly at series level, to other, often more detailed, but unpublished, finding aids. There was no logical analogue for this element within EAD beta but we felt it would best be placed as another sub-element of <add>.

In the Core Executive we overcame these problems by using a series of <note> tags with appropriate text labels for these elements. This was of course unsatisfactory as important data for us was not as fully structured as we would like. We, therefore, proposed that in version 1.0 <add> should be available from both <archdesc> and <c> tags and that it should have a new Other Finding Aid (<otherfindaid>) sub-element. These proposals were duly accepted.

Having mapped our data elements to EAD beta we then created a template in our SGML editing software with the seven levels of our hierarchy representing a single department. When pulling the data together for the larger of the departments within the Core Executive we ran into a major problem: the resulting files were going to be too large. First, we found that our SGML authoring software was having problems parsing files over 1.1 megabytes. Other parsers were investigated, including James Clark's *NSGMLS,* which overcame this problem but the file size issue had wider implications. It became obvious that large files would take too long to download on the Internet.

After some discussion of the issue, much of which centered on the principle that there should only be a single EAD instance for each "collection," we pragmatically made the decision to split the files. In terms both of file size and the centrality of the series, the most sensible arrangement was to have the seven department files linked from our second (division) level to separate series files, of which there would now be nearly three hundred. We took advice from Daniel Pitti, who has been very supportive in all our endeavors. Links were achieved by the use of <archref> tags with the file name of the series file as the value of the href attribute. The link was activated by a processing instruction (?ATTLINK) declared in each file, which worked so long as each series file that was referred to from a department file was also a declared entity in that file.

We found this worked well but left us with a further problem to resolve. The data below series level had been encoded for us by contractors. We had supplied them with a copy of our EAD template, which mimicked the whole catalog hierarchy. The idea was that we would integrate each of the returned series-level files into the appropriate department file. In the file the contractors returned, however, the series-level data appeared at the third level, the sub-series data at the fourth level, and so on. As we were now going to have a separate EAD file for each series, the series-level data needed to be at the top (<archdesc>) level. A program written in C was then developed to move the data up to the appropriate level to give us a validated EAD file for each series.

We now found that some of the larger of these series files, those with over about five thousand record descriptions, were still too large to be mounted as single files. Consequently, we had to split these up into two or three separate files, which were linked together in the same way as the departmental and series files.

A final issue relating to the size of our series was raised when we looked at providing navigation for the user. As noted, many of the series have thousands of orderable units, or pieces and items, and we wanted to provide logical table of contents entries to enable readers to go straight to the part of an inventory they wished. Initially, we thought we would be able to use the sub-series title as an entry in the table of contents. Our series are problematic, however, as they do not always have sub-series and even if they do all pieces may not automatically belong to a sub-series. We came up with the very pragmatic solution of adding <head> tags with reference to a range of fifty pieces, which were then brought over into the table of contents. This was far from ideal, however, especially as it involved a lot of time-consuming manual intervention; we have yet to develop a better solution.

After a partial launch of the Core Executive Catalog in April 1998, we successfully made the whole mini catalog available online in September 1998; access to it will be found on the PRO's Web site *<http://www.pro.gov.uk/>*.

TOPCAT AND EAD 1.0: BACKGROUND

The TOPCAT project was established to provide an interim holding environment for the higher-level catalog data of the *PRO Guide* until it eventually becomes the "top" of the new online PRO catalog, PROCAT. TOPCAT is more than just a storehouse, however; it holds dynamic data that will require ongoing editorial restructuring prior to its full implementation within PROCAT.

The source data for the print edition of the *PRO Guide* has been stored and maintained since 1994 in a custom-built Oracle 6.0 relational database application. But it was decided that the most appropriate new environment for TOPCAT would be an SGML database based around the recently developed SGML structured standard for finding aids, *Encoded Archival Description* (EAD). This would provide both a convenient editorial environment for the large amount of highly textual restructuring required of the data, and also form the basis of a customizable display medium for its online delivery.

EAD 1.0

After the official release of Version 1.0 of the EAD Document Type Definition (DTD) in August 1998, a series of analytical reports were gathered from the DTD with the help of the SGML::DTD perl module from Earl Hood's freely-available *PerlSGML* library: <*http://www.oac.uci.edu/indiv/ehood/perlSGML.html*>. The SGML::DTD module provides different means of interpreting the information in a DTD by building up data structures that represent the information contained within it.

Another piece of freeware also to be found in the *PerlSGML* library is *dtd2html,* a program that generates a multi-file HTML document that documents a DTD and allows logical hypertext navigation around it. The program has already been run against Version 1.0 of the EAD DTD by The Medieval Miniature Compendium Project in Mexico; the results can be seen at: <*http://mmc.unam.mx:1999/eaddoc/DTD-HOME.html*>.

Version 1.0 of the EAD DTD now encompasses nearly 160 SGML elements. Not all of these available elements would be required to accommodate the TOPCAT data structure, and on the basis of the analytical reports gathered above, an appropriate EAD template for TOPCAT was devised See Appendix 1. It currently utilizes around a third of the full EAD tag set, with the option to include any of the remaining available elements as needed.

FROM LEGACY SYSTEM TO EAD

A system was now required to fetch data from the appropriate tables within the Oracle relational database structure and build it up into a series of SGML-encoded files. A few options were considered, but the most versatile was to use DBI, a freely available perl-based Database Interface which allows access to multiple database types and utilizes Open Database Connectivity (ODBC): <*http://forteviot.symbolstone.org/technology/perl/DBI*>. A further advantage is the fact that DBI programming is done in perl (using embedded SQL to access data in relational tables) and the excellent text-processing functions of perl are ideal for a task that ultimately involved the creation of a set of text files.

With an agreed design for the TOPCAT EAD template established, a set of mapping files were created to identify the appropriate sequence and SGML location for each section of the original *PRO Guide* data. The basic design for the program was then to fetch each appropriate data field from each appropriate table in the relational database, bolt it into its appropriate element of SGML EAD-encoding, and assemble all the elements in the right order according to the mapping files, the template design, and the underlying schema (DTD) which defines EAD itself.

The end result was a dataset of over three hundred SGML-encoded text files, each one representing top level EAD finding aid description for the records of one government department or agency. Since the data is now held in SGML, its validity and integrity can be verified against the EAD DTD with the aid of an SGML parser; the one used here is James Clark's NSGMLS which is widely regarded as the best in its field and is freely available as part of his SGML processing suite, SP: *<http://www.jclark.com/sp>*.

Editing

The ongoing editorial restructuring of TOPCAT prior to its implementation within PROCAT is being carried out at the PRO using Interleaf's SGML editing suite Author/Editor 3.5. Like all out-of-the-box authoring systems, this provides a user-friendly environment for archivists to manipulate their finding aids without having to get too deeply involved with the technical complexities of the underlying EAD SGML and DTD themselves. There are many other SGML authoring systems available on the market; for coverage of the main contenders, see: *<http://www.infotek.no/sgmltool/editetc.htm>*.

Internal Access: SGML

The next issue facing the PRO was to develop a system for providing access to the data in its new format. Initially, the intention was to provide electronic access to the data on the PRO's intranet. Since the master data is undergoing daily editorial revision, it was decided that a duplicate dataset would be preferable for display purposes. This could be regenerated regularly from the master set to be more or less up-to-date and would prevent public access to data that is in a state of flux.

The software chosen to interpret the SGML for on-screen delivery was the Panorama Viewer 2.0, a Web browser plug-in for Netscape/Internet Explorer. This is a versatile and relatively inexpensive product that provides all the basic features expected of online document delivery (navigation tool, hypertext support, free-text search engine, ability to print, and so on: *<http://www.interleaf.com/Panorama/page3.html>*.

The design of display and navigation by the Panorama Viewer is controlled through the use of auxiliary files (style-sheets and navigation files), thus providing a versatile platform for presentation style. This ranges from having basic control over font size and color to more sophisticated features. In the case of TOPCAT, this included being able to suppress (hide) elements of the data that are still incomplete (a benefit made possible by exploiting the structural nature of SGML in order to be context-aware at any point within a document's "tree").

The contentious issue regarding the online delivery of large files was not encountered here: Panorama Viewer is easily able to handle our largest files (approximately 1.5Mb) and size or speed is not really an issue within an institutional *intranet* such as ours. Indeed, being able to provide a complete instance of an individual finding aid allows the user convenient features, such as fast internal hyperlinking, the full scope of the finding aid available within the navigator, or the ability to search or print the finding aid in its entirety. In the context of *Internet* delivery however, there is a serious trade-off against such convenience with other factors such as speed and system performance, but more on this below.

The front page index into TOPCAT consists of an HTML table which lists the three hundred or so government departments and provides links to the finding aid for each. As links to SGML (EAD) files, these automatically invoke the Panorama Viewer plug-in, but HTML frames are also invoked from the front page in order to maintain a top frame link to the original HTML index whilst Panorama Viewer runs alongside in the lower half of the screen.

Certain illustrations exist within the finding aids (e.g., departmental diagrams) which are too complicated to capture or render with SGML; the simplest solution for these was to scan them from the paper version of the *PRO Guide,* and display them as GIF images accessed via embedded links within the SGML.

External Access: HTML, XML

In addition to its availability across the PRO's intranet, access to TOPCAT data over the Internet was provided in May 1999. In the longer term, an ideal implementation of EAD-based finding aids might be to serve them directly to XML-compliant browsers as XML instances supported by XSL stylesheets governing their appearance. In the interim, in order to serve the vast majority of the WWW community, we must continue to look at EAD to HTML conversion. Various methods exist to achieve this, including using word-processor macros, the creation of customized programs using a scripting language like perl, or dynamic server-side transformations via a proprietary publishing package such as that provided by DynaWeb.

One of the stated purposes of the Extensible Stylesheet Language, XSL, was to be able to perform transformations from one encoding scheme to another, and indeed this has since developed into a W3C recommendation of its own: XSL for Transformation, XSLT. With a regard to the increasing importance of XML/XSL technologies, we decided to attempt our EAD (as XML) to HTML transformation using XSL. We first converted our EAD-encoded finding aids into valid XML documents using James Clark's freely available SGML to XML converter, SX, and designed accompanying XSL stylesheets to outline the exact EAD to HTML transformation we wanted to achieve from them. Then, with the help of James Clark's XSL processor XT (others are also freely available, e.g. IBM's LotusXSL), we pre-generated our deliverable HTML instances ready to be served to users on the WWW.

One of the drawbacks to this approach is the situation where individual finding aid instances happily stored on a server as large EAD text objects also need to be delivered to WWW clients requesting them. A variety of contributing factors can govern Internet access speed (bandwidth, type of connection, modem capacity, time of day) but to be WWW-friendly to the majority of users, it is not really acceptable to contemplate regularly serving individual HTML instances larger than 500Kb or so.

There are solutions to this problem, but these invariably involve developing expensive proprietary systems to enable dynamic data "chunking" before delivery. An alternative method is to break the original finding down into artificial mini-deliverable instances which are in some way linked together to recreate the continuity or hierarchy of the finding aid, e.g., using Frames with hyperlinked Navigation and Full-Text panels vertically divided on-screen. But this is not an ideal situation as it can entail the careful data management of multiple datasets and, anyway, it is contrary to the notion of the standard structural medium, EAD itself.

STORAGE AND MAINTENANCE: NOT EAD?

One potential solution to the issues surrounding the data management and online delivery of large finding aids is the use of a Relational Database Management System (RDBMS). The logical components of the finding aid, identifiable as the individual elements that make up EAD, are stored together as linked units in a dynamic system of tables and table fields. Any particular unit can be produced, along with other associated units if required. With a well-designed, user-friendly GUI, these can be delivered per se as nothing more than straight HTML pages. Alternatively, the RDBMS structure can be "reconstructed" on-the-fly into whole instances of complete EAD which have been ordered and compiled according to the syntax of the EAD DTD itself. This might be the method chosen to produce standard EAD for purposes of data exchange. In fact, an RDBMS will sit at the heart of the PRO's full online catalog, PROCAT, when it becomes available.

SEARCHING

The RDBMS also provides an environment that allows the comprehensive indexing and thus rapid search access to any chosen part of the database, usually under a range of search criteria. This is arguably harder to implement across a dataset that is basically a set of EAD text objects. Several commercial free-text search engines exist, such as Verity or OpenText, which have excellent reputations based around sophisticated indexing and the utilization of free-text retrieval technology such as Boolean and proximity searching. The addition of SGML-aware retrieval capabilities adds to the effectiveness of these engines, allowing, for example EAD-specific searching; OpenText 5.0 builds an indexed version of the database with "regions" which represent the SGML and which can be searched, like an RDBMS, under a range of search criteria.

The reality behind all of this, however, is that different institutions use different systems. What is ultimately required is a search engine that can operate independent of any proprietary system. An attempt in this direction is Z39.50, an information retrieval protocol which can enable complex search and retrieval from *distributed* databases and information resources. If "attribute sets" or data labels are used which are commonly agreed upon, Z39.50 can enable finding aid descriptions to be navigated from collection level down to specific files. The Implementation Group for Z39.50 (ZIG) is currently drafting a formal architecture for these attribute sets, and of course the role of EAD in this architecture will be vital, but several questions remain to be resolved. For instance, who will develop and "own" the EAD attribute? And who will ensure that guidelines and best practices for an EAD attribute set are created and disseminated? Again, different institutions conform to different format standards (like MARC-AMC or TEI) and it will be necessary for archivists to establish a precise relationship between these and EAD, not to mention overseeing the coordination of any development amongst the different communities.

PROCAT AND EAD

The major new development at the PRO where EAD will have a prominent role is PROCAT. The main aim here is to make the key finding aid to the Office's archives available remotely from the main record office at Kew and to as wide an audience as possible through use of the Internet. This will enable us to provide a much higher availability of our catalog with access not restricted to Office opening hours.

We are combining both the management of the archives catalog within the Office and its presentation to readers over the Web into one integrated system. PROCAT will allow the Office to carry out its key business activity of managing and maintaining its catalog in a more automated way, leading to improvements in efficiency and quality and allowing a more timely delivery of information to readers. With respect to presentation we shall be able to provide a comprehensive online system searchable by both those visiting Kew and by remote users. This service will allow historians, genealogists, researchers, and others to have much improved mechanisms for locating the particular records they wish to consult.

PROCAT will also include links to other related systems. These will be both in-house and other institutions' offerings, both national and international, all of which will greatly enhance the wealth of knowledge available to the reader for his or her research activity. From the in-house point of view these will permit easy ordering of documents for production to view, provide direct access to supplementary finding aids such as online databases, or provide access to reader assistance through information notices. However, the key component of the new system is to provide, as an integrated whole, the previously supplied separate components of the *PRO Guide* and the individual class lists, together with information leaflets supplied to aid users with their research.

Current work, and earlier pilot work, on standards for archival cataloging and usage of EAD, together with experience gained from the Core Executive pilot, the TOPCAT project, and others, have all fed into the design for PROCAT. The public interface will employ technology similar to the Internet browser approach and the use of EAD will be a core concept within the operation of the system.

PROCAT will have to store and manipulate large volumes of information both from a maintenance and a presentational point of view. Current estimates suggest the catalog will contain about eight million entries and that the database itself could be of the order of tens of gigabytes in size. Obviously we will also need to allow capacity for growth. When we assessed the nature of the information within our finding aids we noted two distinct forms. Some of the information is by nature structured, for example a code comprising a fixed number of characters, a numeric value within a given range, a date, and so on. This type of data is well suited to the traditional relational database approach.

However, significant parts of our information contain substantial areas of discursive text. These occur in EAD data elements such as administrative history/biographical history and scope and content. These text blocks can be substantial in size and additionally might display some structure to their content. These areas are not readily manageable using the relational approach and a different technique is needed. Indeed, some form of document management would be more effective in dealing with these. We therefore have a potential dilemma in choosing which technique to handle these two very different types of data. We believed the text blocks could benefit from the application of EAD or more likely a subset DTD.

We realized we could not force one type to be constrained by the needs of the other and thus decided to have the best of both worlds. We have proposed a solution that is a hybrid of both approaches. We recognized that we needed to adopt a basic relational model because of the volume of structured data we had to manage and manipulate. But in PROCAT we also proposed to use EAD to modify, store, and display the large text elements.

Our proposed solution to the management and storage issue is to place the large text elements into a special data type defined within the relational database. Leading Relational Database Management Systems (RDBMS) do have facilities for such requirements. They achieve this by permitting a non-standard data type to be referenced from within the system. This functionality is targeted at those kinds of data that do not fit easily within the confines of the standard types (numbers, dates, fixed length character fields, logical values, and so on). This new data type is aimed at including other, less rigid data forms such as text, image, graphics, and so on, within the database. These kinds of elements within the RDBMS are sometimes referred to as Objects and in our case they would be EAD objects. By referencing the data in this way we could modify the content using an appropriate EAD authoring tool (see previous section).

One way we intend to improve the quality of indexing and referencing to common terms, names, and so on, is through the use of Authority/Keyword Files, and we propose to employ such control over the whole of our catalog. Authority Files will hold authorized terms for four specific areas–namely corporate bodies, persons, places, and subjects. Unlike a thesaurus, an entry in the Authority File will only exist if at least one reference to it exists within the catalog. Such an approach is very structured in nature and efficient facilities for the maintenance and management are not easily provided for by the direct use of EAD. In our case this will be an XML compliant tool.

Editors amending or preparing catalog entries through PROCAT will supply indexing through cross-reference to the appropriate Authority File term ensuring a consistency in the use of such terms, e.g., spelling, name usage, and so on. Such indexing will only be made when the entry is significantly related to the index term. Then, when readers search using the Authority term, they will be presented with entries rich in content to the subject matter they are looking for. It is a challenging task to integrate such Authority control whilst utilizing EAD techniques to the large text elements. The "control access" elements within EAD do not alone provide the necessary uniqueness of storage required for this approach: structured relational tables will be employed to provide the required control.

PROCAT is being designed for import and export of EAD files and the catalog data will be capable of display in EAD form. When an EAD attribute set for Z39.50 is available PROCAT will be in a position to contribute data. Matching to Dublin Core is also possible, though perhaps in the short term more problematic, as Dublin Core presently looks at the electronic finding aid rather than the archival fonds described by the finding aid.

Our work with EAD to date has confirmed its great value as a data structure standard for government, as well as other, archives. The greater richness of EAD 1.0, and its recognition of the potential significance of the component levels, meets all our requirements in terms of hierarchical description and range of data elements available. Its XML compliance is of enormous value for easy user access. The sheer bulk of our holdings and the dynamic nature of the catalog make the full rendering of PROCAT as an integrated EAD document management system not feasible at present. Nevertheless EAD has a significant and continuing role both within PROCAT and as a means of facilitating data exchange with the rest of the world.

NOTE

1. *Encoded Archival Description Tag Library, Version 1.0* (Chicago: Society of American Archivists, 1998), p. 26.

APPENDIX 1. Series Level Template for EAD 1.0

```
<C LEVEL="series" LEGALSTATUS="public" LANGMATERIAL="eng">
  <DID>
    <HEAD></HEAD>
    <UNITID LABEL="Reference"></UNITID>
    <UNITID LABEL="Former Reference"></UNITID>
    <UNITID LABEL="Former Reference (PRO)"></UNITID>
    <UNITTITLE></UNITTITLE>
    <ORIGINATION LABEL="Creator(s)">
      <CORPNAME></CORPNAME>
      <PERSNAME></PERSNAME>
    </ORIGINATION>
    <UNITDATE LABEL="Covering Dates"></UNITDATE>
    <PHYSDESC>
      <EXTENT></EXTENT>
      <GENREFORM></GENREFORM>
      <DIMENSIONS></DIMENSIONS>
      <PHYSFACET></PHYSFACET>
    </PHYSDESC>
    <NOTE LABEL="Scale 1"><P></P></NOTE>
    <REPOSITORY LABEL="Held at"></REPOSITORY>
    <ABSTRACT></ABSTRACT>
```

APPENDIX 1 (continued)

```
</DID>
<ADMININFO>
      <ACCESSRESTRICT>
         <HEAD>Access Conditions</HEAD>
         <P></P>
      </ACCESSRESTRICT>
      <USERESTRICT>
         <HEAD>Restrictions on Use</HEAD>
         <P></P>
      </USERESTRICT>
      <ACQINFO>
         <HEAD>Immediate Source of Acquisition</HEAD>
         <P></P>
      </ACQINFO>
   <CUSTODHIST>
      <HEAD>Custodial History</HEAD>
      <P></P>
   </CUSTODHIST>
   <NOTE LABEL="Accumulation Dates"><P><DATE></DATE></P></NOTE>
   <APPRAISAL>
      <HEAD>Appraisal Information</HEAD>
      <P></P>
   </APPRAISAL>
   <ACCRUALS>
      <HEAD>Accruals Information</HEAD>
      <P></P>
```

```
    </ACCRUALS>
    <ALTFORMAVAIL>
        <HEAD>Location of Originals</HEAD>
        <P></P>
    </ALTFORMAVAIL>
    <ALTFORMAVAIL>
        <HEAD>Copies Information</HEAD>
        <P></P>
    </ALTFORMAVAIL>
</ADMININFO>
<SCOPECONTENT>
    <HEAD>Scope and Content</HEAD>
    <P></P>
</SCOPECONTENT>
<BIOGHIST>
    <HEAD>Administrative History</HEAD>
    <BIOGHIST><P></P></BIOGHIST>
</BIOGHIST>
<ARRANGEMENT>
    <HEAD>Arrangement</HEAD>
    <P></P>
</ARRANGEMENT>
<ADD>
    <BIBLIOGRAPHY>
        <HEAD>Publication Note</HEAD>
        <P></P>
```

APPENDIX 1 (continued)

```
      </BIBLIOGRAPHY>
      <OTHERFINDAID>
         <HEAD>Unpublished Finding Aids</HEAD>
         <P></P>
      </OTHERFINDAID>
      <RELATEDMATERIAL>
         <HEAD>Related Material</HEAD>
         <P></P>
      </RELATEDMATERIAL>
      <SEPARATEDMATERIAL>
         <HEAD>Separated Material</HEAD>
         <P></P>
      </SEPARATEDMATERIAL>
   </ADD>
   <NOTE><P></P></NOTE>
   <CONTROLACCESS>
      <HEAD>Index Terms</HEAD>
      <CORPNAME></CORPNAME>
      <PERSNAME></PERSNAME>
      <GEOGNAME></GEOGNAME>
      <SUBJECT></SUBJECT>
   </CONTROLACCESS>
</C>
```

Cross-Community Applications: The EAD in Museums

Richard Rinehart

SUMMARY. Markup and network technologies present an opportunity for museums to integrate traditional collection and item descriptions and make them available to anyone, anywhere. Encoded Archival Description, while developed in the archival community, appears to provide the means to realize this opportunity. Several museum projects are experimenting with the application of EAD to museum materials to find out what does and does not work. Traditional descriptive practices and standardization efforts within the museum community provide the context for this development. EAD will accommodate many traditional practices while also offering the possibility of new and potentially powerful forms of access. While EAD offers museums many potential benefits, its use also presents challenges. *[Article copies available for a fee from The Haworth Document Delivery Service: 1-800-342-9678. E-mail address: <getinfo@haworthpressinc.com> Website: <http://www.HaworthPress.com> © 2001 by The Haworth Press, Inc. All rights reserved.]*

KEYWORDS. Archival description, Encoded Archival Description, EAD, finding aids, museum access and description, museum standards

---

Richard Rinehart is Director of Digital Media at the University of California, Berkeley Art Museum and Pacific Film Archive, 2625 Durant Avenue, Berkeley, CA, 94720 (E-mail: rinehart@uclink.berkeley.edu).

[Haworth co-indexing entry note]: "Cross-Community Applications: The EAD in Museums." Rinehart, Richard. Co-published simultaneously in *Journal of Internet Cataloging* (The Haworth Information Press, an imprint of The Haworth Press, Inc.) Vol. 4, No. 3/4, 2001, pp. 169-186; and: *Encoded Archival Description on the Internet* (ed: Daniel V. Pitti, and Wendy M. Duff) The Haworth Information Press, an imprint of The Haworth Press, Inc., 2001, pp. 169-186. Single or multiple copies of this article are available for a fee from The Haworth Document Delivery Service [1-800-342-9678, 9:00 a.m. - 5:00 p.m. (EST). E-mail address: getinfo@haworthpressinc.com].

INTRODUCTION

In their traditional exhibitions and publications, museums have provided intellectual and historical contexts to enrich the intellectual and aesthetic understanding of our shared cultural heritage. With the advent of network and digital media technologies, the museum community has begun to consider new models of access. The model discussed here attempts to combine traditional contextual information with item-level information routinely maintained by museum registrars in collection management systems.

Encoded Archival Description (EAD) plays a central role in this model. Even though EAD is optimized for archives and manuscript libraries, there are enough similarities between archival and museum description to suggest that EAD may be an effective tool in combining contextual information with item-level information in a new museum description and access system. Archival description, and by extension, EAD, emphasizes broad contextual description of collections combined with hierarchical analysis and description of subcomponents of collections down to the item level. In addition, EAD makes all descriptive elements available at all levels of analysis and description, which facilitates both detailed collection-level description, and detailed description of items comprising a collection.

Archival description also differs from museum description in many significant ways. In particular, archivists identify collections based on the common provenance of the items that comprise them. While provenance is very significant in museum descriptions, it has a different meaning and role, and does not always define collections. While EAD appears to be a useful tool in defining new museum access and descriptive systems, it remains to be seen whether this and other differences between archive and museum descriptive practices will make use of EAD in museums impractical. With the first efforts underway to test the museum implementation of EAD, we will soon begin to have data to help us evaluate the success of this potentially important experiment in cross-community standards development.

BACKGROUND: ARCHIVES, LIBRARIES, AND MUSEUMS

Libraries, archives, and museums differ in the kind of physical access they provide to their materials. Libraries with circulating collections provide direct access to the books and journals in their collections. Users can borrow books and journals and take them home or on trips–wherever, in fact, they like. Archive and manuscript materials are generally directly available for use, typically under monitored conditions within the confines of the archive or library.

Users thus have direct access to archival materials, though without the freedom to remove them from the archive or library. Special collection libraries, with unique or rare books and journals, typically resemble archives in giving direct physical access, but in a monitored environment. In contrast to archives and libraries, museums rarely provide direct physical access to materials, and then only to documented scholars. Instead, selected holdings are displayed in exhibitions. Users can look at those items being displayed, but cannot touch them.

The nature of the physical access to materials has largely determined the intellectual access that libraries, archives, and museums have provided to users. Because libraries and archives provide physical access to most if not all of their holdings, it is necessary to provide intellectual access to enable users to determine the holdings of a particular library or archive. Libraries have provided such access through public catalogs. Archives, at least in the United States, have also begun to provide access through public catalogs, though more traditionally they have provided access through a variety of printed finding aids. Users in both archives and libraries must have intellectual access to the materials in order to locate and use them.

In contrast to archives and libraries, museums traditionally have not felt a need to provide detailed intellectual access to their holdings. Since museums generally do not entertain requests from the public to use particular items, there is no need for public catalogs and inventories. Instead they provide users with selected access through exhibitions and publications. With few exceptions, the public cannot examine comprehensive listings of all of the items held by a particular museum.

Museum curators and staff, however, do have a need to know what is in the museum collection in order to control and manage it. As soon as affordable computers and database management software became readily available, museums began to create collection management systems to facilitate item-level control. These systems, though, are generally available only to museum staff, and not to the general public.

With the emergence of the Internet and markup technologies, museums, like libraries and archives, have been presented with new opportunities to provide intellectual access to their holdings to anyone, anywhere, with a computer and a connection to the Internet. The advent of visual technology has given museums an even greater incentive to take advantage of the opportunities the Internet has opened to them by making it possible for them to enhance this access with visual representations of their holdings. Advances in three-dimensional technology promise to extend access in ways unimaginable only a few years ago. Thus archives and museums have an unprecedented opportunity to both expand and enhance their public service mission.

Many museums are now beginning to provide the public with online access to information about their collections. Perhaps the most obvious reason for this is that the technology supports it. Technology has advanced sufficiently to allow museums to integrate traditional exhibition and publication information with internal management and control information while at the same time providing access to images, and to make all of this widely and publicly available on the Internet. Given the importance of visual information to museums, it is easy to understand why they did not rush to embrace the pre-image Internet. It was only with the rise of markup and image technologies that the value of the Internet to museums became clear and inescapable.

The public has also quickly grasped the new possibilities. They have begun to expect if not demand Internet access to museum resources. The public, particularly teachers and scholars, have increasingly come to expect broad, electronic access to all kinds of information generated by and held in public agencies, and museums have not escaped this expectation. With respect to government institutions, such access has even become mandatory for certain kinds of information. The U.S. Federal Freedom of Information Act has been extended to cover Web-delivery of public information. These changes in public expectation have come at the end of two decades in which the social and public role of museums has become increasingly prominent.

Although external pressures and expectations have played a significant part in the interest museums are showing in the new methods of access, the primary motivation for embracing the new technologies springs from the desire of museum staff and curators to more effectively fulfill their traditional mission to the public, while expanding it to serve a broader community of users. Museums, like other cultural heritage institutions, are now looking to the Internet to provide opportunities to serve more effectively, and on a scale impossible until now.

To take advantage of these opportunities, many museums are taking their first steps toward creating public catalogs by putting Web interfaces on their collection management systems. While this is surely a good place to start, databases created to provide curators and staff with item-level control were not designed to facilitate public access. Among other deficiencies, these item-level systems frequently lack the contextual information that makes items intelligible and useful to public users. In these systems, for example, there is usually no detailed contextual information about individual items, and no information about their intellectual and historical relations to other items. Typically these systems only provide "tombstone" information, a set of basic information next to an image. The inadequacy of this approach for public users has already come under scrutiny.[1] The proprietary nature of these systems also makes it difficult if not impossible to link or associate related objects when they are held by different museums.

Providing comprehensive, persistent, public access to collection information is an entirely new service for museums, and will require the investigation of new information models. While providing access to the information in collection management systems has been a step forward, it is clear that museums need to reevaluate their descriptive practices in order to take full advantage of new technologies and the opportunities they present. The recognition of this need has driven some museums to explore the possibility of adapting work done in the archives community to develop an Internet-friendly standard for detailed collection descriptions in finding aids. Although, as noted above, museums and archives have developed different descriptive practices based on the different ways they have traditionally provided physical access to their collections, there is clearly enough common ground to suggest that museums may well be able to take advantage of the recent success of the archival community in developing EAD. It is clear, however, that a museum adaptation of EAD cannot be successful unless it is based on a careful consideration of the differences between the ways these two different communities use the key concept of "collection."

COLLECTION vs. ITEM LEVEL ACCESS: MUSEUMS AND COLLECTIONS

It is important to recognize that the term "collection" varies in meaning among the different cultural heritage communities. For archives, collections of items are primarily identified based on a common provenance. Collections of papers or records are the unselfconscious by-products of people living their lives and organizations carrying out their functions. Archivists also frequently work with "artificial" collections. Artificial collections are intentionally created based on one or more selection criteria by either individuals or organizations. Typically the criteria are based on genre, form, or a theme. Artificial collections are similar to many museum collections, though provenance–the collector–remains a significant defining characteristic. Nevertheless, while provenance, as the term is understood by archives, defines some museum collections, far more common are collections identified by form and genre, movement, creator, historical period, and geographic origin. Museum collections thus tend to be more interpretive when describing collections.

Having noted this significant difference in the value museums and archives place on "provenance" as the identifying principle underlying their collections, it is important to recognize that, although EAD was designed to enable provenance-based identification and description of collections, it also accommodates description of collections defined artificially, which is to say, by form and genre, creator, historical period or movement, geographic area, and, indeed, by any criteria. Given this flexibility, it appears that EAD might be useful in museum description.

In addition to provenance, two other characteristics of archival description are noteworthy in the context of museum description. The first of these is that archival description preserves the context of creation, typically by providing biographical and historical information and through detailed scope and content analysis. While archival contextual description provides the information necessary for understanding the origin of the material, it is not difficult to imagine extending it in museum descriptions to provide information necessary for understanding collections related by form, historical period or movement, geographic area, or other criteria. The second noteworthy characteristic is that archival description is also hierarchical, which is to say, it begins by describing the whole, and then proceeds to describe components of the whole, and components of the components, and so on. The components are intellectual rather than physical, and generally are identified on the basis of the function that generated the material or its form or subject matter.

Despite the differences in the way in which archives and museums choose to identify and describe collections, the emphasis on context and hierarchical descriptive analysis as practiced by archivists and embodied in the EAD appears to offer museums a means to integrate traditional item-level descriptive control systems with contextual information. While archivists emphasize provenance and a hierarchical analysis centered on function, form, and subject, EAD does not enforce these descriptive criteria. It will, in fact, permit other criteria, such as those employed in museum description. Whether these features of EAD can be fruitfully adapted and exploited by the museum community to serve its mission is something that can only be discovered through real-world testing.

EAD AND MUSEUM ACCESS AND DESCRIPTION

As we have noted, museums did not consider collection-level information the highest priority when they began using computers to control their collections. Following financial accounting, collection management was often the next function to be automated in museums. Collection management systems were developed to facilitate detailed item-level control of museum objects by curators and other staff. Thus it is not surprising that when the Internet began to interest them, museums began experimenting with making information in these management systems available to public users by developing Web or HTML-based interfaces. Typically the management information in the underlying system was not augmented with additional intellectual analysis and description to enhance its usefulness to the public.

While making this information available to the public would be useful, the sparse information that serves curators and initiated scholars well is frequently insufficient for many public users. It is important for museums to recognize, then, that in their quest to provide meaningful descriptive information to diverse audiences, item-level records represent only one end of the information continuum.[2] The other end is represented by interpretive and historical information that places museum items in the broader context of the collections in which they reside. Collection-level description facilitates greater understanding of individual items, and at the same time, creates greater awareness and understandings of collections themselves.

To provide such description does not require museums to adopt a completely alien way of looking at their holdings. Like archives and library special collections, museums have often based their prestige on the quality of their unique collections as much as on the unique items in them. Museums are collections of collections, and, indeed, a number of museums are currently demonstrating their recognition of the importance of collection-level information by providing descriptive information about their collections to supplement item-level information.

There are already many examples of this trend on museum Web sites: the Los Angles Museum of Contemporary Art presents us with The Panza Collection and The Barry Lowen Collection; the National Gallery of Art's Web site presents Gilbert Stuart, John Singleton Copley, and American Portraits of the Late 1700s and Early 1800s; and the National Museum of American Art hosts The Arvin Gottlieb Collection: Paintings from the American Southwest. These collection-level guides are based on provenance, artist, or period. They typically include a wealth of contextual information. One of the largest museum online databases, the San Francisco Fine Arts Museum's "Thinker" project, has recently added a new feature to the item-search interface. This new feature enables viewers to browse by "collection." Users can ask to see other items in the same collection through predefined searches in the item database. While no collection-level information is supplied, users can at least view related items together.

The Consortium For Interchange of Museum Information (CIMI), among others, has argued in its report on the Dublin Core test bed project for a standard "collection-level record format" for museums to complement item-level description. CIMI states that, while item-by-item subject analysis would greatly improve the success of searching, many museums simply cannot afford such analysis. The report suggests that subject access could be accomplished economically through use of a controlled vocabulary at the collection level. Katherine Martinez of the Research Libraries Group, in an article summarizing standards efforts in the museum community, concluded by proposing that collection-level records would make it easier to represent museum collections in integrated library/archive systems.[3]

While many museum items are meaningful when considered individually, many can only be understood when seen in relation to other items. Works in new genres such as installation art, performance art, and conceptual art exist in the museum collections as both documentation and artifacts. Many of the actual works comprise several pieces. "Artwork" no longer necessarily refers to a single item. Also common in twentieth-century art are runs or series of photographic prints, etchings, sculpture castings, and paintings. For the purposes of collection management and preservation, it is enough to know where and what each item is, with some reference to the fact that several items are related. For intellectual access, however, the relationships become primary, and need documentation to assist in navigation and understanding.

But even when museums have attempted to provide collection-level contextual information on their Web sites, they have been hampered by the limitations of the HTML markup language they employ. Most of the museum online access systems to date have provided item-level information through Web databases, but collection-level information in static HTML, thus excluding this information from sophisticated integration, navigation, and searching. Clearly, museums are in need of a semantically and structurally accurate representation of both item-and collection-level information if the full value of the representation is to be exploited on behalf of users. Any representational schema must be able to accommodate detailed item-level information, as well as full-text description at both the item and collection level. Further, such a schema must integrate both the item-and collection-level descriptive information. Such an approach would facilitate exploiting existing management information, enhance its value through the addition of collection-level information, and feature and enhance the value of collections.

The semantics and structure of EAD suggest that it may provide an adequate vehicle for communicating such collection-level integration. It accommodates collection-level description and, through its hierarchical structure, detailed description down to the item level. EAD thus can be used to represent the full spectrum of museum descriptive information from the item-level record found in existing collection management systems to the detailed collection descriptions, artist biographies, essays, exhibition catalogs, and pedagogical materials produced by curators and scholars. EAD can take an important place in the complex array of descriptive apparatuses employed by museums without negating existing museum description and management systems. EAD can complement a wide range of access tools (e.g., CIMI Z39.50 profile, *Categories for Description of Works of Art,* Dublin Core, Collection Management Systems, MARC records, and so on) and indeed may help to integrate them in the museum's quest to provide online access.

EAD AND THE MUSEUM COMMUNITY: BACKGROUND

The compatibility between EAD and museum descriptive practices is beginning to be recognized. CIMI literature has suggested that libraries and museums should jointly explore the use of EAD as a tool for the description of their collections. In the grant application for CHIO-II made to the National Endowment for the Humanities by CIMI in 1997, CIMI identified, under the heading "Developing Agreement on Standards through Consensus-building," the need "to establish a cooperative link with the very important EAD standard, so that our content can make use of this standard and not compete with it in any way." The use of EAD to describe museum collections in a number of recent consortial projects outlined below is, in part, a response to this call to link library and museum standards development.

In 1995, the Berkeley Art Museum/Pacific Film Archive (BAM/PFA) began investigating the possible use of the FindAid DTD, the predecessor to EAD, for providing online access to three collections: the Theresa Hak Kyung Cha conceptual art collection, the Hans Hofmann paintings, and Images and Ideas: the Berkeley Art Museum Collection. The latter is intended as a repository-level guide to collections. BAM/PFA also began working with three other museums to use EAD for describing conceptual art collections. As a result of the experimentation with EAD Beta, the collaborators in these projects recommended changes in EAD to accommodate important museum descriptive standards. In particular, they recommended enhancements to the element for physical description, <physdesc>, to accommodate detailed item-level physical description, and to include *Categories for Description of Works of Art* to the official list of EAD authorities (alongside AAT, LCSH, and so on). These changes were adopted by the SAA EAD Working Group and incorporated into version 1.0 of EAD.

In 1997, the four museums experimenting with EAD for conceptual art obtained NEA funding for the project and created CIAO (Conceptual and Intermedia Arts Online). CIAO has grown into a collaborative project between The Berkeley Art Museum/Pacific Film Archive, Tate Gallery, the University of Iowa Alternative Traditions in the Contemporary Arts, the Hood Museum of Art at Dartmouth, Franklin Furnace, the National Gallery of Canada, the

Getty Research Institute, Electronic Cafe, Block Museum, Anthology Film Archives, Museu de Arte Contemporânea, Universidade de São Paulo, and the Walker Art Center to create networked access to educational and scholarly material on the broad theme of conceptual and intermedia art, including new works of digital art.[4]

Conceptual art, while a subject of central concern to contemporary art studies, presents problems of access that impede its use by scholars and students, and its exposure to the general public. While there may be literature on and exhibitions of conceptual art, collections access is impeded by the ephemeral, documentary, and multi-part, mixed-media nature of many conceptual artworks. The works often challenge traditional methods of art description and cataloging. Works of this nature require a context in order to be understood; they require complex relationships between objects and groups of objects to be made explicit in both human terms and in machine representation to support navigation. Linking the "objects" with the "archives" is also crucial in that it is often unclear where one stops and the other begins in conceptual artworks, and both contribute to a fuller understanding.

In 1998 several California museums began participating in the Online Archive of California (OAC), the EAD union database for the state of California maintained by the California Digital Library (CDL). Out of these efforts came the Museums and the Online Archive Of California (MOAC), which, under CDL auspices, has launched an IMLS grant project to test the desirability and feasibility of developing a museum implementation of EAD within the OAC union database.[5]

MOAC will use EAD to integrate museum descriptive information with archive and manuscript descriptions in the statewide OAC. Museum, archive, and library descriptions will coexist and be accessible through a single interface and optionally through content-tailored portals. Partners in the initial development include Stanford Cantor Center for Art, Grunwald Center for Graphic Arts at UCLA, Oakland Museum of California, UCR/California Museum of Photography, Fowler Museum of Cultural History at UCLA, Phoebe Hearst Museum of Anthropology, Japanese American National Museum, Berkeley Art Museum/Pacific Film Archive, Berkeley Museum of Paleontology, and the Bancroft Library. MOAC is exploring issues relevant to providing access to object and image data within the EAD on behalf of the OAC. MOAC is also investigating how to best integrate access to collections information from diverse types of museums (art, photography, anthropology, cultural, history) with an even larger set of institutions (archives, historical societies, and libraries). As mentioned above, MOAC will have to address a number of serious issues to determine if EAD can make cross community information resource sharing a reality for users and professionals alike. The real test of any standard is not how well it plays out in theory, but what it enables one to accomplish in the real world.

Clearly MOAC and the other museum EAD projects currently underway will be the first serious test of whether users will profit from the marriage of library, archives, and museum collection description. It will also test whether the archives and museum communities can fruitfully cooperate together on a standards development process. These and other investigations will help determine whether EAD can be usefully applied in museums, and can facilitate integrating access to collections from a variety of cultural heritage institutions.

STANDARDS AND MUSEUMS

The standardization of description and access in the library community has a long history, dating at least to the middle of the nineteenth century. Copy cataloging provided a major economic incentive for librarians to sacrifice individual approaches for community-based standard approaches. Both the archive and museum communities lacked an economic motivation, given the unique natures of their collections. It is only with the emergence of markup and network technologies that a clear motivation for developing standards has emerged in archives and museums.

Markup technologies, specifically Standard Generalized Markup Language (SGML) and Extensible Markup Language (XML), have provided an affordable and flexible means for communities, even small communities, to develop accurate semantic and structural representations of their information. Given that the potential market for SGML and XML is anyone with a document of any kind, the market driving the development of software is large, and this is increasingly leading to a large number of affordable products.

Standard representation of computer information is absolutely essential in the cultural heritage communities. Each has a commitment to the long-term preservation of the materials under their control, and a key component of this commitment in the computer age is to have reasonable assurance that the information in their care and which they create is not dependent on specific computer hardware and software. SGML and XML provide this assurance.

The markup technologies alone, however, probably would not have provided sufficient motivation by themselves for standardization in the archive and museum. The ability to provide remote access by means of the Internet offers archives and museums the opportunity not only to fulfill their mission to provide public access to materials in their care, but also to democratize it. The combination of the two technologies makes it possible to fulfill and extend the mission of archives and museums.

INTEGRATION OF MUSEUM INFORMATION

As a flexible standard for integrated collection and item description, EAD offers the museum community the opportunity to integrate descriptive information in three important ways. First, EAD will facilitate integrating collection-level description and contextual information with item description within a museum. Second, it will enable integrating description of related materials held in different administrative and curatorial units within museums. Finally, EAD will make it possible to integrate museum descriptions with description from other museums, and from other cultural heritage repositories, in particular, libraries and archives.

Museums, as we have seen, employ a variety of description and control apparatuses. To date, while these different apparatuses frequently focus on the same materials, the different kinds of information have existed in distinct and isolated systems. EAD will enable museums to integrate information from a variety of systems such as educational brochures, artist and provenance files, historical analyses, and so on, with item descriptions frequently found in management and control systems. Such integration will enhance the intellectual and educational value of the various kinds of information. Users, for example, will be able to read about an artist, and then browse works by that artist. Or read about a particular artistic movement, and then browse works reflecting that movement.

Frequently, intellectually and historically related materials are dispersed among curatorial and administrative units within a museum. The Berkeley Art Museum/Pacific Film Archive, for example, has two main collections, visual plastic art, and film. Each has its own collection management system, with distinct record structure and semantics based on the standard for the field. Art uses the *Categories for the Descriptions of Works of Art*,[6] represented in a relational database form. MARC and AACR2 are used for description of films. The Oakland Museum of California has separate departments for art, history, and science. The Metropolitan Museum has individual departments for painting, textiles, sculpture, and other genres and forms. While integrating collection management systems is difficult because of unique administrative and curatorial challenges, integration of intellectual and historical description, though not without its own challenges, appears feasible, and would greatly benefit users. EAD can accommodate information from different descriptive systems, and thus provide a common ground on which the different kinds of description can be integrated. By accommodating data from diverse descriptive systems, EAD can serve to provide unified, integrated public access to all collections and items in a museum.

Many museum collections and items are intellectually and historically related to collections and items in other museums and in libraries and archives. By accommodating information from diverse descriptive systems within museums, and from libraries and archives, a shared standard such as EAD can serve to provide union access to cultural heritage resources. For example, the paintings by an individual artist are frequently held in more than one museum. EAD makes it possible to provide union access to all of the paintings, regardless of where they are. If the artist's papers are in an archive or manuscript library, then EAD makes it possible to integrate access to both the papers and paintings. Such integration of access will be of great benefit to public users, who frequently want to locate and use all materials generated or produced by an individual artist; information traditionally provided by expensive and scarce *catalogs raisonne.*

EAD enables integration of diverse descriptive information through a flexible descriptive semantics and structure. While museum and archive description differ in significant ways, they nevertheless share many specific descriptive categories or elements. Collections, collection components, and items generally all have titles, even if in some cases the title is assigned by the curator or archivist, or is explicitly "untitled." Similarly, collections, collection components, and items in museums and archives have creation dates. Thus the EAD elements <unittitle> and <unitdate> can easily be applied in both museum and archival contexts. Many other EAD elements, <origination> (for creator or collector), <unitid>-unit identifier, and <repository>, have similar utility in both archives and museums.

There is a major difference in the evaluation of the physical nature of materials in archives and museums. Archives generally emphasize the intellectual content of materials over their physical qualities. Physical description in archives generally involves providing a statement concerning the extent or quantity of materials, with a general description of their form or genre. Museums, of course, generally provide a detailed description of the physical nature of an object. EAD accommodates both the sparse archival description as well as the detailed descriptions found in museums. The <physdesc>-physical description contains three important subelements that facilitate elaborate description: <dimensions>, <physfacet>-physical facet, and <genreform>. Each of these elements is repeatable within <physdesc>, and in combination can be used to provide a detailed physical description of an object. Both <physfacet> and <genreform> accommodate controlled vocabularies, using an attribute to designate the thesauri employed. For example, the term "paintings" selected from the Art and Architecture Thesaurus would be represented as follows:

```
<genreform source="aat">Paintings</genreform>
```

There are several attributes that can be used to qualify general descriptive elements to provide a more precise or constrained semantics. In particular, the "encodinganalog" attribute, which appears on all descriptive elements, can be used to "link" an element to another encoding scheme, such as MARC. The "type" attribute also appears on <admininfo>-administrative information, <add>-adjunct descriptive data, and the generic <odd>-other descriptive data. The "type" attribute provides a standardized way of providing semantic extensions to the descriptive categories in EAD.

The example in Figure 1 shows how EAD markup can be applied to an average museum item record, and how certain elements of the record map specifically to the *Categories for Descriptions of Works of Art.* In this instance, the CDWA mapping not only provides a community-specific reference, but also acts to refine the EAD record on the item level by distinguishing one <physfacet> element from another, adding the specific record granularity some communities may require at this level.

The museum item-level record in Figure 1 would be included in a larger EAD collection description in the list of items in that collection. It represents the basic "tombstone data," the information found on wall-labels that accompany museum artifacts on public display. This information is also typically found in museum collection systems.

Because EAD was designed to accommodate a nonstandard and therefore diverse past and to provide space for the archival community to negotiate best practices and content standards, with few exceptions, it does not constrain the number and order of elements. This flexibility makes it possible to employ its descriptive apparatus in the manner most appropriate to the materials being described.

Both the CIAO and MOAC projects will serve to illustrate how this flexibility can be employed in museums. Both projects wanted to provide public access to descriptive information in collection management systems in the EAD <dsc>-description of subordinate components. Each item description is contained in a <c>-component description within the <dsc>. Both projects had to decide which elements to export from the management systems into EAD. Clearly some management information is sensitive, such as donor information, and some is of little or no value for the public, such as crate number. Both projects decided to use the fifteen fields defined in the Getty/RLG REACH project as a guide, as it had objectives similar to those in the two projects.

The REACH project set out to investigate whether information about museum objects could be extracted from collection management systems and made useful for research use. Museums and vendors were enlisted; together they identified the access points that would be most useful to researchers. The

FIGURE 1

```
<c01 level="item">
    <did>
        <origination>
            <persname role="artist">Hans Hofmann</persname>
        </origination>
        <unittitle>Painting No. 12</unittitle>
        <unitdate>1945</unitdate>
        <physdesc>
            <physfacet type="materials-description" source="cdwa">oil on canvas</physfacet>
            <physfacet type="materials-processes" source="cdwa">painted with palette
            knife</physfacet>
            <dimensions>40 x 60 inches</dimensions>
        </physdesc>
        <repository>Jonestown Art Museum</repository>
        <unitid>1909.4.45</unitid>
    </did>
    <admininfo>
        <custodhist>
            <p>Gift of Mr and Mrs. McGillicutty</p>
        </custodhist>
    </admininfo>
    <odd type"transcription">
        <p>"To my beautiful Ophelia"</p>
    </odd>
    <odd type="condition">
        <p>Painting is in bad shape, having been painted with a knife and left in the artist's
        basement.</p>
    </odd>
    <controlaccess>
        <subject source="aat">family portraits</subject>
        <genreform source="aat">paintings</genreform>
    </controlaccess>
</c01>
```

resulting set of data elements was to be used for exporting the data from the disparate museum collection management systems.[7]

REACH attempts to define a base set of descriptive elements found in most museum systems that will satisfy most if not all research. After accepting the REACH recommendations, the two projects mapped the descriptive elements into EAD. This mapping is illustrated in Figure 2.

The display order of the elements was chosen based on an informal survey of typical museum wall-labels and Web databases. In this way, the projects were able to craft markup which reflected museum community practice without sacrificing compatibility with other EAD systems. Note that these elements are reflected in the EAD example given in Figure 1.

The fifteen elements chosen represent a "target" set. Some museums may lack some of the elements in the set, and yet others may have additional descriptive information that would be useful in research. Museums having less

FIGURE 2

REACH	EAD
Electronic Location & Access	<dao> or <daoloc>
Creator/Maker	<origination> with <persname> and <corpname> optional
Object Name/Title	<unittitle>
Date of Creation/Date Range	<unitdate>
Place of Origin/Discovery	<geogname>
Medium/Materials	<physfacet> with optional type attribute
Techniques/Process	<physfacet> with optional type attribute
Dimensions	<dimensions>
Current Repository Name	<repository>
Provenance	<custodhist>
Current Object ID Number	<unitid>
Notes	<odd>
Subject Matter	<subject>
Type of Object	<genreform>
Style/Period/Group/Movement/ School	<corpname> with optional role attribute

information can simply omit those elements they lack. Museums having more can extend EAD to accommodate more detailed description. If museums lack any item-level information, they could, in fact, choose to provide only collection-level access to holdings. Another option would be to provide collection-level access, with a link providing direct access to a Web accessible database providing item-level description. In this scenario the museum could contribute the collection-level description in EAD to a union database, and thereby enhance discovery and use of its local resources.

Within the <controlaccess>-controlled access, it is possible to provide extensive access through controlled vocabularies. Access elements for this purpose are <corpname>-corporate name, <famname>-family name, <geogname>-geographic name, <occupation>, <persname>-personal name, <subject>, <genreform>-genre or form, and <function>. While many museums cannot afford to provide detailed controlled access at the item level, it becomes much more economic if provided at the collection level. EAD, in fact, supports providing such access at both the collection and item level. Controlled access terms can greatly facilitate discovery and retrieval.

The flexibility of EAD thus offers museums many options for exploiting existing descriptive information, and extending and enhancing access. These many options make it possible for a wide range of museums, small and large, resource poor and rich, to enhance the visibility, utility, and use of collections. The options are so great, in fact, that it is clear that the museum community will need to explore and experiment with many options, and, based on this experience, develop EAD best practices. While EAD accommodates a wide variety of descriptive content, it does not prescribe optimal descriptive content for either archives or museums. If EAD descriptions from different museums are to coexist in union access systems, some degree of normalized practice will be necessary.

Current museum projects are beginning to research and experiment with various uses of EAD. They are exploring what museum description has in common with archival description, and where it differs. If the differences are profound, then it may be ultimately necessary for the museum community to develop its own structure and content standards, and to explore with the archival community how such standards can be exploited in integrated cultural heritage access systems.

Current experiments with EAD by the Museums and the Online Archive of California and other projects will help determine whether it is possible for the museum community to share EAD with the archival community, and whether it is possible to provide union access to archival and museum descriptions in integrated cultural heritage access systems.

CONCLUSIONS: OPPORTUNITIES AND CHALLENGES

Application of EAD to museum collections is just beginning, and thus there are no firm and final conclusions. Nevertheless, there is sufficient experience on which to base some general observations about the technical, intellectual, and political issues involved in museum use of EAD.

It is clear that EAD is based on the right emerging technologies. The advent of XML, and its rapid embrace by commercial, government, and educational institutions as the fundamental standard for representing and sharing text-based Internet information should give us confidence in the future viability of the technology underlying EAD. If technology were the only issue, EAD would be a clear solution to many descriptive challenges in the museum community. But is EAD the right intellectual solution?

EAD was developed for the archival community, with some informal input from the museum community to date. It attempts, with apparent success, to address hierarchical description that integrates and interrelates both collection and item information. It provides descriptive elements at all levels of description that have much in common with museum descriptive categories, though with some differences. Broad descriptive categories that can be user-specified using attributes provide a means to extend EAD to accommodate museum-specific categories of description. While the early experiments with EAD have been promising, it is only with broad and extended experimentation that the museum community will be able to determine whether EAD is adaptable for its purposes, or whether something similar, though museum-specific, needs to be developed.

Community-based standards are as much political in nature as they are technical and intellectual. The viability of EAD in the museum community will depend also on the ability of the museums to collaborate and cooperate with one another in determining common protocols for applying EAD. And it will also depend on collaboration between the museum community and the archive and library communities in the ongoing development and maintenance of EAD.

While there are unquestionably differences in library, archive, and museum descriptive principles and practice, the user who simply wants to know what they have in their collections or whether a particular item exists, and if so, where, is likely to have little or no interest in or appreciation of these differences. Such a user, it can be argued, would benefit greatly from more seamless access to the truly vast array of cultural materials held collectively by them. If the technical, intellectual, and political challenges can be met, then EAD offers libraries, archives, and museums the possibility of providing integrated access to this global repository of humankind's cultural effort regardless of where it exists and in which kind of repository.

NOTES

1. For more on this discussion see Kevin Donovan, "The Best of Intentions: Public Access, the Web & the Evolution of Museum Automation," at <http://www.archimuse.com/mw97/speak/donovan.htm>.
2. Richard Rinehart, "The Museum Information Continuum," *Spectra: Journal of the Museum Computer Network* 23, no. 1.
3. Katherine Martinez, "RLG's Cultural Heritage Initiatives," *Spectra: Journal of the Museum Computer Network* 25, no. 3.
4. For more on CIAO, see <http://www.bampfa.berkeley.edu/ciao/>.
5. For more on MOAC, see <http://www.bampfa.berkeley.edu/moac/>.
6. For more on the *Categories for the Descriptions of Works of Art,* see <http://www.ahip.getty.edu/cdwa/>.
7. For more on REACH, see <http://www.rlg.org/reach.html>.

Encoded Finding Aids as a Transforming Technology in Archival Reference Service

Richard V. Szary

SUMMARY. Much of the literature dealing with the use of encoded archival finding aids to date has focused on its underlying principles and on methodologies for implementation. This article explores the potential transforming effects that this technology can have for archival reference service, particularly in facilitating user self-sufficiency and staff productivity. The author discusses the technological and communication barriers and expectations that may characterize users of encoded finding aids, the necessity for a critical mass of content, and the potential benefits of standardized identification and presentation of finding aid elements and how these issues provide an opportunity for archivists to rethink archival reference methodology. The availability of a large number of standardized finding aids to a sophisticated user community can support a triage approach to archival reference that allows professional reference archivists to spend more of their time on training, development of systems, and mediating complex inquiries. *[Article copies available for a fee from The Haworth Document Delivery Service: 1-800-342-9678. E-mail address: <getinfo@haworthpressinc.com> Website: <http://www.HaworthPress.com> © 2001 by The Haworth Press, Inc. All rights reserved.]*

Richard V. Szary is Carrie S. Beinecke Director of Manuscripts and Archives, Yale University, P.O. Box 208240, New Haven CT 06520-8240 (E-mail: richard.szary@yale.edu).

[Haworth co-indexing entry note]: "Encoded Finding Aids as a Transforming Technology in Archival Reference Service." Szary, Richard V. Co-published simultaneously in *Journal of Internet Cataloging* (The Haworth Information Press, an imprint of The Haworth Press, Inc.) Vol. 4, No. 3/4, 2001, pp. 187-197; and: *Encoded Archival Description on the Internet* (ed: Daniel V. Pitti, and Wendy M. Duff) The Haworth Information Press, an imprint of The Haworth Press, Inc., 2001, pp. 187-197. Single or multiple copies of this article are available for a fee from The Haworth Document Delivery Service [1-800-342-9678, 9:00 a.m. - 5:00 p.m. (EST). E-mail address: getinfo@haworthpressinc.com].

KEYWORDS. Archival reference service, archives, Encoded Archival Description, EAD, finding aids, users

INTRODUCTION

Much of what has been written and discussed about the development and implementation of the Encoded Archival Description (EAD) document type definition for archival finding aids has focused on the structure, content, and implementation of the new standard.[1] Articles, presentations, and workshops have offered archivists and systems managers a wealth of advice on how to analyze a repository's finding aids in the context of EAD, retrospectively convert legacy finding aids to the new format, select authoring and publishing software, and manage the administrative and technical issues involved. While the main rationale for the development of EAD has been to make finding aids discoverable, searchable, and displayable in a Web environment, little has been said about how the act of making them widely available outside of the repository may affect how archives provide reference services.

As an archival administrator, I have been especially interested in examining how EAD-encoded finding aids might affect the cost-effectiveness of our reference services. As archives continue to pursue our mission of selecting, preserving, and providing access to the primary sources documenting the development of our society and culture, the enormity of that task dwarfs the available resources that we have or are likely to obtain–even in the best of times.[2] Archivists must explore every avenue for improving how we deploy those resources to enhance our ability to fulfill that mission. While I would not suggest that reference services can be re-engineered into a one-size-fits-all, checkout-counter-style operation, we do need to examine the highly informal, idiosyncratic, and personalized approach that characterizes many of the reference programs we now have, to see how to make access to the primary sources entrusted to us more available, comprehensible, and cost-effective.

The emergence of EAD as a standard for encoding and providing systematic access to finding aid information has been of interest primarily as part of the continuing development of the descriptive standards required for enhancing access to archival materials through interchange of descriptive products and by ensuring their migration to new systems over time. In addition, however, it also offers the possibility of improving the cost-effectiveness of reference services by enabling users of archival resources to become more self-sufficient and freeing reference staff to handle complex queries, train users in the discovery and use of primary sources, study user behavior, and help develop improved access methodologies and mechanisms.[3]

When I presented an earlier version of this paper at the 1996 American Society for Information Science conference, I suggested that the initial and primary transformation of research and reference service would take place within the repository, rather than in the research community, because of four factors:

- the small proportion of users who are Web-capable and navigation-skilled,
- the pace of conversion (relating to size and resources of repository),
- lack of interoperable systems that are deployed to make finding aids known and available to users, and
- the nature and quality of finding aids, many of which are sufficiently idiosyncratic to require staff intervention to interpret and use them effectively.

Within a repository, a critical mass must be achieved in the first two factors–user population and holdings coverage–before encoded finding aids can have a major transforming effect on how reference service is provided. While the availability of interoperable systems and greater standardization in finding aid structure and content will also contribute to the effectiveness of an encoded finding aid system, the first two factors are most critical to beginning this transformation.

BUILD IT AND WHO WILL COME?

One of the primary governing factors in how the availability of EAD-encoded finding aids will transform reference to primary sources is whether there is a sufficient body of users who have ready access to, or are interested enough to acquire, the technological resources needed to make effective use of these new tools. Closely related is whether the archival community that allocates its resources to the conversion and maintenance of these tools can develop an effective way of alerting potential users to the availability and content of encoded finding aids and educating them in their use. Finally, it is quite possible that repositories will find themselves increasingly approached by non-traditional users because of the wider availability of encoded finding aids.

Technological Barriers

Most researchers who use primary source materials come from historical or humanities-based disciplines whose members are not well-positioned to take advantage of new technological tools. This situation can be characterized by a number of features:

- The absence of a technological basis or support structure that is indispensable to the effective pursuit of studies in the discipline. Unlike the hard and social sciences where access to machine-readable data and the tools to process it play such a fundamental role, within the humanities most scholars can still function quite successfully without such resources. Classical studies and art history are two areas where this situation may be changing, as most classical texts become available in machine-readable form and where images of objects important for art historical studies are increasingly converted into digital form.
- The lack of professional support for technology-based initiatives. Publication, pedagogical, and research methodologies are still geared primarily to the use of traditional technologies for gathering, presenting, and disseminating the objects of study. The use of electronic technologies in these endeavors is generally incidental or supplementary rather than integral or essential.
- The resulting lack of technological skills and resources. If the methodology of humanities disciplines do not depend on a strong technology base, then there is little incentive for practitioners in these fields to acquire the skill to harness existing technology to professional pursuits or to acquire the material resources (hardware, software, communications) needed.

Marketing encoded finding aids to the historical research community must therefore take into account the level of technical capability currently present in the primary user community. The model for access to the finding aids may initially be repository-based workstations and include instructional programs that can introduce the power and usefulness of the new tools to users who are not otherwise oriented to networked resources and services. Once convinced of the effectiveness of these tools, users may then have a greater incentive to invest in enhancing their own technological capabilities.

Communication Barriers

In addition to a professional culture that encourages an appreciation of the technology and acquiring the skills to use it, the development of a user community for encoded finding aids requires a commitment to the dissemination of information on the availability and content of these tools. While users have become accustomed to using online public catalogs for access to published library holdings, many rely just as heavily on less structured methods (such as footnotes) that rely on work done by other researchers or on direct contact with repositories and their reference staffs to identify primary sources of interest.

To the extent that researchers do identify primary sources through online catalogs, the ability of Web-capable catalogs to support links to other sites and files makes access to encoded finding aids a natural extension of this existing tool. Linking the summary description present in the catalog record with the more detailed finding aid description and inventory–the model that archivists promote as the most effective searching and retrieval methodology–is a major method of alerting users to the existence and availability of encoded finding aids.

Most EAD applications are being developed with Web access as the primary delivery mechanism. The availability of Web-accessible search engines that can reach out and index remote sites, providing local users with ready access to a decentralized universe of finding aids, will provide wide visibility for repositories who make their finding aids available in this way.[4] To the extent that this model is employed, users will not be faced with the need to track a large number of local sites and check each one for materials of interest as they often need to do now with online catalogs.

The mechanisms for effective communication of the availability of these new tools to users who are already accustomed to and make use of online searching, then, are readily available. It will be the integration of EAD finding aid systems into established discovery patterns and the routine reference process, and their inclusion in methodology courses and bibliographic instruction that will most effectively make other users aware of their availability and content.

New Users

Given the current technological capabilities and awareness of the primary user communities for archival and manuscript repositories, and the ease with which many other communities connect to and browse online resources, it is very possible that repositories who place encoded finding aids on Web-accessible systems will find that they receive more inquiries from members of these other communities than from their expected clientele. Given public fascination with the type of historical information and resources that finding aids describe, and the same public's lack of experience or understanding of how primary sources are used, repositories should be prepared for a new stream of questions and greater demands for service than they have had to accommodate in the past.

In assuming that they are dealing with a sophisticated research clientele, most repositories expect that the majority of their users will approach them well-grounded in the secondary literature of their subject. They also assume that users will understand the preservation, security, and privacy concerns that require more controlled access procedures than the local public library. Finally, most experienced users of primary sources understand the limitations of arrangement and descriptive work, and the importance of documents in context, and expect to spend time reviewing boxes of documentation in search of relevant materials, and to understand them.

Technologically sophisticated users who discover and browse archival finding aids, but who have not worked with research collections, are unlikely to be aware of all of these considerations and may expect a level of access and service that repositories are not, and never have been, expected to provide. While the wide availability of encoded finding aids may expose a larger public to the extraordinary primary resources that they were unaware of, repositories must be prepared to educate an inexperienced public in the realities of primary source research. The enormous expense of providing minimal control and description for archival and manuscript materials precludes the level of access that the inexperienced public may assume exists.

WHAT WILL THEY FIND?

Transformation of archival reference service through the use of encoded finding aids is dependent not only on an interested and technologically capable user community, but on a critical mass of content that can supplant existing mechanisms. As long as users must be as aware of and pay as much attention to traditional means of delivering finding aid information as to searching and viewing encoded finding aids, the full extent of the transformation will not be able to take place. At Yale, we continue to struggle with a combined system of catalog cards (representing an older, more structured and detailed description of manuscripts), online bibliographic records, and finding aids to provide intellectual access to our holdings. In the transition from one descriptive methodology to the next, there has never been a comprehensive migration of information into the next system. Without deliberate planning, encoded finding aids run the risk of being yet another ingredient in the mix. A comprehensive and rational architecture for archival descriptive information must be established, at least at the local level, so that users can navigate the various tools with a good understanding of their relationship to each other.

Complicating the introduction of encoded finding aids is the lack of professional standards that have governed the construction of finding aids. Even within repositories, different structures and content standards have been in place, so that a repository with a long history of finding aids can be faced with a wide variety of documents that need to be converted. One of the principles of the Berkeley effort to develop the DTD was the attempt to accommodate rather than prescribe the structure, content, and format of existing finding aid practices.[5] There was no effort to decide on a standard for any of these aspects. As a result, almost anything that walks the earth and is called a finding aid can be encoded, but it remains to be seen if all of these various creatures can coexist in a shared system. One of the outcomes of the EAD initiative is likely to be greater attention to finding aid standards within the archival profession.[6] Of more immediate concern, however, is whether a conversion effort will involve large-scale reconsideration of existing practice at the local level, the development of new local standards, and the retrofitting of existing finding aids to the new standards.[7] If this happens, the cost and time needed for conversion will increase substantially.

The critical mass can be thought of as a particular percentage of existing finding aids that must be encoded before the system becomes a viable alternative to existing mechanisms. The size of the legacy information base will vary from repository to repository but is likely to be vast for many of the institutions with large holdings. In the department of Manuscripts and Archives at Yale, there are an estimated 75,000 pages of existing finding aids to be converted. At least 80% of these are not in machine-readable form and many have handwritten annotations and corrections.

Conversion of legacy information must compete for resources with the need to process materials already here as well as new additions. Manuscripts and Archives has approximately 5,000 linear feet of materials requiring further work, and the department acquires at least 600 linear feet of new materials each year. There are no resources directly allocated for finding aid upgrade (such as word-processing of typed finding aids or addition of handwritten annotations) so funding for conversion must be obtained separately unless resources can be redirected from other activities.

Creation of a critical mass of encoded finding aids–sufficient to support this mechanism as more than a peripheral system–will vary amongst repositories depending on the size of their holdings, the degree to which their finding aids already conform to local structure, content, and format standards, and the extent to which they are available in some sort of machine-readable form.

TRANSFORMATION OF THE REFERENCE FUNCTION

If archivists can meet the challenges of enabling a critical mass of users to use a critical mass of encoded finding aids, then there are a wide range of opportunities for transforming archival reference service. There are five results of a comprehensive program of making encoded finding aids directly available to users that can have a significant effect on how reference will be planned and managed.

Increased Standardization of Finding Aid Information

As noted above, the lack of standards for finding aid structure, content, and format is a major challenge to efficient conversion of existing information. Looked at positively, the need to handle large amounts of finding aid information, whether as a conversion project or as new entry, will generate a need for a level of standardization that will support automated encoding. The ability to target searches to specifically tagged elements will mean that those elements will have to be identified more explicitly than is currently the case. The result will be a more consistent recording and presentation of finding aid information, providing the user with a common base of assumptions that will be consistent across an entire set of finding aids. Moving from one finding aid to another will no longer require reorientation to a unique document type that might require interpretation from reference staff.

Ability to Search Within and Across Finding Aids

Finding aids are often large and complex documents. With current hard-copy delivery mechanisms, users must review tens or hundreds of pages of listings to identify descriptions of materials that might be of interest to their research topic. A momentary lapse of attention may cause the user to miss an important entry. While the arrangement of the entries can give users a clue as to where a particular entry might be found, the transcription of content descriptions (such as folder titles) often leads to entries appearing in unexpected places. While a full-text search engine may be able to identify particular occurrences of a term, the ability to encode structure as well as content is critical to displaying the description within which a term is found in a way that conveys to the user how the described materials fit in the structure of the entire body of materials of which it is a part. For example, knowing that the materials being described are part of a correspondence series rather than a series of personnel files is critical information for proper interpretation of the materials and for deciding whether it is necessary to examine the described materials.

Current practice, based on hard-copy finding aids, allows a researcher to examine one finding aid at a time. By providing a common encoding scheme for all finding aids, searching across finding aids for a particular term–often in a particular context–becomes possible. This is particularly important since the catalog record contains terms for only the most prominent areas documented and finding aids may contain entries for more specific documentation. For example, a catalog record may contain the names of a dozen correspondents in a large collection, but the finding aid may contain an entry for each correspondent represented in the papers. While these finding aid entries may not be controlled by an authority file or thesaurus, structured full-text searching will be able to identify the vast majority of instances where a particular term is recorded.

Integration of Finding Aids with the Catalog

Archivists have a top-down model of information retrieval that assumes that the user will first identify the particular set of records or manuscripts that may be of interest (often through a summary catalog entry), proceed to perusal of a more detailed description and inventory (finding aid) to identify particular subsets to be examined, and finally move to an examination of the materials. In current system architectures, this implies a note within the summary catalog record that indicates the availability of a finding aid. The user must then contact the repository to review or obtain a copy of the finding aid.

With encoded finding aids linked to the catalog, this process becomes much more effective and intuitive. The user is presented with a summary description of the materials and, based on the content of that record, can immediately move to a more detailed description that can provide more information to confirm the relevance of the materials for the topic at hand. In the opposite direction, if the user comes directly to the finding aid through a search of the database of encoded finding aids, he can then move to the more structured catalog record–containing access points from a controlled vocabulary–and redirect a catalog search to discover whether there are similar collections of interest. This is particularly important since the finding aid generally contains transcribed information that has not been subjected to authority control. The link back to the catalog provides a way of cross-collection searching that an encoded full-text database may not support.

Increased User Self-Sufficiency and Staff Productivity

Archival reference service is still very much a serendipitous activity that depends heavily on the knowledge and skill of the reference staff. Reference staff have served as gatekeepers to holdings, not necessarily out of a desire to retain control, but because the access mechanisms have been so idiosyncratic and the detailed knowledge of holdings so specialized that users require guides who can lead them through the labyrinth. As holdings and research use increase, reference staff are increasingly forced to limit the amount of time they can devote to more complex questions because of the sheer volume of the workload.

Making finding aids directly available to users for searching, retrieval, and display has the potential of shifting part of the reference burden, especially the initial stages, from the staff to the user. Combined with the increased standardization of structure and content that this initiative presupposes, users should be able to travel much further in their research unaided before they need to call in the specialized expertise of a reference professional. In such an environment, reference staff are likely to find their time and energies reserved for more esoteric and complex questions that even the best-constructed finding aids may not be able to address, and for educating users in effective methods of discovering and using primary source materials.

Increased Need to Educate Users

In noting the challenges to making encoded finding aids a transforming technology, I mentioned the potential for new classes of users, most of whom are not familiar with or experienced in the use of primary resources or the operation of an archival repository. Coupled with the need to introduce and orient the current user community to a new tool for meeting their needs, archivists will be faced with an instructional demand that goes beyond our current efforts. The Web technology that will provide access to these new access tools will diminish the role of reference staff as gatekeeper to the technology, which we were forced to play in earlier automation efforts. If designed properly, encoded finding aids will be readily available to a wide spectrum of users. Our instructional tasks will need to focus as much on the descriptive architecture we are putting into place, the intended function of a finding aid in that architecture, and the basics of primary sources research, as on the technology that supports that architecture. In particular, we must be prepared to encounter the notion that item-level description is possible and desirable.

CONCLUSION

Encoded archival finding aids have the potential not only to allow repositories to further standardize their descriptive practices and to manage and disseminate information about their holdings more widely and effectively, but also to transform the way in which they provide reference service to potential users. Encoded finding aids will put more information directly into the hands of researchers, foster better finding aid practice, encourage the development of more powerful discovery and retrieval systems, and make the primary source materials that they describe accessible to a wider range of users than their traditional constituents. Each of these developments provide an opportunity for archivists to rethink the methodology or reference service as it is currently practiced. While experienced and knowledgeable reference staffs will always be necessary to help users discover and interpret the myriad primary source materials archival repositories hold, providing direct, standardized access to the descriptive tools that are the essential gateways to locating these materials will be a major step towards a more informed and self-sufficient user community and a more effective and productive reference function.

NOTES

1. The best collection of these papers is in the *American Archivist* 60, nos. 3-4 (Summer and Fall 1997).

2. The enormous challenges facing archivists are well-defined by David Bearman in "Archival methods," *Archives and Museum Informatics Technical Report* 3, no. 1 (Spring 1999).

3. See for example, the discussion of use and user studies (most of which have still not been undertaken) suggested by Lawrence Dowler in "The role of use in defining archival practice and principles: a research agenda for the availability and use of records," *American Archivist* 51, nos. 1-2 (Winter and Spring 1988): 74-86.

4. The best example of this type is the Archival Resources service offered by the Research Libraries Group (www.rlg.org/arrhome.html). Other union finding aid systems are based on all of the encoded finding aids contributed by participants residing on a common server.

5. Daniel Pitti's article "Encoded archival description: the development of an encoding standard for archival finding aids," *American Archivist* 60, no. 3 (Summer 1997): 268-283, is the best introduction to the development history of EAD.

6. The first step toward such standards will be the forthcoming *Application Guidelines* for EAD which will be issued later this year by the Encoded Archival Description Working Group of the Society of American Archivists.

7. Dennis Meissner, "First things first: Reengineering finding aids for implementation of EAD," *American Archivist* 60, no.4 (Fall 1997): 372-387.

Popularizing the Finding Aid: Exploiting EAD to Enhance Online Discovery and Retrieval in Archival Information Systems by Diverse User Groups

Anne J. Gilliland-Swetland

SUMMARY. Encoded Archival Description (EAD) provides a flexible metadata infrastructure that, when coupled with World Wide Web functionality, allows archivists to move beyond simply replicating the physical form of the paper finding aid in the online environment and fundamentally re-conceptualize how archival information systems can facilitate popular use. This paper reviews the descriptive imperatives that have led to the traditional physical and intellectual form of the finding aid, and how those imperatives can be addressed by EAD. It then discusses some of the needs that diverse user practices and cognitive approaches bring to the design of discovery and retrieval in EAD-based archival information systems. Finally, it adapts and extends the search capabilities delineated by Bates for a "berrypicking" search interface, and suggests ten strategies to enhance browsing and retrieval in EAD-based archival information systems. *[Article copies available for a fee from The Haworth Document Delivery Service: 1-800-342-9678. E-mail address: <getinfo@haworthpressinc.com> Website: <http://www.HaworthPress.com> © 2001 by The Haworth Press, Inc. All rights reserved.]*

Anne J. Gilliland-Swetland is Assistant Professor, Department of Information Studies, University of California, Los Angeles, 212 GSE&IS Building, Box 951520, Los Angeles, CA 90095-1520 (E-mail: swetland@ucla.edu).

[Haworth co-indexing entry note]: "Popularizing the Finding Aid: Exploiting EAD to Enhance Online Discovery and Retrieval in Archival Information Systems by Diverse User Groups." Gilliland-Swetland, Anne J. Co-published simultaneously in *Journal of Internet Cataloging* (The Haworth Information Press, an imprint of The Haworth Press, Inc.) Vol. 4, No. 3/4, 2001, pp. 199-225; and: *Encoded Archival Description on the Internet* (ed: Daniel V. Pitti, and Wendy M. Duff) The Haworth Information Press, an imprint of The Haworth Press, Inc., 2001, pp. 199-225. Single or multiple copies of this article are available for a fee from The Haworth Document Delivery Service [1-800-342-9678, 9:00 a.m. - 5:00 p.m. (EST). E-mail address: getinfo@haworthpressinc.com].

KEYWORDS. Archival information systems, archival description, Encoded Archival Description, EAD, finding aids, information seeking and use

INTRODUCTION

The finding aid is the workhorse of archival practice–a complex, multifunctional descriptive tool critical to both management and reference of archival holdings. The form of the finding aid has always closely followed its functions as a documentary and management tool. In general, both archivists and users utilize the same version of the finding aid; abridged versions or alternate views are seldom prepared for public use. While the effectiveness of this form in facilitating use of archival materials has never been systematically examined, all indications are that the finding aid as currently conceived does a pretty poor job of addressing the practices, behaviors, and information needs of the non-scholarly user. Moreover, the flexibility of the finding aid as an information discovery and retrieval tool that might facilitate a range of user practices has been severely constrained by the "fixity" of how the finding aid is presented on paper.[1] Today, however, the implementation of EAD in Internet-based archival information systems brings with it the potential for a considerable increase in flexibility for both searching and displaying finding aid metadata. Just as the development of the codex allowed readers random access to its information content while still making possible the traditional linear access provided by the scroll, so too the development of EAD-based archival information systems makes possible new forms of access to archival metadata while still supporting the hierarchical access provided by the traditional finding aid.

This paper argues that the true potential of EAD does not lie in replicating the physical and intellectual form of the finding aid for online distribution. Rather, EAD allows archivists to contemplate how their encoded finding aids might collectively populate a metadata infrastructure for more broadly conceived archival information systems. Such archival information systems would also contain digitized versions of archival materials, full-text versions of ancillary materials, and extensive linkages to other online archival and bibliographic information systems.[2] The paper also argues that at the core of such a re-conceptualization should be a consideration of how best to exploit this EAD metadata infrastructure in order to meet the diverse range of information needs and associated information-seeking behaviors and practices exhibited by Internet users.

In support of these arguments, the paper first reviews the descriptive imperatives that have led to the current physical and intellectual form of the finding aid and the ways in which these can be satisfied by EAD without imposing constraints on the utility of encoded finding aids for information discovery and retrieval. Recognizing that an increasingly heterogeneous user population will purposefully or serendipitously encounter archival information systems on the Web, it then examines some of the archival information needs and practices of representative academic, occupational, and avocational user groups. The paper argues that such a diversity of needs and practices would be best addressed by a metadata structure and system design that supports multiple information discovery and retrieval strategies. By adapting and extending search capabilities delineated by Marcia Bates for a "berrypicking" search interface for online hypermedia information systems, the paper concludes by suggesting ten browsing and retrieval strategies and associated design features that would facilitate more effective popular use of EAD-based archival information systems.

THE MANY ROLES OF THE FINDING AID

To understand why the intellectual and physical form of the finding aid has evolved in the way that it has, and how that form might be re-conceptualized using EAD to enhance the discovery and retrieval of archival information, it is necessary first to understand what imperatives drive archival description. Archival materials[3] stand as evidence of organizational or personal actions and, more broadly speaking, the conduct of everyday life. This evidence is used to hold organizations accountable for their actions and, again more broadly, as collective memory. Materials generated by the same activity exhibit complex organic inter-relationships that often make it more illuminating to examine them as a whole than to focus on a single item. The quality of evidence associated with any given archival materials is a factor of the degree of contextualization and documentation of these inter-relationships that exists for those materials. For certain kinds of research (although by no means all), the usability of archival materials is directly correlated to the extent to which quality evidence elucidates their trustworthiness, authenticity, and completeness. While the discrete informational value of archival materials may be important, it is often not the key reason they are maintained. Indeed, as sources of factual information, archival materials contain the subjectivity inherent in their creators and circumstances of creation. Describing these materials is, therefore, first and foremost a delicate exercise in preserving evidence and making evidential values apparent to archival users in time and over time–making the materials intellectually available for interpretation, yet not providing that interpretation. Secondarily, it is about providing intellectual access to the factual information that archival materials contain on persons, places, and subjects contained in those materials.

In sum then, archivists seek through description "to preserve, perpetuate, and authenticate meaning over time so that it is available and comprehensible to all users–present and potential."[4] The tool they use to do so has traditionally been the finding aid, which has assumed three primary roles. Firstly, it is a *tool that meets the needs of the archival materials being described* by authenticating and documenting them as archival collections.[5] Secondly, it is *a collections management tool* for use by the archivists. Thirdly, it is an *information discovery and retrieval tool* for making the evidence and information contained in archival collections available and comprehensible by archivists and users alike.

It is useful to review each of these roles in order to understand the underlying imperatives for archival description and the ways in which they can be addressed in less constraining terms by EAD.

The Role of the Finding Aid in Authenticating and Documenting Archival Collections

While archival collections inherently reflect the biases and perspectives of their creators, they nevertheless serve as authentic, accurate, and impartial evidence of the activities of those creators to the extent that they have been securely housed and appropriately described by archivists–activities that Jenkinson terms the "physical and moral defence" of archives. As Jenkinson states:

> The perfect Archive is *ex hypothesi* an evidence which cannot lie to us: we may through laziness or other imperfection of our own misinterpret its statements or implications, but itself it makes no attempt to convince us of fact or error, to persuade or dissuade: it just tells us. That is, it does so *always provided that it has come to us in exactly the state in which its original creators left it.* Here then, is the supreme and most difficult task of the Archivist–to hand on the documents as nearly as possible in the state in which he received them, without adding or taking away, physically or morally, anything: to preserve unviolated, without the possibility of a suspicion of violation, every element in them, every quality they possessed when they came to him, while at the same time permitting and facilitating handling and use.[6]

The finding aid documents the provenance of the archival materials and the original order in which they were arranged, often manifested through some form of hierarchy. The materials themselves can subsequently be compared against the finding aid in order to establish that the arrangement and collectivity of the materials have not been altered in any undocumented way after entering into archival custody. The paper finding aid serves as a mirror, therefore, of the arrangement of the archival materials within collections, and insofar as the physical arrangement and intellectual inter-relationships of those materials remain stable, so too does the arrangement of the finding aid. The finding aid should also document any actions performed upon archival collections, such as adding new accruals, deaccessioning materials no longer deemed to be of continuing archival value, or reformatting materials for preservation purposes.

The imperative to document the circumstances of creation of archival materials and the inter-relationships between materials of the same provenance has also supported the hierarchical structure of archival finding aids. Finding aids proceed from the general–an overview description of a collection–to the specific–a description at the lowest level of analysis, most commonly the file level but potentially the individual document (i.e., item level)–all the while reflecting the native arrangement of the archival materials. The description should be sufficiently granular to be able to document, when necessary, the existence and nature of specific materials within the collection. The use of hierarchy, as well as cross-references both vertically within the collection hierarchy and laterally to provenantially related collections, indicates inter-relationships that may exist within and between groups of materials acquired from the same provenance.

The Use of Encoded Archival Description in Authenticating and Documenting Archival Collections

EAD meets the above imperatives for authenticating and documenting the collectivity of archival collections by identifying and delineating finding aid elements that address those aspects of archival description. Figure 1 indicates several examples of ways, comparable to those used in the traditional finding aid, in which EAD can be used to establish the authenticity and completeness of archival materials.

Features inherent in the use of EAD in automated systems also enable moving beyond what was possible in the traditional finding aid in terms of documenting authenticity. EAD proffers several mechanisms for automatic validation of the integrity of the finding aid itself. For example:

- In an SGML-based system, the EAD Document Type Definition (DTD) can be automatically enforced, thus checking the structural integrity of an encoded finding aid in terms of its compliance with the DTD.

- In most automated systems, the completeness and consistency of finding aids can be partially enforced through the use of templates that automatically insert generic header and formatting metadata. Such templates can also require archivists to complete data elements that are mandated by applicable descriptive standards (for example, the *Rules for Archival Description* or the *General International Standard for Archival Description).*[7]
- The Revision Description (<revisiondesc>) element provides version control for description by ensuring documentation of any changes made to the finding aid over time that reflect corrections, deaccessioning of part of the materials it describes, or accessioning of new accruals from the same provenance.

FIGURE 1. Examples of How EAD Can Be Used to Authenticate Archival Materials and Document Their Collectivity.

EAD Element	**Function**
Custodial History <custodhist>	Indicates the chain of custody for the materials being described up until the point when they were accessioned into the archives
Acquisition Information <acqinfo>	Indicates the circumstances under which the materials were accessioned
Appraisal <appraisal> and Arrangement <arrangement>	Indicate different aspects relating to the arrangement of the materials when they were accessioned
Processing Information <processinfo>	The most prominent of several elements that indicate actions performed on the materials during the processes of arrangement, description, and preservation
Physical Description <physdesc> at any level of description within Descriptive Identification <did>	Allows for a physical description of the materials at whatever is the appropriate level of granularity for identification purposes
Origination <origination> and Biography or History <bioghist>	Provide contextual information about the circumstances of creation, collection, and use of the materials prior to their accession by the archives in order to "preserve the value of records as evidence of transactions"[1]
Accruals <accruals> and Organization <organization>	Reflect the organic nature of the archival materials by indicating how the archival materials within a collection relate to each other
Related Material <relatedmaterial> and Separated Material <separatedmaterial>	Indicate how the archival materials being described relate to materials contained in other archival or library collections, or information elsewhere.

[1]Wendy Duff, "Will Metadata Replace Archival Description: A Commentary," *Archivaria* 39 (1995): 33-36; Luciana Duranti, "The Archival Body of Knowledge: Archival Theory, Method, and Practice, and Graduate and Continuing Education," *Journal of Education for Library and Information Science* 34, no.1 (Winter 1993): 13.

In terms of documenting collectivity, EAD has also expanded upon what was possible in the traditional finding aid. For example, the availability of the Archival Reference (<archref>) element has increased the amount of linkage realistically feasible to incorporate into a paper finding aid. <archref> provides for an almost infinite number of inter-relationships to be established during encoding between materials that derive from the same provenance or functional activity. The ease of revision in the EAD environment also allows for the insertion of additional <archref> tags as new relationships are discovered between materials or as new accruals are added to a collection.

The ultimate EAD enhancement, however, is that it is no longer essential, because of authentication and documentation requirements, for the finding aid to retain its traditional physical form for every kind of use. Once the appropriate elements have been completed and their structural inter-relationships (which reflect the intellectual relationships of the materials described by the elements) are established and documented, the content of those elements can be physically rendered in any number of ways, according to user needs or preferences. This makes it possible to generate a variety of alternate user views of the metadata held within the archival information system. It also allows for individual elements, or groups of related elements that have informational value independent of their role within the finding aid, to be combined into searchable databases of contextual information. For example, an element such as Biography or History <bioghist>, which provides contextual information relevant to a collection, is often consulted by users as a source of factual information about an organization or creator. To facilitate such use, this element could be automatically extracted from the finding aid and stored in a separate, browsable database, being replaced in the finding aid by a pointer from the appropriate place.

The Role of the Finding Aid as a Collections Management Tool

Much of the information that archivists require to manage their holdings and to ensure appropriate access to, and use of those holdings is dispersed throughout the finding aid. Firstly, there are high-level elements that address global collections-management aspects such as date(s) of accession, donor information, processing information, and restrictions of access. Secondly, there is collections-management information that needs to be associated only with portions of the materials being described, such as items that are restricted for legal or preservation reasons, or that have been removed for treatment or exhibition. Some of this information, such as access and use restrictions, is relevant for users, while some, such as donor information, may not be.

The Use of Encoded Archival Description as a Collections Management Tool

In EAD some, although not all, of the kinds of elements that facilitate collections management are grouped within the Administrative Information (<admininfo>) component of the finding aid (for example, Restrictions on Access {<accessrestrict>} and Restrictions on Use {<userestrict>}, as well as Acquisition Information {<acqinfo>}, Accruals {<accruals>}, and Processing Information {<processinfo>}). If there is specific collections-management information associated with only a portion of the materials being described, this can be achieved by using the appropriate <admininfo> elements at the relevant level and component of the Archival Description <archdesc>. For example, users who are working at the item level can be alerted to information about any restrictions on use or access that specifically pertain to that item. Similarly, the element <physloc> that indicates the physical location of an item within the repository is available within the Descriptive Identification <did> element within <archdesc> in order to facilitate associating a location directly with the archival materials being referenced. This latter feature could be further exploited in an archival information system that supports online ordering by users of actual materials or copies of materials from the repository, although in cases where digital facsimiles of the materials themselves are also available, the physical location of the material becomes less relevant and should only be viewable upon user request.

It can be confusing for users to be exposed to administrative elements not directly relevant to their needs, especially when such elements are not clearly grouped together within a single administrative information component. Again, as with the imperative to authenticate and document the archival collections being described, there is no longer a need with an EAD-based archival information system to adhere to the physical form of the finding aid. Users' confusion can be eased by presenting them primarily with contextual and content information, with an option to display a virtual grouping of administrative information associated only with the materials which they are interested in consulting. Within that grouping, irrelevant or sensitive elements of administrative information could also be switched off from public view by using the "internal" value on the audience attribute available on most EAD elements. The ability to switch off, or otherwise automatically mask certain EAD elements from public view also helps archivists deal with the dilemma of whether or not to include descriptions of classified or otherwise restricted materials that are part of an archival collection.

The Role of the Finding Aid as an Information Discovery and Retrieval Tool

The finding aid plays a third and vital role as a tool used by archivists and by primary and secondary users of archival materials for discovering what materials exist and where they are located, for browsing likely collections and making decisions about which materials might potentially meet their needs, and for retrieving identified material either on or offline. Consideration of user needs in terms of effectively carrying out these activities has not traditionally been factored into the design of the finding aids. As the preceding discussion demonstrates, archivists have historically been materials-centric rather than user-centric in their descriptive practices, resulting in the finding aid assuming a form quite unlike the concise bibliographic description with name and subject access most users are accustomed to using in other information systems such as library catalogs, abstracts, and indexes. A recap of the characteristics of the finding aid resulting from meeting the needs of the materials (and of those who manage them) reveals that these are frequently at cross-purposes with the characteristics needed for the finding aid to facilitate broad-based, unmediated use:

- The finding aid is arranged according to the provenance and original order of the materials. An important limitation for archival users is the lack of alternative access points for secondary use: "archives are normally used by posterity for purposes quite different from those which caused their compilation and . . . more often than not, users approach the reference archivist with a subject or name-based query."[8]
- The finding aid contains considerable contextual description of the circumstances surrounding the creation of its materials. The users for whom this is most critical are those who come to the finding aid with little or no background knowledge but who need to be able to understand the historical or administrative context of materials contained in the collection (for example, graduate students writing term papers). Users who are particularly concerned about context, such as academic users, usually come to the finding aid with a considerable amount of pre-existing contextual knowledge, and while they may require additional reassurances of the extent to which the materials they are examining are trustworthy,[9] it may not be necessary for them to have quite so much contextual information immediately available. Most importantly, however, not all users or uses require or desire contextualization (for example, institutional records creators seeking to retrieve a known item from the archives, or a teacher wishing to demonstrate to a class what a glass slide looks like), and yet

the traditional finding aid makes direct, de-contextualized access to archival materials close to impossible.

- The finding aid describes material collectively and hierarchically and there is frequently little or no item-level description. Many users want item-level access, for example, to locate a known item quickly, to check a citation to a particular document, or to establish in advance of a visit to a repository that a particular item is contained in a collection. [10] Moreover, some users may want to invert the hierarchical method of information discovery and retrieval supported by the traditional finding aid. For example, K-12 teachers looking for specific images to use in support of a curricular activity may well first locate a digital image online, and then wish to backtrack through the image's metadata to the item description in the finding aid, from there working up the hierarchy to discover background information about the image and any related images or narratives.
- The finding aid has administrative information woven throughout. As discussed earlier, such information is not always relevant or appropriate for the user and it can lead to user confusion when working with the finding aid.[11]
- The finding aid is designed to be used in an environment where archivists not only mediate between the user and the materials in the closed stacks, but also between the user and the finding aid. Archivists work closely with users to explain what a finding aid is and how it works. They also assist users in identifying the most likely finding aids to work with by drawing upon their own contextual knowledge and reformulating users' subject queries into provenance-based queries that can then be mapped onto the ways in which their archival holdings are arranged and described.[12] When users encounter finding aids outside of a repository, either in HTML form on the Internet or in publications of finding aids such as the *National Inventory of Documentary Sources in the United States,*[13] no reference archivist is available as a mediator and the arcane and often inconsistent form of the finding aid can be bewildering to the uninitiated user.

This recap would appear to indicate that the role of finding aids as tools that facilitate discovery and retrieval of archival materials has been treated by archivists as secondary to the other roles already discussed. The reality is somewhat more complex, however. There are significant intellectual challenges that arise out of the nature of the archival materials being described that have made it difficult for archivists to address user needs more fully.

- *Archival collections tend to contain heterogeneous materials* in terms of the subjects they address (what Jenkinson terms the "universality" of archives[14]), their intellectual forms, and their physical formats, making it difficult to assign sufficient, consistent, and appropriately granular subject descriptors. The need for, and the intellectual problems associated with providing subject as well as provenantial access to heterogeneous archival materials has been the subject of numerous articles in both the archival and the library and information science literature.[15] Several archivists have also argued that subject access alone is insufficient, and that additional access points such as occupation, time period, geographic coordinates, form-of-material, and function should be provided.[16]
- *Archival materials contain the technical language of their creators.* This issue is closely associated with that of how to provide and enhance subject access to archival materials. Technical language is most evident in the folder or file titles assigned by their creator and usually retained by the archivist in the finding aid, although it will sometimes also be used in subject descriptors. It can be hard for the non-expert user to identify or understand the terminology used by the creator in the course of business, professional, academic, or personal activity, especially if the terminology is now archaic (for example, scientific papers arranged according to superceded taxonomic classifications). As a result, users conducting a natural language online search are unlikely to use the same terminology used in documents. Users conducting a controlled vocabulary search have to be able to identify the correct modern equivalent of the technical or archaic concept in which they are interested and hope that this was also the term selected by the person who added the subject headings for the finding aid. Again, the solution appears to lie in increasing the number of access points rather than in attempting to achieve more consistency in indexing.[17] Gilliland-Swetland et al. argue that archivists may need to map technical terminology used as subject access points within archival finding aids to a less technical vocabulary in order to facilitate resource discovery by non-expert secondary users such as K-12 students.[18] It is worth noting here too that archival finding aids employ not only the technical terminology of the creators of the archival materials, but also that of archival description. The use of technical archival terms to label components of a finding aid can make it difficult for users to predict what a given data element might contain. Meissner suggests that this problem might be addressed through more user-friendly labeling of data elements within encoded finding aids.[19]
- *Archival materials tend to be voluminous and unsynthesized.* Archival description has sometimes been criticized as expediency chasing theory,

and indeed archivists' devotion to hierarchical description is not only grounded in the need to authenticate and document collections. It is also an expedient practice designed to yield optimum levels of control over materials based upon an assessment of a collection's physical extent and perceived intellectual density. Several high-level notes summarize the scope and content of the materials as well as the circumstances of their creation, and administrative information such as restrictions on use and access. Following the notes are often lengthy file or folder title lists, sometimes using indentation to give visual clues to relationships between folders. The limitations of these features are that the file lists are unwieldy to navigate and can lose some of their meaning if they are reformatted or the user loses track of how many levels of indentation have occurred. Another drawback is that the description of the item is physically distanced in the finding aid from the high-level notes relating to it, requiring the user to jump backwards and forwards through a large amount of text to identify important contextual or administrative information.

FACILITATING INFORMATION DISCOVERY AND RETRIEVAL BY DIVERSE USER GROUPS

Nowhere is the potential of EAD more apparent than in addressing the role of the finding aid as an information discovery and retrieval tool. Indeed, it has been the desire to enhance information discovery and retrieval by more users for a more diverse range of needs that has largely driven the development of EAD and EAD-based archival information systems. The materials-centric, evidence-based approach that is integral to archival theory and practice has developed, it could be argued, not only because of the needs of the material, but also because of archivists' professional beliefs about how archival materials *ought* to be used, rather than reflecting how many users *actually* use, or *want to* use those materials (a user-centric approach). This materials-centric approach has come under increasing fire, not only from users, but also from within the archival profession itself, for not sufficiently accommodating the range of practices and needs exhibited by diverse user groups.[20] The materials-centric and the user-centric approaches can now be simultaneously addressed, if not reconciled, through thoughtful design of EAD-based archival information systems.

By better understanding the range of information-seeking practices and needs associated with certain categories of archival users, it is possible to tailor the indexing and searching capabilities of the system, as well as the presentation of metadata, more closely. Conway's research at the U.S. National Archives identified four major categories of archival user: academic, occupational, avocational, and personal.[21] User groups within each of these categories come with different information-seeking and use practices derived from the methods and needs of their disciplinary, professional, or business circumstances. A brief review of the practices of some representative user groups–academic historians, institutional administrators, genealogists, and K-12 teachers–illustrates the diversity of practices that need to be accommodated by a broadly accessible archival information system.

Academic Historians

Academic historians are probably the preeminent example of the academic user of archives. Archival descriptive practices are often criticized for privileging the needs of the academic historian, and indeed, archival descriptive practices developed in close association with the rise of modern objective or scientific history. The scientific method of historical investigation advanced by Prussian historian Leopold von Ranke in the nineteenth century called for historians to conduct exhaustive archival research using contemporary records and accounts in order to establish objective fact. This school of history was largely responsible for creating the demand for the availability of archival materials for scholarly analysis.[22] For these historians, it is critical to assess the provenance and wider context of the materials they are examining, and their practices, therefore, map more closely to the nature of the traditional archival finding aid than those of any other user group.[23] In the latter part of the twentieth century, however, these historical practices underwent profound change. From the 1960s onwards, the rise of social history bred a new kind of historian, one who was interested in the ordinary individual, and in understanding phenomena such as social structures and the nature of communities, rather than in the bureaucratic activities of mainstream institutions or social elites. Provenantial access and collective description is, therefore, less useful to the social historian.[24] Social historians might also be assisted by the provision of links to related primary source materials such as demographic datasets and transcriptions of oral histories.

Research conducted by Tibbo[25] with historians and by Bates with humanities scholars suggest several intellectual access points that might assist academic historians in their research using archival materials. These include chronological, geographical, individual/group, personal names, discipline terms, and topical subjects. Studies by Stevens and Maher both found that word-of-mouth and citations were primary sources through which historians discover and locate archival materials.[26] Conway, however, in his 1986 user study conducted at four presidential libraries, found that a scholarly "grapevine," rather than any published sources, was the most important way in which academic researchers found out about archival holdings.[27]

Institutional Administrators

Institutional administrators are those users who work for the institution that created the archival material, and as such represent major occupational archive users. Sometimes institutional administrators are the actual creators of those materials, sometimes they need to consult materials created elsewhere in the institution. In general, institutional administrators wish to use archival materials for one of four reasons: (1) they need to reference specific documents or files they created that have subsequently been transferred to the archives; (2) the institution needs to locate documents or files that are required for legal purposes, such as substantiating a legal claim or satisfying an FOIA request; (3) the institution wishes to use its own records for the purpose of knowledge management (for example, market development or fund-raising); or (4) they need to answer a factual question (for example, the date when an event occurred). Often, rather than look for archival materials themselves, institutional administrators will call the archivist with a request and have him or her respond.

Increasingly, however, institutional administrators are seeking to have access to archival information and holdings on their desktops as a function of the knowledge management activities of their institutions. Such access requires that the archival information system provides fast and effective ways to locate and deliver known items (i.e., ways that do not involve navigating through a lot of contextual information), to access key institutional information such as administrative histories of major offices, chronological lists of key events, and to search by genre, date, and table of contents (for example, corporate newsletter or annual report), or by format (for example, galleries of institutional images searchable by subject).[28]

K-12 Teachers

Teachers present a very different example of the occupational user. Increasingly, state and national curricular frameworks are encouraging the use of primary sources in the classroom as a way of enriching learning and building information literacy skills in children. This development is coupled with strong external incentives for the archival community to use technological developments such as Web-based archival information systems containing digitized archival content as a way to enfranchise the K-12 community which traditionally has been considerably restricted in its access to archival repositories and materials. As a result, teachers and their students may well become one of the most populous user groups for Web-based archival information systems.

Most teachers have not been trained in how to locate, evaluate, and select from large volumes of unsynthesized archival materials and find the process to be time-consuming and bewildering. Ongoing research indicates that teachers are seldom interested in context, but wish to locate and contrast specific items from several collections of archival materials that exhibit characteristics that are representative of a genre, format, period, or event. In other words, in many instances, teachers are interested in using archival materials because of their artifactual and other intrinsic properties, rather than for their documentary value.[29] Because students, especially those in elementary grades, may have difficulty reading handwritten documents or large passages of text, teachers often prefer to work with visual material. The characteristics they seek from an archival information system, therefore, include the ability to rapidly identify and locate the actual materials online (rather than just descriptions of those materials), especially visual materials; to be able to make copies of those materials and cut and paste text contained in digitized documents; to be able to display a range of digitized materials drawn from a variety of collections in order to compare and select from among them; and to be able to locate related non-archival materials, such as biographies and magazine articles, with ease.

Genealogists

Avocational users are those who use archives to pursue their own interests, particularly hobbies, but do so on a regular and fairly knowledgeable basis. Examples include those who are interested in Civil War re-enactment, railroad history, or antique car restoration. The most prevalent avocational use of archives is, without doubt, genealogy. Genealogists need to know enough administrative history to be able to identify where they might most likely find the records they need, and the form that those records would be likely to take. Printed genealogical guides often assist genealogists in this endeavor, as do online bulletin boards where genealogical tips and information are exchanged. Most genealogists want to be able to search and retrieve actual documents by name at the item level–a genealogist who wanted to obtain a copy of his or her great-grandfather's certificate of naturalization would not be satisfied with that of any representative immigrant who entered the country by the same immigration route during the same period! Other access points that are useful are dates and geographic location, which can help to narrow a search when there are multiple instances, or several variants, of the same name.

Any design of an information system also needs to consider that individual users exhibit different cognitive behaviors and capabilities. Cognitive approaches vary enormously according to the individual user's developmental level, spatial or textual orientation, and the mental model which the user constructs and constantly reformulates during the search process. Considerations of developmental level raise issues including a user's ability to articulate and refine a need, to read, to understand and negotiate hierarchies, to relate materials from disparate sources, and to grasp complex concepts embedded in the use of historical documentation such as the implications of the passage of time. Considerations of textual or spatial orientation have implications for how (and how much) information is presented textually and visually to a user in order to be most effectively received. Such considerations have implications for both how archival materials are represented through their descriptive metadata, and how such metadata are presented through the user interface.

Conway's research at the National Archives, one of the few extensive archival user studies to date, also indicates that the "search/retrieval process is not necessarily linear nor straightforward and may involve back and forth movement (physically and intellectually) among archivists, finding aids, and the materials themselves."[30] This lack of linearity in searching and retrieval is an aspect of information-seeking that has been examined in much more depth in library and information science research. Marcia Bates's work, in particular, has considered how user satisfaction might be increased in the hypermedia environment through the interaction of indexing, self-indexing, and cognitive aspects of an information system in order to facilitate multiple ways to enhance upon traditional ways of searching for materials.[31] Bates argues that users employ a variety of strategies when seeking information and continuously modify their strategies as their searches and needs evolve even within the same search session. Each strategy may retrieve certain pieces of information which cumulate in a process Bates refers to as "berrypicking." Her conclusion, therefore, and one that would appear to be borne out by the diversity of practices and needs discussed above, is that browsing and berrypicking, and in a larger sense, discovery and retrieval in an information system, could be made more effective by facilitating more user strategies in its design.

EXTENDING SEARCH CAPABILITIES IN EAD-BASED ARCHIVAL INFORMATION SYSTEMS

Based on an analysis of over forty years of research and observation in information-seeking and retrieval, Bates developed a model for a search interface that delineates a set of six of the most commonly used strategies for browsing and berrypicking. These strategies are footnote chasing (backward chaining); citation searching (forward chaining); journal run; area scanning; subject searches in bibliographies and abstracting and indexing services; and author searching. For each of these strategies, Bates gives several *key design features* that indicate ways in which it might be facilitated through the search interface of an online information system.

The power of Bates's model for archival applications lies in how it reconciles a range of known user practices with a vision of new forms of access that might be facilitated in heterogeneous hypermedia information environments such as the World Wide Web. While some of the strategies Bates identifies (such as journal run) are necessarily associated with the content of bibliographic information systems, and there are important strategies specifically associated with archival information seeking and use that do not feature in the Bates model, it nevertheless provides a useful framework within which to conceptualize how discovery and retrieval might be extended in EAD-based archival information systems.

The following discussion adapts and extends the search capabilities delineated in the Bates model for archival use by outlining ten major strategies and associated design features to enhance information discovery and retrieval in EAD-based archival information systems for a range of uses: footnote chasing, function scanning, repository scanning, subject searching, name searching, date searching, geographic location searching, physical form and genre searching, top-down searching, and bottom-up searching. The *sine qua non* for supporting such strategies is the availability of consistent, richly encoded EAD metadata as the infrastructure supporting the archival information system (although it must be recognized that it is unlikely that in reality the metadata infrastructure of any one archival information system would be able to support all of the proposed strategies). Some of the strategies presuppose that a gateway exists between the archival information system and bibliographic information systems, such as online catalogs and full-text databases of journal articles or specialized bibliographies. Some of the strategies presuppose that selective digital facsimiles of archival materials being described by the finding aids are available within the same archival information system, and that these facsimiles will have their own metadata associated with them (such as Dublin Core metadata).

Strategy 1: Footnote Chasing (Backward Chaining)

Footnotes play a critical role, for academic users in particular, in locating archival materials. They are also an important means within a finding aid of identifying the source of contetxual information. This strategy, therefore, has two potential manifestations:

1. Working backwards from footnotes contained in contextualizing EAD elements such as <bioghist> in order to identify citations to materials used by the archivist to compile those data elements.
2. Working backwards from footnotes in secondary publications in order to identify archival collections used by the author of those publications, or to identify the work of other scholars working in the same area.

Key Design Features

a. Availability of full text of secondary documents and references.
b. Ability to jump back and forth between footnotes in elements such as <bioghist> and the source materials being cited, e.g., Board of Trustees proceedings, corporate annual reports, curriculum vitae of the creator of the materials.
c. Ability to jump back and forth between references in secondary publications and the finding aid for the archival materials being cited.
d. Ability to jump from a reference in a secondary publication to the published work of other scholars working in the same subject area.

Strategy 2: Function Scanning

This strategy exploits the provenantial base of archival description in that a user identifies an organizational unit or function, or individual activity that is highly relevant to his or her research, and then scans administrative histories related to that function and/or scope and content notes for archival materials within collections generated by that function.

Key Design Features

a. Ability to browse a pull-down list of <function> elements automatically extracted from encoded finding aids in order to identify major functions such as law enforcing, teaching, or accrediting that generate archival materials. Use of a controlled vocabulary during tagging to describe major functions represented by the archival materials being described would enhance the effectiveness of browsing by disambiguation and controlling for terminological variances.
b. Ability to search the <function> element at any level in the finding aid hierarchy for a specific function, and to delimit the search by date span.
c. Easy jumps between identified <function> elements and a display of the <scopecontent> elements summarizing the content of collections or record series described as having those elements.

d. Ability to browse a file of <bioghist> elements containing administrative histories and biographical information in order to identify activities relevant to the information being sought. Chronological (i.e., <chronlist> format) rather than narrative layouts of these elements would facilitate browsing by date.
e. Easy jumps between identified <bioghist> elements and a display of the <scopecontent> elements for any archival collection generated as the result of a function or activity of that institution or individual.

Strategy 3: Repository Scanning

This strategy involves identifying a repository that collects materials in the area of the user's interest and then scanning summaries of that repository's holdings to ascertain their nature and scope.

Key Design Features

a. Ability to generate a pull-down list of repositories contributing finding aids to a union database together with the addresses of those repositories, using the <repository> element and any included sub-elements such as <address>.
b. Ability to link from a repository name to a browsable list of <unittitle> and <scopecontent> elements for all archival collections or record series held by that repository.
c. Easy jumps between repositories identified from the pull-down list and Web pages containing additional information on the repository.

Strategy 4: Subject Searching

This strategy involves a user conducting a variety of subject searches across and within finding aids and digitized archival content in a union database; in specialized bibliographies; and in online catalogs.

Key Design Features

a. Ability to browse an automatically updated keyword list derived from the <unittitle> as well as the Corporate Name (<corpname>), Family Name (<famname>), Function (<function>), Genre or Format (<genreform>), Geographical Name (<geogname>), Name (<name>), Occupation (<occupation>), Personal Name (<persname>), Subject (<subject>), and Title (<title>) elements used anywhere in finding aids; and comparable elements used in metadata associated with digitized archival materials contained in the archival information system. Ability to click on a keyword, initiate a search, and highlight the keyword wherever it is located in the search results screen.

b. Ability to browse an online thesaurus that maps technical, archaic, or jurisdictionally-bound terms used in <controlaccess> elements to contemporary or less technical terms. Ability to initiate searches using any term and have it map to the term used in the <controlaccess> element.
c. Ability to browse a list of authorized subject headings (e.g., *Library of Congress Subject Headings, Art and Architecture Thesaurus*) and initiate a search on a chosen subject term across the archival information system, the full-text of relevant specialized bibliographies, and institutional online catalogs.
d. Ability to conduct natural language keyword searches within major contextualizing or summarizing elements such as <title>, <scopecontent>, and <bioghist> delimited by specified Component <c> element or other specification of level within the finding aid or by span dates associated with the <scopecontent> element for that level.
e. Ability to stem words to be used in keyword searches to facilitate searching for word variants.
f. Highlight all located keywords and, where available, dates associated with the element in which the name is located.

Strategy 5: Name Searching

This strategy involves using a personal or corporate name to identify a creator of archival materials, the subject of the archival materials, or published work by or about such persons or institutions.

Key Design Features

a. Include bibliographies of the works of individuals creating collections of personal papers and manuscripts. Facilitate easy jumps between the <bibliography> element and the <bioghist> element, as well as between the <bibref> elements in <bibliography>, the online catalog record, and the full text of the published works.
b. Ability to browse a name list derived from the <name>, <famname>, <persname>, <corpname>, and <title> elements used anywhere in finding aids, and comparable elements used in metadata associated with digitized archival materials contained in the archival information system. If a date is associated with a name, it should be displayed in the name list to assist users in distinguishing between individuals with the same or similar names. Ability to click on a name, initiate a search, and highlight the name wherever it is located in the search results screen.

c. Ability to conduct name searches within major contextualizing or summarizing elements such as <title>, <scopecontent>, and <bioghist>, delimited by <c> or other indication of level within the finding aid or by span dates associated with the <scopecontent> element for that level.
d. Ability to stem names to be used in name searches to facilitate searching for name variants.
e. Highlight all retrieved names and, where available, dates associated with the element in which the name is located.

Strategy 6: Date Searching

This strategy involves searching for archival materials associated with a specific range of dates or time period.

Key Design Features

a. Ability to browse a list of designations of temporal period, select a period, and initiate a search on <bioghist>, <scopecontent>, and <controlaccess> fields.
b. Ability to create chronological indexes on the fly using the <date> element, select a date, and then initiate a date search across the archival information system.
c. Highlight all retrieved dates in the context that they have been used.

Strategy 7: Geographic Location Searching

This strategy involves searching for archival materials associated with a specific geographic location.

Key Design Features

a. Ability to browse an online thesaurus that maps colloquial, archaic, or jurisdictionally-bound terms used in <geogname> elements to alternate or contemporary names. Ability to initiate searches on any term, having it map to the form of the term used in the <geogname> element within the archival information system.
b. Ability to conduct natural language geographic keyword searches within major contextualizing or summarizing elements such as <title>, <scopecontent>, and <bioghist>, delimited by <c> or other indication of level within the finding aid or by span dates associated with the <scopecontent> element for that level.
c. Ability to stem words to be used in geographic keyword searches to facilitate searching for variants.

d. Highlight all located geographic locations and any associated dates within the context in which they were used.

Strategy 8: Physical Form or Genre Searching

This strategy benefits users searching for individual items or collections of items based on their physical form or genre.

Key Design Features

a. Ability to browse a pull-down list of <genreform> terms automatically generated from encoded finding aids in order to identify specific types of materials, e.g., account books, architectural drawings, diaries, or photographs.
b. Ability to initiate a search on a selected <genreform> term at any level in the EAD hierarchy, and to delimit the search by date span.
c. Easy jumps between <genreform> elements included in <scopecontent> elements indicating the presence in a collection of items such photographs, and the most granular descriptions of those items.
d. Associate meaningful symbols with item-level descriptions of forms or genres such as photographs, films, or oral histories. Easy jumps between the description of items and digital images of those items.

Strategy 9: Top-Down Searching

This strategy is essentially the kind of searching currently facilitated by the finding aid. It involves starting with contextual information relating to the circumstances under which the archival materials were created and overviews of the collection scope, content, and availability, to identify whether or not the collection contains any materials worth consulting. The user then works his or her way down the descriptive hierarchy to the most granular description(s) of relevant materials, and from that point generates a request to view those materials (online, in the repository, or as photocopies).

Key Design Strategies

a. Browse files of <abstract>, <scopecontent>, and <bioghist> elements in order to decide whether to go deeper into the associated finding aid.
b. Display a frame containing a "table of contents" indicating major elements within the descriptive hierarchy for each collection, highlighting the user's current location within the hierarchy.

c. Easy jumps between <abstract>, <scopecontent>, <bioghist>, and other elements within the table of contents.
d. Facilitate online ordering of copies of selected items directly from the relevant repository.

Strategy 10: Bottom-Up Searching

This strategy is the inverse of top-down searching and facilitates known-item searching. It also facilitates the user's ability to search for a digital image of an item in which he or she is interested and, having found the desired item, to broaden a search by back-tracking from the metadata that might exist in an image header to the related item-level EAD metadata, and from there back up the descriptive hierarchy to look for related or similar materials and contextualizing metadata.

Key Design Features

a. Search across the entire archival information system for particular digitized images, using image header metadata such as Dublin Core metadata.
b. Easy jumps from image header metadata to the EAD description of an item within its parent collection, and from there recursively to the next levels of <scopecontent> and <bioghist> elements for the collection.
c. Display galleries of thumbnails of digital images retrieved by a name or subject search with links back to the EAD metadata for the collections from which they are drawn. Display use and reproduction information upon request for any selected image.
d. Facilitate downloading of selected digital images, together with caption information containing the appropriate archival citation (drawn from the <unittitle> element) and the image title and date (drawn either from the image header metadata or from item-level EAD metadata).
e. Facilitate online ordering of copies of selected digital images directly from the relevant repository.

CONCLUSION

The model expounded above for enhancing archival information discovery and retrieval exploits the rich EAD metadata structure that archivists are already required to create in order to satisfy other descriptive imperatives of the finding aid. In order to exploit the potential of EAD most fully, however, archivists must look beyond the current intellectual and physical form of the finding aid to a fundamental re-conceptualization of the role of archival metadata within more inclusive archival information systems. Such a re-conceptualization will require archivists to think more about how archival description and the materials being described are intellectually related, and how those relationships are understood by online users. It also raises the question of whether it is time for archivists to think further about the relative merits of item-level description of archival collections, and to examine what, if any, metadata they are going to create for individual digitized image files. The richer the EAD metadata that exists at the individual document level, and in the header for individual images, the more ways that are potentially available for an archival information system to meet the needs of a range of users and to interface with other information systems. At the same time, however, the creation of such item-level metadata is likely to prove prohibitively expensive in many settings, and intellectually unnecessary with many kinds of administrative records.

Archivists must also be prepared to develop thorough EAD metadata that adheres wherever possible to data content as well as structure standards rather than simply doing basic encoding that reifies local descriptive idiosyncrasies. Without doubt, the more intensive the use of EAD in terms of types of elements used as well as the numbers of levels to which materials are encoded the more functionality that can be asked of the finding aid. Moreover, the use of content standards facilitates interoperability with other types of metadata such as Dublin Core and MARC. Although more tools will gradually become available to assist in automatic mark-up of finding aids, as already stated, this level of rich metadata development is very resource intensive (both in terms of financial cost and descriptive expertise), and archives will have to consider the benefits to users based on rigorous evaluation of user needs and experiences. Experimental as well as applied research will also prove critical in identifying and evaluating the viability, effectiveness, social benefits, cost-effectiveness, and cost-benefits associated with the representation structures and use-strategies outlined in this paper.

NOTES

1. The trend toward using databases in the preparation of finding aids reflects archivists' attempts to circumvent some of the inflexibility of paper finding aids in terms of facilitating alternate views of, and access points to, the finding aids. EAD, however, takes this approach to a more systematic and standardized level.

2. The term "archival information system" is used in this paper to refer to databases of archival descriptive information that may also include digitized materials and their associated metadata.

3. The term "archival materials" is used in this paper to refer to the official records, personal papers and manuscripts, audio and visual materials, and realia commonly found in archival holdings.

4. Heather MacNeil, "Metadata Strategies and Archival Description: Comparing Apples to Oranges," *Archivaria* 39 (1995): 30.

5. The term "archival collections" is used in this paper to refer to aggregates of archival materials such as fonds, record series, and manuscript collections that are addressed as organic units by archival activities such as arrangement and description.

6. Hilary Jenkinson, "Reflections of an Archivist," *Contemporary Review* 165 (June 1944): 355-361.

7. Bureau of Canadian Archivists, Planning Committee on Descriptive Standards, *Rules for Archival Description* [revised by the Canadian Committee on Archival Description, May 1998] (Ottawa, Ontario: Bureau of Canadian Archivists, 1990); International Council on Archives, *General International Standard on Archival Description (ISAD(G)*, Revised: August 18, 1995. URL: http://www.archives.ca/ica/isad.html.

8. Jenkinson, "Reflections of an Archivist," ibid.

9. See, for example, Philip C. Brooks, *Research in Archives The Use of Unpublished Sources* (Chicago: University of Chicago Press, 1969); Freeman, ibid.; and Barbara Orbach, "The View from the Researcher's Desk: Historians' Perceptions of Research and Repositories," *American Archivist* 54, no.1 (Winter 1991): 28-43.

10. See, for example, the results of the Digital Portfolio Archives in Learning Project in terms of understanding the needs of elementary school teachers and children. Anne Gilliland-Swetland, Yasmin B. Kafai, and William E. Landis, "Application of Dublin Core Metadata in the Description of Digital Primary Sources in Elementary School Classrooms" (paper submitted for review); and Anne Gilliland-Swetland, Yasmin Kafai, and William E. Landis, "Integrating Digitized Primary Sources into the Elementary School Classroom: A Case Study" (paper submitted for review).

11. See, for example, efforts undertaken by the Minnesota Historical Society to streamline where and how much administrative information is made available to the user in EAD-encoded finding aids. Dennis Meissner, "First Things First: Reengineering Finding Aids for Implementation of EAD," *American Archivist* 60 (Fall 1997): 372-387.

12. David Bearman, "Authority Control Issues and Prospects," *American Archivist* 52 (Summer 1989): 282-299; Mary Jo Pugh, "The Illusion of Omniscience: Subject Access and the Reference Archivist," *American Archivist* 45 (Winter 1982): 33-40. As Roper observes, "it is incumbent on the archivist to be an administrative historian and to explain to users the administrative background to records in his archives and the arrangement which they have acquired as a consequence . . . [most users] find the arrangement of archives in accordance with the agencies which created them rather than by subjects difficult to grasp and this has become especially so as administration has become more complex and has extended into areas of new activity." See Michael Roper, "The Academic Use of Archives," *Archivum* (1980): 33.

13. *National Inventory of Documentary Sources in the United States (NIDS-US)* (Teaneck, NJ: Chadwyck-Healey, Inc. 1983-).

14. Jenkinson, ibid.

15. See, for example, Avra Michelson, "Description and Reference in the Age of Automation," *American Archivist* 50 (Spring 1987): 192-210; Jackie Dooley, "Subject Indexing in Context," *American Archivist* 55 (Spring 1992): 344-54.

16. Bearman, "Authority Control Issues and Prospects," ibid.; and Kathleen D. Roe, "The Automation Odyssey: Library and Archives System Design Considerations." In *Beyond the MARC Format* (Haworth Press: 1990), 145-162.

17. Bearman, "Authority Control," ibid.

18. Gilliland-Swetland et al., "Application of Dublin Core Metadata" ibid.

19. Meissner, ibid.

20. Randall C. Jimerson, "Redefining Archival Identity: Meeting User Needs in the Information Society," *American Archivist* 52 (Summer 1989): 332-340; Elsie T. Freeman, "In the Eye of the Beholder: Archives Administration from the User's Point of View," *American Archivist* 47 (Spring 1984): 111-123; Barbara Craig, "What are the Clients? Who are the Products? The Future of Archival Public Services in Perspective," *Archivaria* 31 (Winter 1990-1991): 135-141.

21. Paul Conway, *Partners in Research: Improving Access to the Nation's Archive* (Pittsburgh: Archives & Museum Informatics, 1994), 50.

22. Maynard J. Brichford, "The Origins of European Archival Theory," *The Midwestern Archivist* 7, no.2 (1982): 91.

23. Apart from archivists themselves, who are probably the most intensive of all users of finding aids.

24. William Joyce, "Archivists and Research Use," *American Archivist* 47, no.2 (Spring 1984): 124-133; Fredric M. Miller, "Social History and Archival Practice," *American Archivist* 44 (Spring 1981): 113-124.

25. Helen R. Tibbo, *Abstracting, Information Retrieval and the Humanities: Providing Access to Historical Literature* (Chicago: American Library Association, 1993); Marcia J. Bates, Deborah N. Wilde, and Susan Siegfried, "An Analysis of Search Terminology Used by Humanities Scholars: The Getty Online Searching Project Report Number 1," *Library Quarterly* 63 (January 1993): 1-39.

26. Michael E. Stevens, "The Historian and Archival Finding Aids," *Georgia Archives* 5 (Winter 1977): 64-74; and William J. Maher, "The Use of User Studies," *Midwestern Archivist* 11, no.1 (1986): 15-26.

27. Paul Conway, "Research in Presidential Libraries: A User Survey," *Midwestern Archivist* 11, no. 1 (1986): 33-56.

28. See Elizabeth Yakel and Laura L. Bost, "Understanding Administrative Use and Users in University Archives," *American Archivist* 57 (Fall 1994): 596-615 for a recent study of administrative use of archives.

29. Several projects at the University of California, Los Angeles and Berkeley have been examining the needs of teachers and children using archival materials. These include the Online Archive of California Evaluation Project, the Berkeley Interactive University Cultural Heritage Pilot Project, the Digital Portfolio Archives Project, and the UCLA Institute for Primary Resources. See Anne Gilliland-Swetland, "Evaluation Design for Large-Scale, Collaborative Online Archives: Interim Report of the Online Archive of California Evaluation Project" (paper submitted for publication); Gilliland-Swetland et al., *Digital Portfolio Archives in Learning,* ibid.; Kafai, Yasmin, and Anne Gilliland-Swetland, "Integrating Historical Source Materials into Elementary Science Classroom

Activities," (paper submitted for publication); and Gilliland-Swetland, "An Exploration of K-12 user Needs for Digital Primary Source Materials," *American Archivist* 61, no. 1 (Winter/Spring 1998): 136-157.

30. Conway, ibid. p.52.

31. Marcia J. Bates, "The Design of Browsing and Berrypicking Techniques for the Online Search Interface." *Online Review* 13, no. 5 (1989): 407-424; Marcia J. Bates, "Rethinking Subject Cataloging in the Online Environment." *Library Resources & Technical Services* 33 no. 4 (1989). 400-412; Bates, "Where Should the Person Stop and the Information Search Interface Start?" *Information Processing & Management* 26, no.5 (1990): 575-591.

Index

Page numbers followed by "n" indicate notes.